THE NEGLECTED DUTY

The Neglected Duty

The Creed of Sadat's Assassins and Islamic Resurgence in the Middle East

JOHANNES J.G. JANSEN

MACMILLAN PUBLISHING COMPANY
NEW YORK

Collier Macmillan Publishers
LONDON

Macmillan Publishing Company
866 Third Avenue, New York, N. Y. 10022

Collier Macmillan Canada, Inc.

Library of Congress Catalog Card Number: 86-3045

Printed in the United States of America

printing number
1 2 3 4 5 6 7 8 9 10

Library of Congress Cataloging-in-Publication Data

Jansen, Johannes J. G.
The neglected duty.

Includes English translation of: al-Farīḍah al-ghā'ibah.
Includes bibliographies and indexes.
1. Islam and politics—Egypt. 2. Jam īyat al-Ikhwān al-Muslimin (Egypt) 3. Egypt—Politics and government—1952– 4. Islam—Egypt. 5. Jihad. I. Faraj, Muḥammad ᶜAbd al-Salām. Farīḍh al-ghā'ibah. English. 1986. II. Title.
BP182.J36 1986 297'.1977 86-3045
ISBN 0-02-916340-4

Contents

Foreword

For more than a century the people of the Islamic world have been engaged in a searching, at times heated, and always painful debate about the situation of the Muslim community in the world. The discussion continues unabated in our own day, having, in fact, become even more intense under the spur of events such as the Iranian Revolution, the occupation of the Great Mosque in Mecca in 1979, the attack of American Marine barracks in Beirut in October, 1983, and numerous other incidents of religiously motivated political violence and terrorism. In this book a new and ominous phase of the debate is presented.

The document, entitled "The Neglected Duty," which is the focus of this book, draws upon classical Muslim ideas and the experience of the recent past to reach the radical conclusion that there can be no true Islam apart from the espousal of revolutionary force to overthrow existing governments and to establish an Islamic state or states. The document is a call for Muslims to take up arms in fulfillment of their religious duty to submit to the will of God and to bring the world into subjection to Him. Insofar as its message strikes a sympathetic note in any large number of contemporary Muslim minds — as the evidence seems to suggest it does — the document points to an element in present-day Muslim life that is highly disturbing and that holds the threat of even greater instability and violence in the troubled regions of the Muslim world than we have so far seen.

The roots of the debate that has led to twentieth century Muslim radicalism lie in the eighteenth century; they sprang from a sense of malaise in many Muslim minds, a feeling that the community had slipped, gradually but inexorably, into decline, losing its hold upon those great religious principles that had once made it an instrument of the divine purpose and brought it to glory. In an attempt to reverse the trend, concerned individuals in different parts of the Muslim world launched determined reform efforts aimed at restoring the spiritual health and the strength of the community. Reasoning that Islam was the basis of the Muslims' former power and that its abandonment was the cause of latter-day weakness, the reformers primarily sought to eliminate innovations and non-Islamic elements in popular religion and restore the original purity of Islamic teaching and practice as they were conceived to have existed in the earliest period of the community's history. Thus, they set themselves against much in Islam as it was traditionally practiced, and in doing so, precipitated an intense scrutiny of the community's spiritual foundations and the true source of its strength. Inevitably, many familiar aspects of established Islam, both at the popular and at the high cultural level, came under radical question.

The reforms were not limited to theological considerations, however; they also had a social and political dimension. Movements that grew from the reform impulse did not hesitate to employ armed forces to accomplish their purposes, even when that meant fighting against other Muslims. Indeed, among their objectives was the establishment of theocratic states prepared to employ their full powers to insure that the law of Islam reigned supreme in their territories. The caliphates of West Africa, the Sanūsī "state within a state" in Cyrenaica, the Wahhābī "kingdom" of Central Arabia and the short-lived theocracy created by Sayyid Aḥmad of Rā'ē Barēlī on the northwest frontier of India — to mention only the most important ones — all exemplify the integral nature of the reform movements as political-cum-religious entities. This aspect of their nature prefigures contemporary Islamic radicalism. Then, as now, it inspired fear and opposition in the established Muslim states which were compelled to take up the defense of their territory and their legitimacy as well.

Motivations for the reform movements of the eighteenth and early nineteenth centuries seem to have arisen from within the Muslim community itself as the response of sensitive religious people to their reflections upon the problems of the various Muslim societies. It is significant that all of the groups mentioned above grew up on the peripheries of the great metropolitan centers of Islamic civilization among peoples, many of them nomadic and some of them half pagan, who lived in relatively isolated societies organized on a tribal basis. None of the regions where these movements flourished had as yet been directly or strongly touched by the intrusive foreign influences soon to come, nor does the thought of the reform leaders reflect a response to external pressure or threats.

As the nineteenth century wore on, however, the debate entered a new phase and took on an entirely novel dimension. The determinative factor in giving a new focus to the discussion was the massive weight of European imperialism which came to bear upon the Muslim countries. Area after area formerly ruled by Muslims fell under European control. Their political arrangements were swept away to be replaced by European governance, and the way was opened to the operation of foreign entrepreneurs and the invasion of alien ideas, cultural values, and institutions. In those countries where Muslim rulers remained, such as Iran and Turkey, their rule was often merely nominal as they were subject to constant and heavy-handed European interference in their affairs and seizures of their territory. By the end of World War I, the only significant areas of Muslim population in the world that retained a degree of real independence were the Yemen, Afghanistan, and Central Arabia. That they were yet free was due either to the fact that they served some convenient purpose of the imperial powers, as in the case of Afghanistan as a buffer to Russia, or to the oil which attracted the imperialists' attention, as in the case of Central Arabia.

One consequence of imperialism, once its impact was fully felt, was to breed a consuming sense of crisis throughout the Muslim world, one both more deep-seated and more far-reaching than that which had stimulated the reform movements of the previous century. The evidence of Muslim military and political impotence and of economic and technological backwardness was to be seen on every hand. In addition, as time went on, these weaknesses of the Muslim world increasingly posed the danger of a complete loss of Islamic identity and culture under the assault of foreign cultural values. For Muslims, who were the heirs of a proud imperial and cultural tradition of their own and who, based on Qur'anic teaching, lived in the conviction that their way of life, ordained by the Sovereign Creator of the universe, should lead to worldy success as well as eternal bliss, the new situation of frustation and seeming helplessness caused agonizing soul-searching. What were the causes of the manifest Muslim decline? Did the problem lie, as some alleged, in the very foundations of the community's life and culture itself, in Islam? Was Islam the barrier to progress that had caused Muslim backwardness? Why was it so easily possible for the distant Europeans to subdue the numerically far larger Muslim population to their will? How was lost strength to be regained and departed glory and prestige reasserted? These and a host of related questions became the preoccupation of Muslim leaders and thinkers; they form the background and framework of all contemporary Muslim thought and pose the issues being debated today just as they did for the fathers and grandfathers of the present generation.

Among the intellectual and political elites of the Muslim world the reaction to European power and influence that eventually came to predominate was one of accommodation to the values which these thinkers held responsible for Europe's success and strength. Some were outright Westernizers who saw the salvation of their societies in becoming like the Europeans to the extent possible, but others, the majority, sought to retain traditional Islamic identity while interpreting it a manner commensurate with science, progress, and modern civilization. At an early stage, in reply to the charge that Islam is the cause of backwardness, they endeavored to show that genuine and original Islam, in contrast with its distorted medieval expressions, in fact places no obstacles in the way of the full and free exercise of human reason and those attitudes which have led to the accomplishments of modern science and technology. In a further development of this same line of reasoning, a later series of more positively assertive writers and thinkers presented Islam as the origin and inspiration of all civilization and progress, holding that the Europeans had gained their insights into the principles and methods of science and even their awareness of the basic values of liberal society from contacts with Muslims in medieval times. Thus, for Muslims to pursue science and to take their place among the advanced nations of the world in other ways, far from being a betrayal of Islam, was but the fulfillment of the demand Islam places upon humankind and the reappropriation of what the Muslims had originally given to the world, though it had been lost to them for a time. In the perspective of Islamic modernism, as this view is known, there is no conflict between Islam and the modern world; to be truly modern is also to be truly Islamic.

Intellectually, these arguments were part of a lively apologetic for Islam called forth by the threatening situation in which Muslims found themselves, an attempt to demonstrate the enduring truth and relevance of the Islamic heritage and to reaffirm the community's identity. Such a defense of Islam against implied or explicit criticism continues to be a basic component of Muslim thought to this day. Its existence is a testimony to the persistence of the Muslim sense of being threatened by the dominant modern civilization.

The need to be modern also provided the ideological justification for a sweeping program of practical reform in the Muslim countries in such fields as law, education, and political and economic institutions. Under the leadership of elites, strongly influenced by European ideals, the major countries of the Muslim world were thus gradually but firmly set upon the road to modernization. With the collapse of colonialism and the achievement of independence by most Muslim countries after World War II the pace of change accelerated enormously. Spurred by ebullient expectations of a bright future of freedom and prosperity, the Muslim ruling classes, like those in other developing nations, set economic development and the mobilization of resources as their principal goals. The massive social transformation which these Westernized governing groups thought necessary in order to recoup the fortunes of their peoples inevitably entailed the disruption of time-honored ways of life and traumatic dislocations in society. Disruption was only increased towards the middle of the twentieth century, when oil wealth put vast new possibilities for change into some Muslim hands. New concepts and ideas that were introduced and called upon as justifications for the modernizing drive, such as constitutionalism, popular sovereignty, patriotism, women's rights, and most powerful of all, nationalism, since they were alien to the classical Islamic tradition, raised questions about the legitimacy of what was afoot and stimulated the ongoing debate about the community's situation. Opposition to the general trend of the secularization and Westernization of the Muslim societies arose among traditional groups and vested interests, and the common people often did not support or even understand what their leadership was attempting to do. Change and the forms it took, while beneficial in some ways, also brought doubt and distress. To many it seemed that in the struggle to preseve their own identity, Muslims were being forced to take on the very qualities of those whom they sought to stand against. For all of the turmoil that it may have produced, the drive to reshape society in the modern mold and, thus, to restore power and dignity to the Muslim community has been the dominant motif of Muslim life in the twentieth century. For most thinking Muslims it seems is little choice for the community but to modernize if it is to survive as a distinct entity.

Beginning as early as the 1930s in some areas but coming to a climax in the 1970s, however, there has been a ground swell of disillusionment with the path that most Muslim societies have traversed in the modern period and a demand for a new direction. There is widespread rejection of Western civilization as a model for Muslims to emulate, and in its place has come a search for indigenous values that reflect the traditional culture of Muslims. In consequence the debate about the place of Islam in the world has taken still another, in this instance dramatic, turn. The strongest expression of discontent may be seen in the rise of militant, religiously based political organizations, such as Muslim Brotherhood, which hold as the basic tenet of their ideology that true Islam demands the creation of an Islamic society and Islamic state in addition to individual conformity to the requirements of religion. These groups present Islam as an alternative to the modern Muslim experiments in liberalism, democracy, republicanism, socialism, economic planning, military dictatorship, and so on, all of which they consider to have foreign origins and to be discredited by their lack of an Islamic basis and their failure to alleviate the fundamental problems of the Muslim societies. Their wrath is directed, not at modernization as such, but at the things which have accompanied it and the people who have led it: the increasing dependence upon alien values, continuing military impotence (resulting in part from the strength of U.S.-supported Israel and economic subjugation to foreign powers, the always-growing secularization of society and its institutions, and the exploitativeness and ineffectiveness of allegedly corrupt and inefficient leadership. Such movements have arisen from one end of the Muslim world to the other; their cause has derived powerful hope and new buoyancy from the Iranian Revolution, which has dramatically demonstrated the capacity of an Islamic movement to prevail over one of the richest, best entrenched and most powerful régimes in the entire Muslim world. Islamic resurgence or fundamentalism, as the movements in question are sometimes called, is a significant and growing factor in both the internal politics of Muslim countries and on the international stage. Since they grow out of Muslim experience in modern times and, indeed, represent the culmination of important forces at work there, it seems certain that the resurgence movements will remain with us for some decades to come. As the case of Iran has shown, given favorable conditions and strong leadership, resurgence movements hold the potential of effecting a radical restructuring of the world political order. The questions which these movements raise for the great Islamic debate of modern times are far from being laid to rest.

Despite its importance, however, and the attention that it attracts when some representative of the resurgence outlook carries out a particularly dramatic action, such as the assassination of Anwar al-Sādāt, Islamic resurgence is little understood by outsiders. In the press and other public communications media it is most often seen as religious fanaticism, simple anti-Westernism, reactionary longing for the past, or mindless terrorism. Almost always it is evaluated in harshly negative terms with little or no effort made to comprehend the deep discontents that have produced it or the internal logic of the stand that it upholds. However little one may like what happens, there must, after all, be compelling reasons for men to behave as they do even, and especially, when they react radically. To neglect the visions in men's minds or their motivations, as is most often the case with commentators on the resurgence movements, is to erect an insuperable barrier to understanding them. Admittedly, the opportunity to study resurgence groups at close range is rare and may require great dedication, but more and better information about these movements is a vital concern for scholars, government officials, diplomats and even the general public if we are to respond intelligently to this important and potentially disruptive force of our time.

The great value of Dr. Jansen's study of the creed of al-Sādāt's assassins lies precisely in its provision of the kind of detailed, exact and authoritative information needed for the assessment of the Islamic resurgence movements. To be sure, his study concentrates on only one group in one country, but in its meticulous monographic approach it exemplifies the method that must be adopted with respect to other exemplars of the phenomenon. A series of such sharply focused studies holds the best promise for accumulating the data required for a proper grasp of what is now happening among our Muslim contemporaries. The timeliness and usefulness of the insight offered by the present study, therefore, can scarcely be exaggerated.

Jansen's book is all the more valuable because it deals with the views of one of the more radical resurgence groups. In general terms, these movements may be distinguished into two types: moderate and radical. The former tend to operate within the framework of existing law and political structures and to seek gradual reform; the latter advocate, and sometimes practice, revolutionary violence to effect the charges they desire. Both types are feared and closely watched by governments, but for obvious reasons radicals are a particular cause of unease to the authorities everywhere. Whenever the existence of such a faction becomes known, governments act quickly to suppress it; leaders are imprisoned or dealt with by even harsher methods. For this reason the more radical resurgence movements must operate clandestinely, concealing their activities from public view until the moment comes for them to act. Apart from the need to protect themselves it is in any case part of their psychology to shun close association with those who do not share their opinions and objectives; neither they nor the authorities welcome the inquiries and attention of outsiders. Consequently, it is exceedingly difficult to gain direct and reliable information about the ways in which Islamic radicals think.

In the present instance we have the good fortune that the manifesto of an important radical group in Egypt has been published. This fact poses a perhaps unique opportunity that Dr. Jansen has seized in the present book by translating the manifesto and minutely analyzing its declarations and implications. Although the document originates in the group responsible for the murder of the Egyptian president in October, 1981, as part of the defense for their actions, its significance extends far beyond the light it sheds on this one small group of radical Egyptian Muslims and on the tragedy of al-Sādāt's death. *The Neglected Duty* is the only authentic and extended statement of radical Muslim resurgence views known to this writer. It presents the radical world view in a forceful and vividly clear way, and it also lays out the ongoing conversation between the radicals and other elements in the Egyptian Muslim community. Like radicalism itself, the alternative Muslim opinions against which the manifesto argues are found elsewhere in the Muslim countries. In spite of differences determined by local situations, the debate in Egypt is broadly similar to the one taking place in the wider community. The document is, therefore, a key to understanding Islamic radicalism wherever it may be found; in any event we have no other source of information of comparable authenticity and depth—hence, its great importance.

Jansen's concern to present the reactions of other religious groups and individuals in Egypt to the radicals' manifesto adds another dimension of great value to his study. The discussion is based on wide reading in the Arabic language periodicals which these other groups and religious leaders publish. Such materials are seldom exploited for the richness they can yield. Often these kinds of materials are inaccessible to even the most interested persons, sometimes for reasons of language, or if Arabic is not an obstacle, then because of the inaccessibility of this kind of publication outside of Egypt. The discussion reveals the nature of the debate about the role of Islam in political and social life as it is carried on among the Egyptians themselves with all of its variations and nuances. The analysis sets into relief the issues that preoccupy religiously inclined Egyptians and that separate them from one another. Who the principal participants in the debate are and what they stand for also becomes clear. None of the various groups and religious leaders discussed agrees outright with the radical demands that they take up jihād and be willing to sacrifice their lives for the forceful imposition of an Islamic order or the elimination of allegedly un-Islamic and unjust rulers, but at the same time there is often ambiguity in their stance, giving reason to suspect that their sympathy for radicalism may go deeper than their explicit arguments suggest. It is clearly difficult for Egyptians who themselves have a strong religious drive to reject completely the efforts of those, radicals though they be, who strive to remake society into an Islamic image. This study, thus, casts important light on the degree and nature of the support which radicalism enjoys in one of the major Muslim countries. In any case the presentation of the sometimes contending, sometimes overlapping positions offers a rare and fascinating glimpse of the give and take of religious discussion in a Muslim society. Such a focused view of Muslim opinion about an important religious issue or one so rich in concrete detail is difficult to discover. This study, therefore, has much to offer both the student of religion and the student of politics. As for "The Neglected Duty," the views that it expresses may prove eventually to be among the most significant expressions of Muslim thought in the twentieth century.

Charles J. Adams
Williamsburg, Virginia.
March, 1986

Preface and Acknowledgments

SADAT WAS MURDERED by Muslim extremists in October 1981. His murderers left behind a pamphlet, "The Neglected Duty," which their lawyers regarded as a valid, Islamic defense of their act of terrorism. This pamphlet was published for the first time in December 1981.[1] For a long time to come, so a certain Jamāl al-Bannā writes in a book published in March 1984, this pamphlet, called in Arabic *Al-Farīḍah al-Ghā'ibah,* will dominate the discussions on fundamentalist and extremist Islam.[2] Jamāl al-Bannā derives his prestige when writing about these matters partly from his close family relationship to Ḥasan al-Bannā, the founder of the Muslim Brotherhood.[3] The preface and the cover of his book on the creed of Sadat's assassins explicitly mention that he is a son of ᶜAbd al-Raḥmān al-Bannā, a brother of Ḥasan al-Bannā.

But even if Jamāl al-Bannā had not been a member of the family of the founder of the Muslim Brotherhood, there would be no reason to doubt the truth of his words. No one reading the text of "The Neglected Duty" can fail to be impressed by its coherence and the force of its logic. Even if its author had not been a member of the group that killed President Sadat, the pamphlet would have had great value on its own. Even if Sadat had not been killed by the group that is for all times associated with this pamphlet, the pamphlet would have had value, not as a historical document about the assassination of a Nobel Prize winner, but as the portrait of a mentality that exists and probably has existed for a long time, and that will not be exterminated by whatever stern and harsh measures governments quite justifiably take against it.

In writing about the creed of Sadat's assassins, I have taken it for granted—perhaps without sufficient sociological proof—that Egyptian society can be divided into three sociologically distinguishable groups. The first is the poor who own very little except their children and who have undergone little intellectual influence from the West. It is from this group that the quietist Ṣūfī movement (which represents the mystical tendencies of Islam) recruits most of its followers, although it is certainly not true that all members of the Ṣūfī Brotherhoods come from this sector.

The second group has undergone Western influence; it is partly demoralized by the alleged superiority of Western ideas, institutions, appliances, and so forth, and is perhaps a little less poor than the first group. Most university graduates fall into this second classification. Society has little to offer these graduates: jobs and prosperity are, to most members of this group, definitely out of reach. To these Egyptians the title of *muhandis,* engineer, is infinitely more prestigious than the traditional Islamic title of shaykh. The resurgence of Islam, however, is one of the few possibilities this number has to make their lives more worth living. Yet it is again not true that all Muslim activists come from this group.

The third division, the ruling rich, is small. Its members have a military background, or they are the descendants of the traditional élite of landowners. They are multilingual, well educated, and cosmopolitan. They have little religious or ideological interests. They are simply in charge and have to keep things running. In doing so they are sometimes not very sensitive to the demands of those they regard as their inferiors, not even when these demands are religious, or are presented as religious.

None of these three groups is unaffected by the presence in Cairo of the prestigious Azhar University, traditionally regarded as the intellectual bulwark of Islam. Al-Azhar supplies these groups with its religious cadre, which results in the Ṣūfīs, the activists, and the élite all having their own Azhar experts who preach Islam to their own people. Although al-Azhar and its graduates are essentially loyal to whatever government rules Egypt, al-Azhar is a constant source of "calm pressure" in the direction of a further Islamization of society.

The success of a great preacher like Shaykh Kishk can probably be explained by the way in which he appeals to both the activists and the Ṣūfīs; his message has many Ṣūfī traits but sounds activist. The success of Shaykh Al-Shaᶜrāwī is more difficult to understand. His merit, in the eyes of the Egyptian masses who see him on television, is probably that he manages to make Islam seem all-important; this counts heavily in his favor since many members of the middle and upper classes have definitely started to doubt whether Islam is really the determining factor in their lives, their society, their country.

Those people in Cairo who regard themselves as professional members of that much-quoted class of "usually well-informed circles" (e.g., diplomats, journalists, foreign experts) suspect Shaykh Al-Shaᶜrāwī of being the John the Baptist of the extremists: Shaykh Al-Shaᶜrāwī, so they allege, is simply preparing the way for He Who Comes, or, in more accurate phrasing, for They Who Come. It is doubtful whether this is true. The evidence to prove or disprove such allegations can, by the nature of the offense, only be circumstantial.

The pages that follow will every now and then betray that their writer lived in Cairo in the period under discussion. This no doubt has affected his perspective. It is regrettable, however, that even living in Cairo, in spite of the advantages it offers, does not guarantee that one sees, hears, and reads everything.

Some of the material on which the following chapters are based I have used before: this applies especially to the middle part of the chapter on Shaykh Kishk and to the first chapter, which was published in a slightly different form in the journal *Welt des Islams,* N.S. vol. XXV, 1985, pp. 1–30.

Qur'ān quotations are given in a translation which is adapted from the translation by Richard Bell.

I am greatly indebted to Peri Bearman for her assistance, especially for her preparatory work on the translation of §76 – 91 and §106 – 143 of the text of "The Neglected Duty," *Al-Farīḍah al-Ghā'ibah.*

I thank all those, both far away and close by, who made it possible for me to publish this book.

Johannes J.G. Jansen
Leiden, October 1985

NOTES

1. I published a first article on *Al-Farīdah al-Ghā'ibah* in a Dutch weekly, *Intermediair,* January 28, 1983.
2. JAMĀL AL-BANNĀ, *Al-Farīḍah al-Ghā'ibah: Jihād al-Sayf . . . am Jihād al-ᶜAql?,* Cairo (Dār Thābit), 1984, 170 pp.
3. On the Muslim Brothers and Ḥasan al-Bannā: R.P. MITCHELL, *The Society of the Muslim Brotherhood,* Oxford University Press, 1969; and O. CARRÉ and G. MICHAUD, *Les Frères Musulmanes 1928 – 1982,* Paris, 1983.

Introduction

THE OTHER PERSON'S RELIGION causes intellectual and moral offense. Christianity is "unto the Jews a stumblingblock, and unto the Greeks foolishness,"[1] but Islam, too, may be a disturbing and annoying religion. Western writers who give accounts of Islam to a Western public often do not stress those elements in Islam that would be offensive or nonsense in the eyes of their Western readers. They rather see it as their duty to present Islam in as acceptable a light as possible to the West. They state the case of Islam with as much coherence as possible and construct the most feasible explanation for various Islamic aspirations. In general, they take on the role of a counsel for the defense. Yet Muslims usually think that Western Islamicists are enemies of Islam who maliciously convey an inaccurate impression of the Islamic creed, ritual, ethics, and so forth, to their (Western) public. How can this state of affairs be explained?

Islam, like all religions, is under attack. Many people will agree that anything or anyone under attack is entitled to a defense. Frequently factual mistakes in polemical writings on Islam compel

Islamicists to join the discussion, and by force of their expert knowledge they usually side with the defense. It would indeed not be pleasant to be an expert on something that is illogical, inconsistent, or even nonsensical. Hence, whatever may have been said to the contrary, Western Islamicists have a healthy interest in putting forward what their public would consider to be the positive sides of Islam.

Two characteristics of Islam are particularly offensive to the general Western reader: its totalitarian claim to universal validity and its theocratic demands. "Our lawgiver . . . did not leave anything, not even the smallest matters, to the freewill decision of those for whom his law was designed," a prominent Jewish writer from the first century AD boasts,[2] and the same worthy and ancient sentiment is found innumerable times among Muslim thinkers.[3] The smallest details of daily life are subject to the provisions of Islamic law, not excluding personal hygiene and metabolism. Muslims, it is well known, identify all prescripts of Islamic Law totally and vehemently with the Command of God.

It is probably this identification that lies at the basis of the Western misappellation of Islamic law: very often, at least in the West, Islamic Law is referred to as Qur'anic law, whereas there is a substantial difference between the legal rulings of the Qur'ān and the rulings of Islamic Law. The scholars of Islam have dealt with these differences in a highly specialized branch of theological knowledge, the Islamic science of the *uṣūl al-fiqh,* especially in its chapters on *naskh,* a term that can be roughly equated with "abrogation." People in the West, knowing that Muslims regard the Qur'ān as God's direct revelation, and noticing that Muslims regard Muslim law also as divine and revealed, have become confused, at least in their terminology, and have started to talk of "Qur'anic Law"—a misappellation that in its way reflects the respect Muslims have for Islamic law, but which is not the correct term.

The sanctification of Islamic Law and its rulings has, of course, more important consequences: if the Law is divine, only God can change it. Humans who criticize the Law, for example, because of its harshness and cruelty, are actually criticizing the Almighty Himself, which is sacrilege. Also, improbable minutiae of the Law that in the West have no religious significance at all may irreversibly separate Muslims from non-Muslims, and could possibly make the one despise the other.

The theocratic demands of Islam no doubt had their equivalents in the history of Christendom. However, since the Enlightenment, the separation between matters of state and matters of religion in the Western world has become almost complete. Moreover, religion, at least in the Western understanding of the word, is almost universally reduced to belief,[4] and many Westerners have great difficulty in realizing that a religion is not exclusively faith, but also comprises ritual, ethics, and a form of religious organization.

Given that this is so, it will not easily occur to the general Western reader that most Muslims—not only those the West calls fundamentalists—welcome the establishment of an Islamic state where the laws, which according to Muslims were given by God, are universally applied. To many, moreover, it is not immediately obvious that the rule of Islamic Law as the law of the land implies the use of force in order to implement a religion, namely, Islam, since no state can exist if it rejects the use of force in order to compel the observance of its laws. Once this is clear, questions about the status of lax Muslims, of non-Muslims, and of ex-Muslims who live in Muslim territory inevitably arise.

The rulers and governments that, perhaps, ought to be replaced by the rule of Islam are usually not very much in favor of their own substitution by an Islamic theocracy. In as far as they control the printing press and the mosque sermons, they are able to prevent the Islamic theocratic sentiment from being expressed too openly. Since this sentiment is fundamental to Islam, it is nevertheless expressed, but only in veiled ways. Autocratic governments in Muslim countries only allow their subjects to contemplate the purities of an Islamic theocracy "through a glass darkly." The theocratic ideal is not always discussed in an atmosphere that is completely free from censorship—hence, an outsider can easily overlook it if he wants to.

The offensiveness of the utopian and revolutionary aspects of Islam and the desire of Islamicists to bring Islam closer to their Western public both play their part in the overemphasis on metaphysics and theology in Western descriptions of Islam. Muslims feel strongly that this emphasis by Westerners on theology is wrong. When Western journalists or scholars picture Islam as a system that is as open-minded, liberal, vague, and humanist as their own Western systems, Muslims assume foul play. To them, modern Islam is not "a search for cultural identity," but a search for the Kingdom of God, which to them means the search for an Islamic state.

Since Muslims themselves are not at all embarrassed by the political aspirations of their religion they fail to see why others should be. To Muslims today it may sometimes seem as if there were a conspiracy between their own governments and those they call "orientalists" to suppress the theocratic demands of Islam. The journalistic or scholarly outsider, as well as the government and its paid public servants, arouse irritation since they all, knowingly or unknowingly, fail to recognize the theocratic claims of true Islam.

It is therefore obvious that the contents of the creed of Sadat's assassins, *Al-Farīḍah al-Ghā'ibah,* can provide a unique source[5] for our knowledge of what many Muslims today really think and believe. The document and the reactions to it strongly suggest that there exists a Muslim consensus that Islamic law has to be applied fully in all spheres of human activity. It is evident that such a consensus can become for Muslims a basis for the legitimization of the use of force.

NOTES

1. I Cor. 1.23.
2. Flavius Josephus, *Against Apion,* ii, §173–74; quoted by W.G. Kümmel, *Theology of the New Testament,* London, 1974, p. 50.
3. E.g., *Majallat al-Azhar,* October 1981, p. 2101.
4. The scriptural basis for this may well be Paul's letter to the Romans, 3.28: "A person is put right with God only through faith, and not by doing what the Law commands." In this translation, the word "only" is, significantly, added by the translator *(The Good News Bible),* and not found in the original Greek text.

5. A certain Dr. Michael Youssef has, as well, recognized the importance of the *Farīḍah* document, since he added several pages to his book entitled *Revolt Against Modernity: Muslim Zealots and the West* (Leiden, 1985) in which he alleges to translate the *Farīḍah*. His translation is, first of all, far from complete. Second, in the sentences and paragraphs that he does not omit Dr. Youssef makes a great number of mistakes, often caused by the confusion of nouns and adjectives with proper names and vice versa. One example: Dr. Youssef translates ". . . when Rashid V became Caliph" (p. 177 of his book) instead of ". . . when the fifth rightly-guided Caliph succeeded to the Caliphate" (§141 of the translation) (Ar. *rāshid:* 'rightly-guided').

CHAPTER 1

The Creed of Sadat's Assassins

SINCE THE ASSASSINATION of President Sadat in October 1981, many observers have argued that this assassination was in reality an attempt to seize power in Egypt and to establish an Islamic fundamentalist régime. One of those who thought so was the famous Egyptian preacher Shaykh Al-Shaᶜrāwī (b. 1911), who declared in an interview with the newspaper *Al-Ahrām* in November 1981: "If God had consented to the assassins' plans, no power, no police, no army could have stopped them . . . but their real aim was not only to assassinate him . . . wasn't the real aim of this whole operation that they wanted to seize power in Egypt?"[1]

Was it? The conspirators responsible for the assassination of President Sadat left a detailed statement on their *Weltanschauung* which was written down by a certain Muḥammad ᶜAbd al-Salām Faraj (1954–1982). This statement is entitled *Al-Farīḍah al-Ghā'ibah,* "The Neglected Duty"—that is, the duty of *jihād,* "war against unbelievers." The seriousness of this small book is made plain not only by its contents but also by the fact that its author was executed on April 15, 1982, together with the four actual assassins of Sadat. No one less than the Muftī of Egypt at that time, Shaykh Jādd al-Ḥaqq ᶜAlī Jādd al-Ḥaqq, wrote an answer to the pamphlet shortly after Sadat's death. Parts of this official answer (*radd,* "refutation") were published in *Al-Ahrām* on December 8, 1981.

Publishing a refutation of the pamphlet's text made the publication of the text itself imaginable. The Cairo newspaper *Al-Aḥrār* did actually take this risk, and in its issue of December 14, 1981, it proudly announces: "*Al-Aḥrār* exclusively publishes the complete text of the constitution of terrorism: The Forgotten Duty." The editor's introduction tries to alert the average Egyptian reader to the dangerous character of the theories proposed in this pamphlet.[2] Not only impious rulers are the aim of the assassinations by Muslim extremists; the man in the street who omits one of the five daily prayer ceremonies, or who does not fast or pay his religious taxes called *zakāt,* or who omits any other Islamic duty may also fall victim to the harshness of the demands of these fanatics. His life, too, so the paper warns, is in danger.

Somehow this editorial warning betrays that there may have been a large and widespread sympathy for the opinions expressed in the *Farīḍah,* if not for the acts committed by the group of which its author was a member. If such a general and vague feeling of sympathy had not existed, it would not have been deemed necessary to utter these solemn warnings. It seems that the late Dr. Richard Mitchell's observation on the Muslim Brothers, the religious "terrorists" of the Nasser era (1952–1970), is still valid: Dr. Mitchell noted that a high proportion of the active members of the Muslim Brothers belonged to white-collar professions, wore Western suits, and had had some form of Western-style education.[3] They were, in short, recruited from the same group of Egyptians from which *Al-Aḥrār* recruits its readers. (*Al-Aḥrār* is the newspaper of the *ḥizb al-aḥrār,* a leftist opposition party).

After the editorial introduction, the complete text of *Al-Farīḍah al-Ghā'ibah* follows. The lawyers of the men who were accused of the assassination of President Sadat would have had all opportunity to protest privately or publicly had this text misrepresented the beliefs of their clients, or had it been altered fraudulently, but nothing is known of such protests. It can hence safely be assumed that the *Farīḍah* is what it professes to be: the self-justification of Sadat's murderers.

The text of the *Farīḍah* as published in *Al-Aḥrār* in 1981 is most probably based on the copy of the *Farīḍah* that was in the possession of the author's lawyer. This *Aḥrār* version became the basis of a hasty reprint[4] which appeared, without mention of a date or place of publication, after the execution of its author (on p. 3 of this edition, Muḥammad ᶜAbd al-Salām Faraj is called *shahīd,* "martyr"). This version was certainly not printed in Egypt, since in its preface the Egyptian authorities are addressed with coarse invectives. According to Professor Stefan Wild (Bonn) in a personal letter, this edition was printed in Amman. The Amman and the *Aḥrār* editions have mistakes[5] and omissions[6] in common, but the Amman version added so many misprints[7] of its own that it is sometimes next to impossible to understand from this edition what the *Farīḍah* is about.

A third version of the *Farīḍah* appeared in 1983 in Cairo, at the end of fascicle 31 of the series of *fatwās* which is being published[8] by the Egyptian Ministry of *Awqāf.*[9] This *Awqāf* edition (reprinted in 1984) is by far the best edition available at present. It adds the full text of the *Farīḍah*[10] as an appendix to the *fatwā*[11] by Shaykh Jādd al-Ḥaqq ᶜAlī Jādd al-Ḥaqq in which the contents of the *Farīḍah* are refuted. The *Awqāf* edition contains fewer misprints than the *Aḥrār* edition but it does not in any important way differ from it. The *Awqāf* edition contains phrases that no doubt belong in the original[12] but that the two other editions do not have. It is strange that some mistakes in the text are common to all three printed versions.[13]

The text as it circulated among the activists seems to have contained 54 pages. Shaykh Jādd al-Ḥaqq professes to have consulted a photocopy of this version.[14] It is probably the same 54-page version that was used by Dr. Muḥammad ᶜAmmārah for his book *Al-Farīḍah al-Ghā'ibah: ᶜArḍ wa-Ḥiwār wa-Taqyīm* (The Forgotten Duty: An Exposition, Dialogue, and Evaluation), which appeared in Cairo in 1982. In this small book Dr. Muḥammad ᶜAmmārah complains about the many printing errors that the *Farīḍah* contains,[15] and a remark made by Shaykh Jādd al-Ḥaqq also indicates that the original text of the *Farīḍah* had been written or typed with little care.[16]

Yet even in this imperfect form the text greatly impressed outsiders and more moderate Muslims, as discussions in the Egyptian weekly *Al-Liwā' al-Islāmī* demonstrate. This weekly, which intends to replace once-widely read fundamentalist periodicals like *Al-Daᶜwah* and *Al-Iᶜtiṣām*, appeared for the first time on January 28, 1982. From the very beginning its successive issues contained allusions to the contents of the *Farīḍah*. On pages 8 and 9 of the issue that appeared on February 25, 1982, we read an explicit discussion of the *Farīḍah* and its theories which was to be continued in the following numbers of the weekly. The way in which the author of the *Farīḍah* invokes the authority of the writings of Ibn Taymīyah (d. 1328) seems especially to have severely shocked and deeply impressed the Egyptian Muslim readers of the pamphlet. In the *Al-Liwā' al-Islāmī* articles in which the *Farīḍah* is discussed, great care is taken to show that the writings of Ibn Taymīyah have their own historical context and that Ibn Taymīyah's teachings cannot be mechanically transposed to twentieth-century circumstances.

Dr. Muḥammad ᶜAmmārah, in his above-mentioned short study of the *Farīḍah,* devotes a considerable part of his book to printing in full the passages by Ibn Taymīyah from which the *Farīḍah* quoted fragments only, thus attempting to demonstrate that the author of the *Farīḍah* cannot claim Ibn Taymīyah's considerable authority in support of his own twentieth-century extremist ideas. Although in this context a neutral and disinterested academic discussion of the contents of the *Farīḍah* is hardly to be expected, Dr. ᶜAmmārah gives a fair summary of the *Farīḍah* and makes some critical remarks about it. Its style he calls weak (*rakākat al-uslūb,* lit., "colorlessness of style").[17] The essential mistake, *al-khaṭa' al-jawharī,*[18] in the theories expounded in the *Farīḍah* is (according to Dr. ᶜAmmārah) the similarity that the *Farīḍah* sees between the modern rulers and the Mongols of the days of Ibn Taymīyah, or, in less diplomatic terms: the essential mistake in the *Farīḍah* is to equate Sadat with Genghis Khan and his successors, and to equate the Egyptian government and its bureaucracy with the Mongol hordes.

Nonmilitants like Dr. ᶜAmmārah may have been impressed by the arguments presented by the author of the *Farīḍah;* many of the latter's combatants, however, were not. To them, it must all have seemed to be commonplace. One of them, so Dr. Gilles Kepel reports,[19] even declared that the *Farīḍah* contained nothing new and consisted of quotations only. Such a remark tends to confirm that the *Farīḍah,* whatever its defects, does indeed give a true picture of the thinking of the extremist militant Muslims. Hence it is an important text.

In his *Le Prophète et Pharaon* (Paris, 1984), Dr. Gilles Kepel analyzes Egyptian Islamic activism in the last decades, and he, of course, discusses the *Farīḍah* too, at the end of his book.[20] Dr. Kepel gives lines from the first half of the *Farīḍah* in translation, but much has to be added to what Dr. Kepel writes. For instance, the author of the *Farīḍah* amply discusses the arguments that less militant Egyptian Muslims have brought forward against the viewpoints of the extremists. It is important to try and identify correctly to which groups of people these arguments actually belong since this will give a clear picture of the tendencies at work within Egyptian modern Islam. Also, when Dr. Kepel lightly remarks, almost in passing, that the text of the *Farīḍah* starts with *"les eulogies (. . .) d'usage,"*[19] he fails to see the specific significance of the phrasing of the opening eulogies of the *Farīḍah*.

The *Farīḍah* (§1 of the translation) opens with a verse from the Qur'ān in which the tensions of modern Islamic activism become clearly visible. On the one hand violent attacks in the name of Islam are something relatively new, while, on the other hand, the perpetrators of such acts of violence claim to personify true Islam. This implies a contradiction: why have Muslims of earlier generations not understood the need for organized violence? It is in this light that one should read the opening verse of the *Farīḍah:*

> *Is it not high time for those who have believed*
> *to humble their hearts to the Reminder of God*
> *and to the truth which He hath sent down;*
> *and that they should not be like those*
> *to whom the Book was formerly given*
> *and for whom the time was long,*
> *so that their hearts became hard,*
> *and many of them are reprobates?* (Qur'ān 57.16)[21]

As far as the *Farīḍah* is concerned, the injunction not to be like earlier generations is the central element in this verse. In the eulogies on God and His Apostle (§2 of the translation) which also precede the body of the text, we are again confronted with this problem. Every deviation from Muḥammad's way of life, so we read, is a mistaken innovation, *bidᶜah*, which will in the end lead its perpetrator to Hell. In its context, this articulate statement means, of course, that the docile masses and their lax rulers are committing "mistaken innovations," and not the members of the *Farīḍah* group.

The first paragraph of the text itself (§3) states that the duty of *jihād*, "war against unbelievers," has fallen into neglect. Yet, so the text continues, traditions from the time of the Prophet prove that only the sword can remove the *ṭawāghīt*, the idols of this world (§4). In the understanding of the *Farīḍah*, the idols of pagan Mecca in the seventh-century AD are to be equated with the rulers and their governments in the twentieth century. Muḥammad "never flattered the heathen Meccan idols"—in the same way, a Muslim in the twentieth century should not bow to his government.

The next topic is the establishment of an Islamic state and the reintroduction of the Caliphate (§7). Four Traditions in which the Prophet foretells this are adduced (§§8–13). The third of these (§10) is particularly interesting to a Western reader: in it the Prophet is reported to foretell the conquest of Constantinople and Rome, the two Christian patriarchal sees not yet conquered by the Muslims in the seventh century (Alexandria was conquered in 642, Antioch in 637). To this tradition the *Farīḍah* (§11) adds a short commentary: "The conquest of Constantinople came about more than 800 years after the Prophet's prediction. And also the conquest of Rome will be realized."

After these optimistic speculations, the author of the *Farīḍah* turns to a problem of urgent importance (§14): many have fallen into despair and do not believe that these great things will come about. "They say: what difference does it all make, isn't it a waste of time and effort on dreams?" It is from remarks like this that the real character of the *Farīḍah* becomes apparent. It is not a manifesto that addresses outsiders, nor is it an apology or a justification of one single assassination—Sadat's name is not even mentioned in it—it is rather an internal discussion paper that circulated among congenial strict Muslims. This discussion paper attempts to meet their objections and doubts, and hence it is of extreme interest to students of Islam. It is one of the very few publications that does not attempt to make itself palatable to a possible censor by omitting offensive subject matter. It is not coded in order to spare the feelings of the more sensitive employees of the secret political police. It gives an outsider a unique opportunity to listen in on what really occupies the minds of many Muslim militants and activists. Many obscure pages written by modern Muslims become meaningful when decoded with the help of the clarity of the *Farīḍah*.

Some Muslims, so the *Farīḍah* teaches, deny that the establishment of a Muslim state is a Muslim duty, and other Muslims neglect this duty, although they do not deny the principle of its obligatory character. Yet, according to the *Farīḍah,* it is the Qur'ān itself that prescribes this duty, for instance, in Surah 5, in the famous verse 48: "Whosoever does not rule (Ar. *yaḥkum*) by what God hath sent down — they are the unbelievers."[22] The author of the *Farīḍah* seems to feel that his appeal to the Qur'ān is not sufficient to justify this radical insistence on the foundation of an Islamic modern state, and he adds an argument that is logically deducible from Islamic Law as sanctified by the Muslim community: "If the religious obligations of Islam cannot be carried out in their entirety without the support of an Islamic State, then the establishment of such a state is a religious obligation too. If such a state cannot be established without war, then this war is a Muslim religious obligation as well" (§16).

The next step in the line of argument that the *Farīḍah* follows is the discussion of the question, "Do we live in an Islamic State?" *(Hal naḥnu naʿīsh fī dawlah islāmīyah?).* The answer that the *Farīḍah* gives to this question is, of course, negative. This negative answer is supported by quotations from Abū Ḥanīfah (d. 767) and Ibn Taymīyah (d. 1328), taken from passages in which these two scholars try to define the difference between *dār al-islām,* the house of Islam, and *dār al-kufr,* the house of Unbelief (§18 – 20). The identification of the house of Islam with the omnipresent and omnipotent modern state gives no difficulty to the author of the *Farīḍah*.

The ruler of such a non-Islamic state, so the *Farīḍah* continues

(§21), cannot be called a Muslim, even if his subjects may be Muslims, as again Qur'ān 5.48 demonstrates: whosoever does not rule according to the laws of Islam is an unbeliever. Since, however, Sadat was born as a Muslim, he became guilty of apostasy—at least in the eyes of the author of the *Farīḍah*—the very moment he started to rule. Muslim law punishes apostasy with death.

The text of the *Farīḍah* spells it all out: the rulers of the Muslims in this century "are in apostasy," *ḥukkām al-muslimīn fī riddah ʿani-'l-islām*. They all (so we read) collaborate with Crusaderism (the pejorative Muslim name for the Western Christian World), with Communism, or with Zionism. "They carry nothing from Islam but a name, even if they perform prayer ceremonies, or fast, or pretend to be Muslim" (§25). Again Ibn Taymīyah's reflections on the wars against the Mongols *(Al-Tatār)* who once invaded Syria supply the point of reference: the Mongols under their leader Ghāzān—who had converted to Islam in 1295—followed Mongol law, the so-called Yāsā, a "mixture of Jewish, Christian and Muslim laws, to which their private fancies were added." To the *Farīḍah* it is obvious that the position of the modern Egyptian Muslims is much worse than that of these Mongols, since Egyptian Muslims live at present under laws that are further away from Muslim law than the Mongol Yāsā, to which Islamic law had at least contributed: "There is no doubt that the Mongol Yāsā is less of a sin than the laws which the West has imposed on countries like Egypt and which have no connection with Islam or with any other revealed religion" (§29). It is noteworthy that the *Farīḍah*, as this paragraph shows, regards the laws of the Muslim world as imposed by the West, and not as indigenous. Elaborate quotations from Ibn Taymīyah follow (§§30–46). The question of how one should consider Muslim scholars and Muslim mystics who served at the Mongol court gets special attention.

The self-confidence of the author of the *Farīḍah*, and his rock-like faith in his own cause, become evident when we see how he himself first makes his point, amply quoting from well-known Muslim authorities like Ibn Kathīr (d. 1373) and Ibn Taymīyah, and then lists at least seventeen objections against his own views. These objections are introduced by formulas like, "There are those who say . . . ," or "There are those who argue . . ." and so on. The objections are not imaginary. They are real objections, raised by real people in real discussions, and they concern the essence of the dilemmas that confront Muslims in the twentieth century of the Christian Era.

The first objection concerns the benevolent societies, *al-jam^ciyāt al-khayrīyah,* of which there are thousands in Egypt (§48). Does not the foundation of such societies, which urge people to do good works, to perform the prayer ceremonies, to pay the religious taxes, and so on, further the cause of Islam? The counter-question which the *Farīḍah* poses is, "Do such well-meaning societies bring about the foundation of an Islamic State?" Moreover, the *Farīḍah* warns, such societies are subject to the State, registered in its files, and have to follow its instructions. This, needless to say, totally disqualifies these societies in the eyes of the author of the *Farīḍah,* even though the number of Egyptians involved in, or affected by, these benevolent societies probably runs into the millions.

The next objection seems to be directed at those Muslims who put private and personal piety above concern for the public cause (§49). "Some say," so we read, "that we should occupy ourselves with obedience to God, with educating *(tarbiyah)* the Muslims, and with exerting ourselves in acts of devotion." Here the author of the *Farīḍah* seems first of all to refer to the Egyptian Ṣūfī movement. The official journal of the Egyptian Ṣūfīs does not talk of educating but of "cultivating" *(tathqīf)* the Muslim masses; however, this difference in phraseology does not entail a difference in meaning. Moreover, the multiple small or large Ṣūfī Brotherhoods, which tend toward a quietist understanding of Islam, are the second religious mass movement, next to the more general Muslim benevolent societies, *jam^cīyāt khayrīyah,* which the *Farīḍah* dealt with in the preceding paragraph.

The *Farīḍah* summarizes the aims of the Ṣūfī movement as insistence on obedience to God, on education, and on an "abundance" *(kathrah)* of acts of devotion—"because our backwardness *(dhull)* is due to our sins." The implication of the wording that the *Farīḍah* chooses seems to be that many Muslims, amongst them the Ṣūfīs, think that the "backwardness" of the Muslim world will disappear automatically when each and every Muslim privately leads a life of Islamic perfection. To this the *Farīḍah* does, of course, not agree.

The response that the *Farīḍah* gives is somewhat predictable. The highest form of obedience to God, so we are told, and the highest form of devotion, is *jihād,* the holy struggle for Islam, and political activism, "provided the other "pillars" (prayer, fasting, etc.) are not neglected" (§50). It should be noted that, in the answer which the author of the *Farīḍah* proffers, the theme of education does not even occur. The possibility that education may serve the cause of Islam is not even considered. This fits in with the low esteem in which the *Farīḍah* holds *ᶜilm,* "knowledge" or "science," and the realistic pessimism with which it regards the possibilities for conversion to its views by peaceful persuasion, as we shall see later on.

Some say, so the *Farīḍah* now continues (§51), that preoccupation with politics hardens the heart and keeps men away from remembering God, *dhikr Allāh.* This is the philosophy[23] of people, so we are now told, who either do not understand Islam, or do not wish to stand firmly by the rule of God, *ḥukm Allāh.* The opposition *dhikr Allāh* versus *ḥukm Allāh* points again in the direction of the Ṣūfīs, not because the meetings of the Ṣūfīs are usually called *dhikr,* but because they are often accused of being lax in implementing the specific rules that Islamic Law imposes.

It is not possible to render into English the common Arabic expression *ḥukm Allāh* which the *Farīḍah* uses here without losing some of its implications. It not only can be translated as "theocracy" but also as "legal regulation(s) coming from God"—the kind of regulations with which a new convert to Islam, like the Mongol King Ghāzān who continued to drink alcohol after his conversion, would perhaps not have cared to comply. It should, in this context, not be overlooked that the spread of Islam (especially among the Mongols who are so frequently discussed by the *Farīḍah*) has been mainly the merit of the quietist, "lax," and unpolitical Ṣūfī Brotherhoods.

Some Muslims, so the *Farīḍah* tells us (§52), want to establish an Islamic political party.[24] Approvingly the author of the *Farīḍah* writes that a party is at least better than a benevolent society since a party *yatakallam fi-'l-siyāsah,* "talks about politics." A political party, so the *Farīḍah* teaches, always collaborates with the state in which it is active. If such a state is an evil heathen state, such collaboration is not good since such states should be destroyed. Moreover, the *Farīḍah* perceives, the establishment of a party will have as its inevitable consequence the membership of legislative councils that enact laws without consideration for God's laws or even in contradiction to these. So much for the Islamic political party.

Another argument, which the *Farīḍah* admits looks attractive (§53), is formulated as follows: "The Muslims should do their best in order to obtain important positions in society. More Muslim doctors, more Muslim engineers, and the existing order will automatically perish. . . ." According to the *Farīḍah,* there are not only no scriptural arguments to support this view, but also reality shows it to be wrong. Those Muslim doctors and those Muslim engineers, so we are told, would be working within a state that is evil and un-Islamic, which disqualifies their efforts. Moreover, each and every Muslim personality who ever got to an important post like Cabinet Minister has always been a 100 percent supporter of the status quo, so the *Farīḍah* complains. Would an Egyptian reader of these lines be able not to think of Shaykh Al-Sha^c^rāwī, Cabinet Minister for *Awqāf* from 1976 till 1978, and similar Muslim dignitaries? The line of reasoning that the *Farīḍah* here follows is also to be met in internal discussions in the West-European Left. If only, many moderates have thought, the influential posts in state and society would be occupied by their sympathizers, state and society will more or less automatically be reformed. However, the radicals felt that they knew better.

An Islamic State has to be established by peaceful means, so some seem to believe. The *Farīḍah* tells us (§54) that for certain people this has been a reason not to join the *jihād* movement or even to withdraw from it. These deserters, so we read, thought that by propaganda and missionary activities *(da^c^wah)* it would be possible to create a broad base from which an Islamic state could be founded. The *Farīḍah,* however, thinks that the Islamic state can by its very nature only be founded by a minority. Does not the Qur'ān say that few among God's servants are thankful (Qur'ān

34.12)? And how could propaganda possibly be successful when all means of communication are in the hands of an evil anti-Islamic state, so the author of the *Farīḍah* asks. The only possibility for success that he sees is to liberate the mass media from the hands of the unbelievers, because when that has happened, people will "enter into the religion of God in crowds" (Qur'ān 110.2).

It cannot be denied that in the Third World the influence of the state on the mass media is far-reaching. Nevertheless, some dissident Muslims have managed to make their voices heard in spite of this state control of the official media as, for instance, Shaykh Kishk who was never even mentioned in the Egyptian media up to September 1981 when (together with many others) he was arrested on the eve of the assassination of Sadat. The mere fact that his name was on that occasion singled out on the front page of *Al-Ahrām* proves that he had indeed managed to become famous without media help. Shaykh Kishk's verbal and vocal virtuosity is extremely effective on a simple cassette tape — a modern means of communication that can be multiplied cheaply and that by its very character is not controllable by the modern state.[25]

The need for missionary activities compels the author of the *Farīḍah* to mention two more points. The first point is that Islamic law should, according to some, only be applied to those people who (as a result of missionary activities) have become Muslims and want that law to be applied to them (§58). This the *Farīḍah* rejects. Pagan laws are now being applied to Muslims and pagans alike. In a similar way, Islamic law, so the author of the *Farīḍah* thinks, will have to be applied to Muslims and non-Muslims alike, which is a step forward, so he writes, since Muslim law is all justice, *kulluhu ᶜadl*.

The second point is formulated in an exceptionally personal way: "Some have misunderstood what I say *(kalāmī hādhā)* and have taken it to mean that we should refrain from propaganda and missionary activities altogether" (§59). He continues by explaining that it is basic to realize when discussing these problems that people should be persuaded to accept the whole of Islam *(al-islām ka-kull)*, and that hence *jihād*, political and religious struggle, has to be included. Attempts to form a "broad base," *qāᶜidah ᶜarīḍah*, so we read, are not sufficient. In the Egyptian context, such a remark can only be addressed to the successful group of people who published the monthly *Al-Da^c^wah* from 1976 until September 1981. The mass readership of this monthly represented a "broad base" indeed. Moreover, the very title of the monthly, *Al-Da^c^wah,* has to be translated as "propaganda," "missionary activity," or "call to Islam."

Some people think, so we read in the *Farīḍah* (§60), that the true road to the establishment of an Islamic state is the separation from society as it is and emigration (hijrah) to another locality in order to establish out there, without alien interference, the true Islamic state. The next steps in this strategy are the victorious return and triumphant conquest of the old society. It is, of course, impossible to discuss the hijrah strategy without referring to Islamic history, first of all to the Prophet's own Hijrah from Mecca to Medina in 622 AD. Needless to say, such a discussion is presented to the reader.

Although there seems to be a certain similarity between the hijrah strategy and the plans of the *Farīḍah* group, this similarity is only superficial. Moreover, the author of the *Farīḍah* already knows that the hijrah strategy is bound to fail, or at least did fail. In the summer of 1977 a group of extremists suddenly became notorious, after having assassinated Shaykh Muḥammad Ḥusayn Al-Dhahabī, a former Cabinet Minister of Religious Affairs. This group had called itself *jamā^c^at al-hijrah,* the group of "separation." Isolation and separation had indeed been their most distinctive characteristic until—after the food riots of January 1977—the government forced a confrontation upon them.[26] Five members of the group, among them their leader Shukrī Muṣṭafā, were executed in March 1978.

In all three published printed versions of the *Farīḍah* these paragraphs on separation and emigration contain misprints, but allusions to the fate of the group of Shukrī Muṣṭafā are unmistakable. The conclusion, moreover, is clear: "All this nonsense (about going out to the desert and confronting the tyranny of the state) only results from having renounced the right way to establish an Islamic state. What is the only true method to do this? God told it clearly: 'Fighting is prescribed for you,' and 'Fight them until there is no dissension, and religion becomes God's . . .'" (Qur'ān

2.216 and 2.193). The hijrah strategy, so the *Farīḍah* notes (§62), is not effective, no matter how much space the Egyptian desert has to offer.

Dr. Muḥammad Ḥusayn Al-Dhahabī, the most prominent victim of the violence of Shukrī Muṣṭafā's hijrah group, was an Azhar scholar. He embodied the traditions of polite cooperation and collaboration with those in power that is characteristic for this venerable center of Islamic Higher Learning. The paragraphs of the *Farīḍah* that now follow may be more generally applicable, but both their content and their place in the line of the *Farīḍah*'s argument indicate that it is al-Azhar that the *Farīḍah* is now talking about.

The author of the *Farīḍah* opens the discussion again by stating the view of his opponents: "Some say that the quest for knowledge, *ṭalab al-ᶜilm*, is the way. How can we fight when we have no knowledge? The quest for knowledge is a religious obligation too" (§63). To this the *Farīḍah* objects that, while being occupied with the quest for knowledge, a Muslim should not omit to pray and fast— or be lax in his other religious duties, of which *jihād* is one. *Jihād*, we are once more assured, is armed struggle, and armed struggle only.

Some clever scholastics, so the *Farīḍah* tells us (§63), have tried to interpret the Arabic term *jihād*, "struggle," as "struggle to obtain knowledge." Here, however, the *Farīḍah* points to the verse from the Qur'ān, "Prescribed for you is fighting," which has been quoted previously, and which the author of the *Farīḍah* holds to be decisive for the proper understanding of *jihād*. To this verse from the Qur'ān is added the Tradition of a man who converted to Islam in the presence of the Prophet, went out to battle, and got killed without ever having carried out one of the more peaceful duties of Islam. His works were few, but his reward is great, the Prophet is reported to have said on this occasion. In a way that is almost a parody of a formalistic Azhar argument, the *Farīḍah* now tells us (§64) that whoever is taught how to pray should from then on pray. Whoever is taught how to fast should from then on fast. The conclusion is obvious: whoever is taught how to fight should from then on—fight.

Al-Azhar scholars in the days of Napoleon managed to prove

from the scriptures that attempts at resisting the French army, which wanted to occupy Egypt, were wrong and against God's will. The irreverent joy with which some orientalists tell this story can of course not be shared by the author of the *Farīḍah*. He bitterly remarks that the al-Azhar scholars did not have much profit from their knowledge and scholarship when the French army entered Egypt (§64). Also, he tells, the generals of the first Muslim armies that conquered the world "from Spain to India" seem not to have been great scholars. All this demonstrates that scholarship is not the decisive weapon in the struggle against the unbelievers. Does not the Qur'ān itself say, "Fight them and God will punish them at your hands . . . God will make you victorious over them. . . ." (Qur'ān 9.14)? This can only mean, so we should understand, that violence, not scholarship, can bring about the ultimate victory of Islam over the unbelievers. The author of the *Farīḍah* continues (§64) by assuring the scholars among his readers that he does not despise scholarship or scholars. He only wants to urge scholars not to be lax in the fulfillment of the duties that God has imposed, of which *jihād* is one.

Before entering upon the next subject, the author of the *Farīḍah* feels that he has to make a small digression on the interpretation of the verse from the Qur'ān that was quoted in the previous paragraph. After the assassination of President Sadat many observers have noted that—although it is extremely difficult to be certain about such sensitive matters—it looked as if the murderers had not made any arrangement about the things that had to be done after the assassination. Some concluded that this could be explained as a sign of their great faith in God who would take care of events after the assassination. Others thought that it pointed not only to a basic misunderstanding of how a coup d'état has to be carried out but also to a lack of practical insight into the nature of modern society. However this may be, the *Farīḍah* (§65) now connects this lack of preparation for the future after a possible successful assassination with the verse from the Qur'ān quoted before: "Fight them and God will punish them *at your hands. God* will make you victorious." The *wortlaut* of this verse is adduced by the author of the *Farīḍah* to convince his combatants that such (human) preparations are unnecessary, since God himself will take care of everything once the Muslims have taken the initiative to obey his command to *jihād* and have opened fire on the unbelievers. In previous ages, so we read, God repeatedly changed the laws of nature in order to punish unbelievers (here we have to think of the destruction of Sodom and Gomorrah and similar Qur'anic stories) — and he will do the same for Muslims going to battle for Islam today.

The vague feeling that the terrorists who killed President Sadat had not worked out a detailed plan for further supplementary action hence seems to be accurate. It can be demonstrated from their own testimony as written down in the *Farīḍah* that they did not think such preparations to be necessary. The text of the *Farīḍah* establishes beyond any reasonable doubt that the assassins of President Sadat were obsessed by their passion for the foundation of an Islamic state, *iqāmat dawlah islāmīyah*. The publication of the text of the *Farīḍah* no doubt became possible partly because the text of the *Farīḍah* itself constituted a clear proof that the assassins had failed in this one great ambition of theirs. Yet, at the same time, both superficial observation by outsiders, as well as the published text of the *Farīḍah*, make it plausible that no specific plan of action existed. It is difficult to explain this contradiction.

The examination by the *Farīḍah* of the questions pertaining to the relationship between *jihād* ("struggle") and *ᶜilm* ("knowledge") is in reality, as has been shown, an attempt to convince Azhar-trained Muslims of the justice of the cause of the activists who want to go to arms to do battle for the cause of Islam. The Azhar establishment has, at all levels, always been rather loyal to whatever régime ruled Egypt. Some have even used the word sycophancy to describe the attitude of the average Azhar scholar toward his government. This traditional loyalty necessitates the examination of the question: under which specific circumstances does Islam justify — or even prescribe — revolt against the powers that be, *al-khurūj ᶜalā al-ḥākim* (§66)? The course of the argument of the *Farīḍah* compels its author to address this concern before he comes to the end of the paragraphs that he devotes to the Azharīs. The customary introduction ("There are some who say . . .") does not precede the discussion of this theme, since it is not a new group of people that is being addressed. The author has continued his dialogue with the Azharīs.

The author of the *Farīḍah* now attempts (§§66–67) to convince Azhar-trained readers and others, with learned quotations from the volumes of Prophetic Traditions and from the commentaries on these volumes, that Muslim scholars agree that the duties of leadership cannot be executed by an unbeliever *(kāfir)*. More important, this consensus is also said to imply specifically that, when a leader suddenly becomes an unbeliever *(ṭara'a ᶜalayhi al-kufr)*, his leadership has come to an end, even if this leader publicly presents himself as a Muslim. With some delicacy the *Farīḍah* makes it clear that the failure of a leader to perform the prescribed five daily prayer ceremonies, or to call upon others to perform these prayers, also qualifies him as an unbeliever. Few pious Muslim readers will have to think long about how to qualify a leader who drinks a glass of champagne in public, and the *Farīḍah* does not even mention such unthinkable horrors. Again, great authorities are quoted, such as Muslim (d. 875), Al-Nawawī (d. 1227) and, of course, Ibn Taymīyah in his polemics against King Ghāzān, who was nominally a Muslim, and his Mongol armies.

The discussion is closed with a practical consideration that is of relevance to the examination of the leadership problem. Some have objected, so the *Farīḍah* discloses, that it is not permitted to fight without a caliph or a commander having authority over the army, *lā yajūz al-qitāl illā taḥt khalīfah aw amīr*. The author of the *Farīḍah* thinks that this objection is answered by the contents of Muslim's chapter on *jihād* in his canonical collection of Prophetic Traditions. Already, however, the Arabic words in which this objection has been phrased indicate that it is not a theological but a practical military consideration. It has no doubt been brought to the attention of the group of the *Farīḍah* that without proper military organization they were not likely to receive in this world any reward for their *jihād*. The very words *taḥt khalīfah aw amīr* seems to point to a milieu of origin for this Arabic phrase that is Westernized, at least as far as its language is concerned; in a more classical Arabic, "under the command of" would have been expressed by *taḥt amr fulān*, and not by the simple preposition *taḥt*. However, it is also arguable that such an excuse for not joining the *jihād* movement of the *Farīḍah* is brought forward not only by Westernized military men, but also by Muslims who in principle agree with the theories of the *Farīḍah* but who have no personal inclination to accept the consequences of this insight as long as such *Farīḍah*-like movements have no obvious charismatic or authoritative leader. If such groups do exist and are large, it is difficult to predict the future of Egypt.

Another practical objection with which the activists of the *Farīḍah* were confronted concerns the existence of the State of Israel. It seems that it had been argued in discussions within the activist movement that the first goal of *jihād* should be the liberation of Jerusalem and the Holy Land (§68). The *Farīḍah*, however, answers this objection against its own views with three counter-arguments: one, it is more important to fight an enemy who is near than an enemy who is far away. Two, such a liberation of Jerusalem would necessitate the sacrifice of Muslim blood for the sake of a non-Muslim state (§69). Islam, however, is not served by the territorial extension of a non-Muslim state, so the *Farīḍah* makes clear. Three, the existence of these imperialist centers within the world of Islam *(fī bilād al-islām)* is due to the very leaders the *Farīḍah* wants to see removed. To fight imperialism, so we read in the *Farīḍah* (§70), is a useless waste of time: "We must concentrate on the real problem of Islam, the establishment of God's law, beginning in our own country, *iqāmat sharᶜ Allāh awwalan fī baladnā*."[27]

The *Farīḍah* shares, of course, the Arab view that the present non-Muslim, non-Arab occupation of Jerusalem is an anachronistic manifestation of nineteenth-century "imperialism" and "colonialism."[28] It is interesting to notice that the author of the *Farīḍah* thinks that Jerusalem will automatically be reconquered once Islam is fully implemented in the lands of Islam. This belief can only have evolved from the underlying assumption that the current international military weakness of the Muslims is due to their disobedience to God's laws. It must be remembered that a certain Wā'il ᶜUthmān in 1975 expressed this idea in one of his books (to which Shaykh Al-Shaᶜrāwī wrote the preface) and was sent to prison for it. The similarity between the thoughts expressed in the *Farīḍah* and opinions like those written down by Wā'il ᶜUthmān (and endorsed by Shaykh Al-Shaᶜrāwī) is indeed striking.[29]

The next step that the *Farīḍah* takes is the consideration of a well-known argument often brought forward by apologists for

Islam: *jihād* should always be a Holy War in defense of Islam (§71). The same apologists then continue their argument (necessarily so) by saying that Islam did not spread by the sword. The *Farīḍah* wants to set this right since, according to its author, this is nothing but a misunderstanding. In the discussion of this intricate point, the *Farīḍah* accuses the governments in the Islamic world of having manipulated theologians and historians in order to keep this misunderstanding alive but "it is now the duty of the Muslims to lift their swords under the very eyes of these rulers, who hide the truth and bring nonsense into the open." The author of the *Farīḍah* alleges to find support for his views on this matter in the contents of the letters that Tradition reports the Prophet to have sent to the rulers of Egypt, Persia, and Constantinople, as well as in "similar letters" (§§72–75). Even if these letters may not convince everyone, few will have difficulty in understanding the verses from the Qur'ān that the *Farīḍah* now quotes (§§76–81):

> *Slay the polytheists wherever ye find them,*
> *seize them, beset them, lie in ambush for them everywhere.* (9.5)

and as well the following fragment:

> *So when ye meet those who have disbelieved,*
> *let there be slaughter.* (47.4)

If these verses are not abrogated by other verses from the Qur'ān then they have binding force; hence, a long technical discussion has to follow on the question of whether these verses are abrogated themselves, or abrogate each another, or do themselves abrogate other verses (§§77–81). The conclusion that these verses support the views of the *Farīḍah* on *jihād* is not surprising.

There are, however, more questions of a practical nature that have to be examined. In the glorious days of the early Muslim conquests, the Muslim armies were usually numerically smaller than the non-Muslim armies they defeated (§82). Were such victories the special prerogative *(khuṣūṣīyah)* of the Prophet and his companions in their sacred age, or can Muslims today count on the same miraculous successes, against all numerical odds? Some have argued that they cannot. The *Farīḍah*'s answer to this argument is of a tragic simplicity. Has God not promised victory as long as the heavens and the earth remain? Hence, Muslims may expect, with confidence and faith, to be victorious over the infidels, no matter how strong and numerous the latter are.

Another excuse for not joining the ranks of the activists comes from people who do not disagree in principle when the pious allege that the Egyptian State is an infidel and evil institution. These people, however, argue that Egypt is to be compared to Mecca in the days when the Prophet lived there, before 622 AD (§83). Such an equation of modern Egypt with ancient pre-Islamic Mecca entails some form of peaceful coexistence (and certainly the absence of open warfare) between the government and the "real" Muslims. In this context it should be remembered that both Sayyid Quṭb and the Muslims in the Soviet Union characterize their own governments as *jāhilī,* which in this context can be best translated as "pre-Islamic."

The *Farīḍah,* however, does not accept such objections. It answers (§62) by pointing out that in Mecca before 622, the year the Prophet moved out to Medina, the prayer ceremonies, *Ramaḍān,* the month of fasting, and the prohibition of usury were not part of the system of life of Muḥammad's followers. Yet it is unthinkable that a modern Muslim would not heed these three duties, even though they were not recognized as Islamic duties at that early period in which Muḥammad had started to persuade his fellow Meccans of the truth of his mission. In the same way, *jihād,* armed struggle against the infidels, has nowadays to be regarded as an essential duty of Islam, so the *Farīḍah* maintains, even if this were not so before the *Hijrah* of Muḥammad from Mecca to Medina.

The Meccan situation leads the author back to the claim of some Muslims that *daᶜwah,* missionary activity, is a form of *jihād,* and that hence whosoever is active in trying to persuade his fellow-citizens with peaceful means also fulfills his duty of *jihād* (§84). Again, it is the text of the Qur'ān which is thought to decide the matter: *kutiba ᶜalaykum al-qitāl,* "prescribed for you is fighting," can be read in Qur'ān 2.216, as was pointed out before.

It is well known that Islamic Law makes a distinction between individual and collective duties. The organization of the communal prayer Friday at noon is a good example of a collective duty. In the handbooks of Islamic Law the duty of *jihād* is usually classified as a collective duty. Yet the *Farīḍah* wants to examine whether this really is the case. Its conclusion is that there are three cases in which *jihād* is an individual (and not a collective) duty. One, when a military confrontation is forced upon a Muslim army, in accordance with Qur'ān 8.15, "When ye meet those who have disbelieved moving into battle, turn them not your backs." Two, when the infidels attack a country, its (civilian) inhabitants have individually the duty to fight. Three, when a religious leader *(imām)* calls upon people to fight, it is also their individual duty to obey him, as the Qur'ān prescribes in 9.38–39: "O ye who have believed, what is the matter with you? . . . If ye do not march out He will inflict upon you a painful punishment."

Looking at the Islamic world and considering these three points, the *Farīḍah* concludes (§§84–87) that the enemy is right among the Muslims, even rules them, so *jihād* is an individual duty for all Muslims, "and above all this, *al-jihād al-islāmī,* the fight for Islam, needs a drop of sweat from every Muslim." Here the author of the *Farīḍah* underestimates things that were to come. Not only sweat, but also blood has been spilled abundantly.

The question of whether *jihād* is an individual or a collective duty has tragic overtones. An individual action against an overwhelming majority often is nothing but a suicide mission. There is, however, a practical implication. If *jihād* is classified as an individual duty, together with praying and fasting, young individuals who consider converting to Islamic zealotry do not need to ask the permission of their parents, *isti'dhān al-wālidayn,* when they want to join an activist cell, as the *Farīḍah* does not hesitate to point out (§87). In a society where the parental authority is so decisive a factor as in Egypt, this consideration is of the greatest importance. It must not be left unsaid that the problem of parental authority has also been recognized by other religions, and has sometimes been solved in the same way. For instance, in the New Testament we read: "I came not to send peace but a sword . . . a man's foes shall be they of his own household . . . he that loveth his father or his mother more than me is not worthy of me" (Mt 11:34–39).

After the digression to parental permission, the *Farīḍah* comes back to those who want to interpret the term *jihād* in such a way as to make it meaningless in the eyes of the author of the *Farīḍah.*

Some people, the *Farīḍah* tells us (§§88–90), have based themselves on an analysis of *jihād* by Ibn al-Qayyim, in which *jihād* is divided into three types: *jihād* against (1) the soul, (2) the Devil, and (3) the infidels. These three forms are *marātib,* "aspects" of *jihād,* so the *Farīḍah* insists, and not *marāḥil,* "successive phases," as some seem to have argued. The author of the *Farīḍah* then asks: "Should we refrain from *jihād* against the Devil (the second phase) as long as we are occupied with *jihād* against the wickedness of our own souls (the first phase)?" Of course we should not . . .

Some people, so we must conclude from this part of the *Farīḍah,* think of themselves first of all as soldiers against their own wickedness, or as soldiers against the Devil, rather than as soldiers against their own governments. For this they have claimed the support of Ibn al-Qayyim, and they refuse to fight for Islam in the way that the *Farīḍah* proposes. The *Farīḍah,* however, insists that these people misunderstand Islam. To demonstrate this, the *Farīḍah* adduces the example of recent converts to Islam, and of people who committed grave sins. Such quasi-Muslims joined, in the days of the Prophet, the battles called *jihād.* It is well known, however, that recent converts enjoy certain dispensations as far as their Islamic duties are concerned, and that it is also a point of debate as to whether people who committed grave sins can really be regarded as Muslims. The fact that even such people took part in *jihād* makes it all the clearer how a true Muslim should behave today.

There is, moreover, another way in which people have attacked the understanding of *jihād* as proposed by the *Farīḍah.* A Tradition reports the Prophet to have said, on his return from the battlefield: "We have come home from the small *jihād* to the great *jihād.*" This Tradition, so the *Farīḍah* teaches (§90), is a fabrication, put into circulation in order to belittle the importance of armed battle for the cause of Islam and to distract the Muslims from fighting against infidels and hypocrites. The casual way in which the *Farīḍah* stamps a Tradition as a fabrication is justified again by a reference to Ibn al-Qayyim. This scholar, too, as we are told, regarded this Tradition as untrustworthy.

Some say, so the *Farīḍah* continues in its argument (§91), that we are afraid to establish the Islamic State, because "after a day or two a reaction *(radd fiᶜl muḍādd)* might occur that puts an end to all we have accomplished." The use of the first person plural ("*we* are afraid, *we* have accomplished") again reminds the reader that the discussions described here are not an intellectual exercise, but that the *Farīḍah* is the result of internal debates that actually took place within the activist movement.

The answer to this objection is simple, almost evasive (§91). The establishment of an Islamic State is the execution of a command that God explicitly gave "and we are not answerable for the results, *muṭālabūn bi-'l-natā'ij*." The author of the *Farīḍah* probably wants his readers to supplement the consideration that God is responsible and will take care, a consideration that is so obvious to him that he does not see the need to write it down. It must not be forgotten, so he emphasizes, that once the government has been removed everything will be in the hands of the Muslims, and all will be justice, if only because Islamic Law is capable of taking care of those who cause corruption, *al-mufsidūn fi-'l-arḍ*. It may be perfectly rational to fear failure after a successful coup d'état, yet the author of the *Farīḍah* has nothing but harsh words for timorous Muslims who hesitate to revolt. They are compared to the "hypocrites" who occur in Qur'ān 59.11 and are said to end up in the Fire, abiding therein (Qur'ān 59.17).

Once more the author of the *Farīḍah* goes back to a theme that he discussed previously. For a second time he wants to consider the question of whether or not the lack of a proper leader makes *jihād* impossible "since some make *jihād* dependent on the presence of a commander, *amīr aw khalīfah*" (§92). This time, however, the aim of the discussion is not only to answer practical objections made against the proposals for action which the *Farīḍah* spells out, but also to examine the question of who has to be the leader of the Muslim community, and to what conditions such a leader has to conform.

It is noteworthy that in the discussion of these conditions no mention is made of the descent of the leader. The question as to whether he should be from the Prophet's tribe Quraysh, or from the Prophet's family, or a lineal descendant from the Prophet's two grandsons Ḥasan or Ḥusayn, is not considered at all. It is obvious that such considerations are not relevant to the author of the *Farīḍah* and his combatants.

Commencing the discussion, the *Farīḍah* quotes (§92) the

well-known Tradition that reports the Prophet to have said: "When three go out, make one of them *amīr,* leader." It continues by explaining that the command should always go to the best Muslim, *al-aḥsan islāman,* and the strongest *(al-aqwā)* man available, which is a relative matter *(nasabī)* (§93). This relativity entails, so the *Farīḍah* concludes, that there always must be one who is best suited. Hence the lack of a leader is no valid argument since people should simply appoint the best suited from among themselves as their leader. Sometimes, the *Farīḍah* philosophically reflects, we find a leader who knows all about Muslim law but nothing of the ways of this modern world, of command and organization, and sometimes the opposite is the case — but no matter how this all may be, we are under the obligation to appoint the best man as our leader, and to throw upon his shoulders the two great duties of Islam: *jihād,* in order to bring back Islam to this nation, and the establishment of an Islamic State. The paragraph is concluded with violent remarks about the extermination of the pagan idols that after all are only human (§94). With these words the text of the *Farīḍah* comes perhaps to its most direct reference to the late President Sadat and the personality cult that surrounded him, especially in the last months of his life.

Having settled that there will always be a leader available since in a given group one of its members is always the best one, the *Farīḍah* now wants to examine the nature of the relationship between the leader and his followers (§§95–97). Tradition reports how in the days of the Prophet the promise to obey until death was given, also to those other than the Prophet himself. Hence, such a *bayᶜah ᶜalā-'l-mawt* is allowed, the author of the *Farīḍah* concludes. Also the famous verse from the Qur'ān, "Obey God, and His Messenger, and those of you who have the command," (4.59) came down in a situation that directly concerned *jihād,* so the *Farīḍah* tells us (§97), quoting Ibn ᶜAbbās in support of this view. The phrasing of the text of the *Farīḍah* again makes it obvious that potential supporters of the group had difficulty, at the least, in allowing themselves to be convinced of the necessity of promising to obey the leader of the group until death. The text as a whole leaves a vague impression that potential supporters had several times not been convinced of the necessity of such an oath, had even been frightened away by the demand for such an oath, in spite of a substantial sympathy for the aims and the ideology of the group. If these impressions are correct, the support for opinions like those expressed in the *Farīḍah* could be wider and larger than outsiders now suspect.

It is widely known that the rewards for participation in *jihād* are great. The *Farīḍah,* too, makes it clear that heaven awaits those who fall while performing their duty of *jihād.* Texts from the Prophetic Tradition demonstrate this abundantly (§§98–99). It has to be admitted that eternal bliss in paradise is a powerful incentive (*tahrīḍ* is the word that the *Farīḍah* uses) to people who can have only few rational expectations of bliss in this world. The results of the neglect of this duty are equally momentous. They affect the personal felicity of individuals. Moreover, so the *Farīḍah* maintains, the international "low position," *dhull,* of the Muslims in this world is also a direct consequence of their laxity in performing this essential duty of *jihād* (§§100–102).

Another objection that appears to have been raised in discussions with the zealots of the *Farīḍah* concerns the killing of fellow Muslims which may result from carrying out the duty of *jihād.* Is it allowed to fight an army that consists partially of Muslims, and call such a fight *jihād?* This is the question with which the *Farīḍah* reports to have been confronted. The answer can, of course, be easily reproduced from Ibn Taymīyah's writings (§§103–105). Ibn Taymīyah's examination of this problem, prompted by the mixed armies of Ghāzān that invaded Syria around 1300 AD, supplies the twentieth-century answer. The *Farīḍah,* following the footsteps of Ibn Taymīyah, considers such killings allowed. This, needless to say, ends the discussion.

A question that must have been discussed extensively, although not with the uninitiated, concerns the methods of warfare to be considered legitimate. Time has progressed, we read in the *Farīḍah* (§106), and man has developed. Modern ways of warfare differ considerably from the ways followed in the days of the Prophet. What ways of warfare may Muslims use, and are they free to use their own judgment in this respect, or do they have to follow the Prophet's example? "Or are they free to act according to their own opinions and insight?"

War is deceit, so the *Farīḍah* explains (§§107–109). All Muslim scholars, so the text continues, agree that in a war with non-Muslims deceit *(khidā*ᶜ*)* is allowed except when a treaty *(*ᶜ*ahd)* has been concluded with those non-Muslims. "It is, however, known that there is no treaty between us and them," the *Farīḍah* concludes, the "them" referring to the Egyptian government. "Since they fight God's religion *(dīn Allāh)* Muslims are free to fight back any way they want." The exact tactics to be used are not revealed in the Qur'ān, or prescribed by the Prophet's example, *laysa waḥyan wa-lā sunnah,* so the *Farīḍah* teaches.

The text of the *Farīḍah* now continues by assuring the reader that it is perfectly legal to lie to the enemies of Islam (§109). Without its context such a remark may of course be used in anti-fundamentalist propaganda. In its context it is, however, not an odd remark. The "enemies of Islam" whom the author of the *Farīḍah* has in mind here are the employees of those official and semiofficial agencies that collect information on activities considered to endanger the security of the state. Only few moralists would seriously maintain that lying to, for instance, Gestapo agents is a sin.

After the short digression on lying as a tactic in the fight for true Islam, the author of the *Farīḍah* now presents (§§110–117) three anecdotes on Islamic tactics in war as employed in the days of the Prophet: the story of the murder of Kaᶜb ibn al-Ashraf, the story of a certain ᶜAbdallāh ibn Unays al-Jihnī and Abū Sufyān, and the story of Nuᶜaym ibn Masᶜūd. The author of the *Farīḍah* does, in passing, mention that orientalists and people who have sickness in their heart (§113) regard the murder (by Muslims) of Kaᶜb ibn al-Ashraf as perfidy *(ghadr).* These people are wrong, so the author of the *Farīḍah* assures the readers, because Kaᶜb wanted to harm Islam and the Muslims.

The question of which tactics are allowed to a Muslim who goes out to battle for Islam caused the author of the *Farīḍah* to discuss the permissiblity *(jawāz)* of lying for the cause of Islam. According to the *Farīḍah,* there are six more points of which the permissibility has to be discussed at this point in the argument (§§118–126). They all concern the ethics of war. Except in the case of the fifth point, the paragraphs in which these questions of permissibility are discussed are headed by the word *jawāz*. When the word *jawāz* does not occur in the paragraph's heading, it figures prominently in the text.

The first of these six points is whether it is permitted to a Muslim to serve in a non-Muslim army (§118). The relevance of the question is obvious: some of the murderers of Sadat were officers in the Egyptian army, and, if the militant activists would not allow military converts to their cause to remain in the army, the recruitment of an army officer into one of their cells would be a liability instead of a success. Moreover, as the assassination of Sadat has shown, militant activists who serve in the army may be indispensable when actions are being planned and carried out. It is, then, not surprising that we receive a positive answer: a Muslim may serve in an army of infidels even if this should lead to his death and even if he himself cannot see the benefit of his penetration into the infidel army — so the *Farīḍah* decides, and this on Ibn Taymīyah's authority. It is easy to imagine how army activists were in need of such a pastoral advice. Many of them must at times have wondered whether they should remain where they are, wait for things to come, and hope for the best. If this impression is right, there may be more potentially militant activists in the Egyptian army than anyone suspects. The text of the *Farīḍah,* on the other hand, also suggests that such military activists feel isolated, frustrated, and ineffective.

The second point of military ethics (§119) concerns the question whether Muslims may attack the infidels without warning. Again the relevance of the question is not difficult to see. If guerillas or terrorists had to warn their victims, their way of warfare would be impossible. On the authority of a discussion of this question by Al-Nawawī in his commentary on Muslim, the author of the *Farīḍah* decides that to give such a warning is (only) recommendable, *mustaḥabb.*

This means that he who omits this warning, for example, in the heat of the attack, will not be punished for this omission. It also means that this warning is *not* obligatory. The total secrecy with which the preparations for successful acts of terrorism have to be surrounded receives in this way its legitimization.

The third point of which the permissibility has to be analyzed

(§121) concerns the questions that arise when children or other innocent bystanders are killed during terrorist attacks. The author of the *Farīḍah* solves the problem by referring to a Tradition in which the Prophet is reported to have been consulted about the fate of children of polytheists, who were put to the sword by the Muslims. Was it right to kill these children? The Prophet is reported to have answered that since these children were their fathers' children they were (as far as inheritance, marriage, retaliation, etc. were concerned) subject to the same rules as their fathers. This meant that their extermination was allowed, but it should not be done on purpose without absolute need for it. (Historians of Islam know, of course, that this problem also played its role in the internal discussions of the Khārijī's of early Islam.[30])

Al-Nawawī's commentary on Muslim's collection of Traditions is quoted extensively in the paragraph devoted to this discussion. Yet it does not become clear to the reader that Al-Nawawī's text is more balanced than the excerpt the *Farīḍah* presents. Moreover, the printed versions of this paragraph of the *Farīḍah* contain several mistakes. It seems that the author of the *Farīḍah* wanted to clarify certain Arabic words that were used in the text of the Traditions he quoted. In order to do this, he added (between brackets) explanations of these words in more contemporary Arabic; for example, *tabyīt* is explained by *al-ighārah laylan,* "to attack by night." In two printed versions of the *Farīḍah* this explanatory addition has been added to the text as if it were an integral part of it.[31] The text as it must have looked in the author's own copy may, however, easily be reconstructed by comparing its present printed versions with pages 49 and 50, volume 12, of Al-Nawawī's commentary on Muslim's *Kitāb al-Jihād.*[32]

The fourth point of military ethics that has to be discussed (§122) is whether the killing of women is allowed. The heading of the paragraph mentions not only women, but also monks and old men. However, in the Traditions which the *Farīḍah* quotes from Muslim's commentary only the killing of women is discussed. It is well known that when President Sadat was assassinated, one monk was also accidentally killed: Bishop Samuel, the Coptic Orthodox (i.e., monophysite) Bishop of Cairo. It is improbable that the author of the *Farīḍah* had Bishop Samuel's death in mind when he wrote these lines, because, if he had, this would imply that he wrote the *Farīḍah* after the assassination of Sadat, whereas everything indicates that he gave the *Farīḍah* its final form before the assassination. The "monks and old men" in the heading of this paragraph must hence have been taken mechanically from the text of Al-Nawawī's commentary.

The Prophet, so the *Farīḍah* explains, is reported not to have condoned the killing of women. According to the *Farīḍah* this is not in contradiction with the previous Tradition about his having permitted—at least under certain circumstances—the killing of children, since "the situations described in these two Traditions are not the same," *li-kull minhumā ḥālah takhtalif ʿani-'l-ukhrā.*

The fifth point of military tactical importance (§123) is the question whether Muslim combatants may ask non-Muslims for help in their struggle. The author of the *Farīḍah* gives a positive answer to this question, and finds support for his position in the writings of Al-Shāfiʿī and Al-Nawawī.

The sixth and last question of military ethics (§126) is connected with Qur'ān 59.5, "The fine palms which ye cut down or left standing on their roots—it was by permission of God, and that he might humiliate the reprobate." This verse, and the context in which it is quoted in Al-Nawawī's commentary on Muslim, both serve to justify a policy of total and ruthless destruction of all property of the enemy.

The way of behavior that the *Farīḍah* proposes for a Muslim army does not differ in any important way from the behavior to be expected from a non-Muslim army that is determined to win the war. The importance of these paragraphs is, however, found in the ease with which the *Farīḍah* connects these military considerations with Islamic Traditional scholarship. In contemporary Western eyes the theories of the *Farīḍah* seem a little inconsistent when the author talks of the treatment of women and children, but in the eyes of the author of the *Farīḍah* this is probably a small price to pay for having Islamicized his military thinking.

Rules of personal behavior for the soldiers in the Muslim army have not yet been given, and this is the topic the author of the *Farīḍah* now has to turn to (§§127–129). May Muslim soldiers allow themselves to be taken prisoner or should they fight until death? Examples from the Tradition literature are quoted and, according to the *Farīḍah*, the examples of the companions of the Prophet demonstrate that death is preferable. The text now goes into details of military behavior such as, "Should a Muslim soldier shout when he attacks?" ("No, the Prophet's companions disliked shouting") and, "What day of the week is best suited to start a military expedition?" ("The Prophet went out to the battle of Tabūk on a Thursday").

Admonitions to be sincerely devoted to true *jihād* follow (§130). If one goes to battle for material gains, or in order to be praised for his courage, this must not be seen as true *jihād*, so we read. True *jihād* can have only one aim: *li-takūn kalimat Allāh hiya al-ᶜulyā*, "that the word of God be supreme." This, again, is illustrated by material from the Tradition (§§130–133). Those who refuse to go out in order to fulfill their duty of *jihād* are reproached violently: rebukes uttered by Sayyid Quṭb are repeated to them, in particular a passage from his *Fī Ẓilāl al-Qur'ān* where Sayyid Quṭb exclaims that such people prefer "cheap comfort" *(rāḥah rakhīṣah)* over "noble toil," and "base safety" *(salāmah dhalīlah)* over "sweet danger" *(khaṭar ᶜazīz)* (§135).

Before the author of the *Farīḍah* concludes his essay, he touches upon two problems. The first problem he calls *tanqiyat al-ṣaff*, the cleansing of the ranks (§136). Quotations from Al-Shāfiᶜī and Ibn Qudāmah are followed by Qur'ān 9.46–47, which says about unwilling warriors: "If they intended to go forth they would make some preparation for it. . . . If they were to go forth with you, they would add to you nothing but unsoundness." Unsound soldiers, so we must understand, are better left at home.

The second problem he calls *ghurūr al-faqīh yamnaᶜ ta'mīrahu*, the vanity of a man of religion makes it impossible to give him the command (§140). Not only the soldiers for Islam but also their leaders and commanders must be a carefully selected élite, so we have to understand. Some men of religion, so the *Farīḍah* observes, are prevented from being chosen as commanders in the struggle for Islam because they are vain, they love to be admired, and hence they may harm not only themselves but also the cause. An illustration from the Tradition is given, taken this time from Ibn Ḥajar al-ᶜAsqalānī's *Tahdhīb al-Tahdhīb*.[33] At this point (§141) the printed versions of the *Farīḍah* again contain a large number of misprints which make the text unintelligible but which can all be corrected from volume 12, page 158 of Ibn Ḥajar's *Tahdhīb.* The story told here concerns a certain Abū ᶜUbayd, a man so pious that even the devout Caliph ᶜUmar II did not want to employ him or give him a command. This Abū ᶜUbayd is, however, called *ubbahat al-ᶜāmmah,* the pride of the masses. When the author of the *Farīḍah* read such a phrase in the *Tahdhīb* he was no doubt reminded of those Egyptian preachers today who may be the pride of the masses but who do not join armed battle against the Egyptian government, like Shaykh ᶜAbd al-Ḥamīd Kishk and others. When the *Farīḍah* quotes this passage about the "pride of the masses" from the *Tahdhīb,* this quotation no doubt must also remind the contemporary Egyptian reader of Shaykh Kishk and his likes.

The final lines of the *Farīḍah* (§§142–143) speak directly to the leaders of the Islamic organizations, *qādat al-jamāᶜāt.* These are told that they should strive to obtain immaculate reputations like the reputation of the abovementioned Abū ᶜUbayd. Yet, at the same time, they are asked to understand that they are not on the right path as long as they do not prepare for true *jihād.* The printed versions of the text of the final lines of the *Farīḍah* are, however, not entirely clear.

If the *Farīḍah* gives a reliable picture of the thinking of Sadat's murderers, it is probable that the real aim of the assassination was to establish an Islamic State in Egypt. The spectators' impression at that time, that there was no plan for further action once the assassination attempt had succeeded, seems to have been right. The assassins may have expected large and spontaneous popular action to follow their removal of the man whom they regarded as the "tyrant," the *ḥākim ẓālim,* the Unjust Ruler. In their own words: once they had punished Sadat for his alleged apostasy from Islam, God would do the rest.

The text of the *Farīḍah* shows how the armed activists thought of themselves as a real army at war with Egypt. Their ideology has considerable consistency and invokes the traditions of Islam to justify their every tenet. It is difficult, if not impossible, to determine how much support the *Farīḍah* ideology enjoys in Egypt today.

NOTES

1. These interviews from November 1981 were collected in ṢALĀḤ MUNTAṢIR, *Ḥiwār ma^ca al-Shaykh Al-Sha^crāwī ^cani-'l-Ḥukm wa-'1-^cAdl wa-'1-shabāb,* Cairo (Dār al-Ma^cārif), 1982, *Kitābuka* series, nr. 142. The quotation given here is found on pp. 51 – 52 of this booklet.
2. It follows that on this point there is a difference of opinion in the interpretation of the *Farīḍah* between the editor of *Al-Aḥrār* and Dr. Muḥammad ^cAmmārah who argues that the *Farīḍah* accuses not the masses but the rulers of apostasy, cf. DR. MUḤAMMAD ^cAMMĀRAH, *Al-Farīdah al-Ghā'ibah, ^cArḍ wa-Ḥiwār wa-Taqyīm,* Cairo, 1982, 72 pp., p. 30. See, however, §23 of the translation of the *Farīḍah.*
3. Cf. EDWARD MORTIMER, *Faith and Power, the Politics of Islam,* London, 1982, p. 253. Studies of the social background of the militant activists have a unique source in the list of indicated members of *jamā^cāt* which was published in the Cairo daily *Al-Jumhūrīyah* on May 9, 1982, cf. GILLES KEPEL, *Le Prophète et Pharaon,* Paris, 1984, pp. 205 – 212.
4. MUḤAMMAD ^cABD AL-SALĀM FARAJ, *Al-Jihād, Al-Farīḍah al-Ghā'ibah,* n.p., n.d. (Ammān, 1982?), 32 pp.
5. E.g., *"y.kh.f.,"* which produces no meaning, Ed. Amman, p. 16; Ed. *Awqāf,* p. 3774, reads *"yakhsif,"* which is no doubt correct. Both Amman and *Al-Aḥrār* read *"t.q.n.h.,"* where the *Tahdhīb* (which is quoted here) reads *"nufattinahu,"* Ed. Amman, p. 31. Ed. *Awqāf,* p. 3792, here reads *"fitnah,"* which is also incorrect.
6. Ed. Amman, p. 24, and Ed. *Al-Aḥrār* both omit half of the paragraph heading which is found in full in Ed. *Awqāf,* p. 3784.
7. E.g., *"Al-Imām Muḥammad"* instead of *"Al-Imām Aḥmad,"* p. 8; or *"awzāṣ"* (p. 31) instead of *"Al-Awzā^cī."*
8. *Al-Fatāwā al-Islāmīyah min Dār al-Iftā' al-Miṣrīyah, yushrif ^calā iṣdārihā (1) Jādd al-Ḥaqq ^cAlī Jādd al-Ḥaqq, (2) Ibrāhīm al-Dasūqī, (3) ^cAbd al-Laṭīf Ḥamzah, (4) Jamāl al-Dīn Muḥammad Maḥmūd, Al-Mujallad al-^cĀshir,* (fascicle) 31. The pages of this fascicle are numbered 3681 – 3792 and 1 – 54 (indexes). On the cover we read: *"Al-Majlis al-A^clā li-'l-shu'ūn al-Islāmīyah, Wizārat al-Awqāf, Jumhūrīyat Miṣr al-^cArabīyah,* Cairo 1983."
9. In 1984 eleven volumes (4159 pp.) of this official *fatwā* collection had appeared.
10. *Al-Fatāwā al-Islāmīyah,* pp. 3762 – 92.

11. Ibid., pp. 3726–61.
12. E.g., in the paragraph headings.
13. Especially in quotations from older sources: e.g., "*bayān,*" instead of "*bayāt,*" and "*ya*ᶜ*tadū*" instead of "*ya*ᶜ*tamidū;*" both Ed. Amman, p. 27; Ed. *Awqāf,* p. 3787.
14. *Al-Fatāwā al-Islāmīyah,* p. 3728.
15. ᶜAMMĀRAH, *Al-Farīḍah al-Gha'ibah,* p. 31.
16. *Al-Fatāwā al-Islāmīyah,* p. 3762: "We preferred to give the text the way it was found in the original, without correction of its mistakes, except in verses from the Qur'ān." In a Qur'ān quotation (Qur'ān 5.48) occurring on p. 8 of Ed. Amman, both the *Al-Aḥrār* and the Amman versions have incorrectly "*mā*"; Ed. *Awqāf* has the correct *man,* p. 3764.
17. ᶜAMMĀRAH, *Al-Farīḍah al-Gha'ibah,* p. 31.
18. Ibid., p. 47.
19. KEPEL, *Le Prophète et Pharaon,* p. 186.
20. Ibid., pp. 184–96.
21. Richard Bell's translation.
22. Both in *Majallat al-Taṣawwuf al-Islāmī* for November 1981 (the first number to appear after the assassination) and in his *fatwā* about the *Farīḍah,* p. 3742, Shaykh Jādd al-Ḥaqq points out that in its context this verse addresses rather Christians and Jews, and that the context makes the militant interpretation impossible.
23. In this context, the word "philosophy" is, of course, used in a pejorative way.
24. The section on Islamic political parties has been omitted from Ed. Amman, cf. its p. 15 with Ed. *Awqāf,* p. 3772. The section does occur in Ed. *Al-Aḥrār,* cf. §52 of the translation.
25. Cf. Chapter 4 and my paper "The Voice of Sheikh Kishk (b. 1933)" in IBR. A. EL-SHAYKH, C.A. VAN DEN KOPPEL, and RUDOLPH PETERS, eds., *The Challenge of the Middle East,* Amsterdam, 1982, pp. 57–66; and KEPEL, *Le Prophète et Pharaon,* pp. 165–69.
26. Cf. MORTIMER, *Faith and Power,* p. 291, and KEPEL, *Le Prophète et Pharaon,* pp. 70–100. The most important source on Shukrī Muṣṭafā and his followers is ᶜABD AL-RAḤMĀN ABŪ AL-KHAYR, *Dhikriyātī ma*ᶜ*a Jamā*ᶜ*at al-Muslimīn "Al-Takfīr wa-'l-Hijrah,"* Kuwayt (Dār al-Buḥūth al-ᶜIlmīyah), 1980, 208 pp.
27. *Balad* instead of *bilād* is either a misprint or a colloquialism.

28. Dr. ᶜAmmārah points out (*Al-Farīḍah al-Gha'ibah,* p. 46) that the Egyptian Free Officers in Palestine in 1948 also were of the opinion that the road to the liberation of Palestine *yamurr ᶜabra taḥrīr al-Qāhirah,* "would pass through the liberation of Cairo."
29. Cf. Chapter 5 and my paper "A Little-Known Endorsement by Skeikh As-Shaᶜrāwī," to be published in the proceedings of the 12th Congress of the *Union Européenne d'Arabisants et Islamisants* (Malaga, September 1984).
30. Cf. W. MONTGOMERY WATT, *The Formative Period of Islamic Thought,* Edinburgh, 1973, p. 33.
31. If the omission of *al-ighārah laylan* in Ed. Amman is not accidental, the relationship between the three printed versions may not be what it now seems to be.
32. *Ṣaḥīḥ Muslim bi-Sharḥ al-Nawawī,* Cairo (Muḥ. Tawfīq, Maṭb. Ḥijāzī), 1349, 18 vols.
33. IBN ḤAJAR AL-ᶜASQALĀNĪ, *Tahdhīb al-Tahdhīb,* Hyderabad, 1325–1327, 12 vols.

CHAPTER 2

The Response from Al-Azhar

ISLAM KNOWS NO CLERGY, but it does know "men of religion," *rijāl al-dīn,* who are not ordained into their ministry but who receive a diploma that legally admits them as professional teachers of the Islamic religion. This arrangement implies that Islam does not know suspension, in the ecclesiastical sense, of ordained functionaries. Nevertheless Islam does know of the possibility that a diploma be taken away from its scholarly incumbent.[1] Hence, in the Islamic system, discussions on the qualifications of a religiously controversial writer or scholar may well be the equivalent of Christian ecclesiastical discussions on the question whether a certain priest or preacher has become (by his words or his actions) a heretic or not.[2] A Muslim scholar, one might say, has not to be ordained but to be certified in order to have the right to expound legally the teachings of Islam. The pinnacle of the educational institutions that grant such certificates is the Egyptian Azhar University in Cairo.

Al-Azhar was founded in the tenth century AD, and during its long history it has, of course, gone through many reforms. The reform of 1961 added to its three faculties (Islamic Law, Dogmatics, and the Arabic Language) several faculties and departments for profane sciences (Medicine, Agriculture, etc.), with the proviso[3] that these new faculties not be duplicates of the existing faculties for the same subjects in the other Egyptian universities, but that these new Azhar faculties establish a link between religion and life, *"yūṣil bayn al-dīn wa-'l-ḥayāh."* The additions to al-Azhar that were created by the 1961 reform did, however, not result in a change in al-Azhar's traditional role as the final Islamic scholarly religious authority and beacon.

Graduates from the three traditional Azhar faculties have customarily found employment as *imām* or preacher *(wāᶜiẓ)* in the mosques, and as "spiritual advisers *(murshidīn)* for the masses and in the armed forces." Al-Azhar graduates also have been active as teachers of religion and of the Arabic language, both in public schools and in religious institutes. A group of them has been occupied, in all the relevant functions, in the Sharīᶜah courts as long as these have existed, and in the domain of family law in general, for example, as notaries *(ma'dhūn sharᶜī)* responsible for the registration of marriage and divorce. Many prominent Egyptians were deeply influenced by their Azhar training: not only theologians like Muḥammad ᶜAbduh, but also politicians like Saᶜd Zaghlūl[4] or writers like Ṭaha Ḥusayn.

The prestige that surrounds Azhar graduates is reflected not only by the fact that non-Egyptian Muslims from all over the world study at al-Azhar University, but also by the welcome given in Muslim circles (in the Arab world in general, in Sub-Saharan Africa, and in the Far East) to Azhar graduates, both Egyptians and others. Al-Azhar University is definitely the top of a large pyramid of religious Islamic instruction which encompasses Muslims all over the world. In spite of this undeniable international character, al-Azhar plays an important internal role too: within Egypt, the base of the Islamic educational pyramid is formed by the lower "Azhar institutes," *maᶜāhid azharīyah,* of which (according to statistics supplied by its late Rector Shaykh ᶜAbd al-Ḥalīm Maḥmūd) there were in the year 1974 – 1975, 290 primary, 96 preparatory, and 96 secondary ones.

According to the same source, the number of these lower institutes needed at that time to be heavily increased. Although such statistics — and such aspirations for growth — are difficult to interpret, it is clear that Egyptian Muslims usually find Azhar institutes in their immediate surroundings, and that in this way, too, al-Azhar and its cadre have the ability to affect the intellectual, religious, and political attitudes of large sections of the Muslim population of Egypt.

Al-Azhar affairs fall under the competence of a special ministry, the ministry for Awqāf and Azhar affairs, in Arabic *wizārat al-Awqāf wa-shu'ūn al-Azhar.* This implies that the top Azhar bureaucrats are all government appointees, the Rector of al-Azhar University (the *Shaykh al-Azhar*) not excluded. It follows that the views expressed in the official Azhar monthly, the *Majallat al-Azhar,* are not the views of a religious underground. Rather, the *Majallat al-Azhar* reproduces in a reliable way the *communis opinio* of the religious Islamic establishment on the one hand, and the government's views on the other hand. The relations between the Azhar establishment and the government may not always be clear to outsiders, but outspoken wide divergence of opinion is improbable.

Al-Azhar itself recognizes that this government influence is not always beneficial. The Azhar journal of April 1984 announces,[5] for instance, the establishment of an institute for the study of Islam in Cambridge (England). This academy, so we read, is founded in order to further knowledge which is based on the Qur'ān and the Sunnah, "in confrontation with the secular views which are at present dominant." Why is such an academy founded "in a free Western country," *quṭr gharbī ḥurr?* Such an academy, we are told, should be far removed from the influence, and the direct domination, of any one country, *bi-man'ay ᶜani-'l-nufūdh wa-'l-sayṭarah li-ayyah bilād,* in order to be able to present its studies with neutrality, *bi-tajarrud wa-ḥiyād.* This casual remark must not be understood as a self-condemnation of al-Azhar. It does, however, illustrate that the Azhar scholars fully realize the predicament in which they find themselves.

Official Islam is not only reflected on the pages of the Azhar monthly. It is also incarnated in the numerous *fatwās* (literally *advice*) given by the successive rectors of al-Azhar and by Egypt's successive Muftīs. Starting in 1980 the High Council for Islamic Affairs (a department of the Egyptian ministry of Awqāf and Azhar affairs) has published selections from the archives of the so-called Fatwā Office *(Dār al-Iftā')*, the office of the government-appointed Muftī. It is this series that contained at the end of its tenth volume the text of the *Farīḍah*. In 1984 the series had reached eleven volumes which were divided into three parts: the first part containing fatwās from the years 1895 to 1950; the second part the years 1950 to 1978; the third part 1978 to 1982. This third part contains fatwās given by Shaykh Jādd al-Ḥaqq ᶜAlī Jādd al-Ḥaqq, who was appointed as Egypt's Muftī in August 1978. Moreover, two important fatwā collections by Azhar rectors are available: the collection of fatwās by Shaykh Maḥmūd Shaltūt, of which the third impression appeared in 1967, and the collection by Shaykh ᶜAbd al-Ḥalīm Maḥmūd, in two volumes, published by Dār al-Maᶜārif in 1981. There is hence no lack of printed, published, and widely distributed material on the Azhar way of answering questions on Islam.

A certain Shaykh Ḥasanayn Muḥammad Makhlūf twice fulfilled the office of Muftī of Egypt, the first time from 1946 till 1950, the second time from 1952 till 1954. The collection of his fatwās[6] from the early fifties contains little or no material that can be understood to refer or allude to the theories of the modern Islamic extremists. When Shaykh Makhlūf talks about *jihād* the context makes it obvious that he mainly thinks of struggle against imperialist and colonialist enemies of Islam.[7] Those who are negligent in performing the duties of Islam are called *ᶜuṣāh mudhnibīn*, disobedient sinners,[8] and in the same vein the Shaykh expresses his regrets that people's religious laxity has become so widespread, but the theme of *takfīr*, "to believe someone to be an infidel apostate," so common in more recent discussions, is not touched upon. Also, in the same fatwā collection Communism is discussed, along with the Bahā'ī and the Ismā'īlī movements, and is judged solely on its theological merits.[9] This fatwā collection represents an earlier phase in the development of modern Islam. It also contains no specific discussions on the position of someone who as judge applies laws other than Muslim Law.

In the fatwā collection by Shaykh Shaltūt, which dates from a decade later, a completely different picture emerges.[10] Shaykh Shaltūt discusses[11] explicitly the question of whether a judge who pronounces a sentence that is not in accordance with Muslim law should be regarded as an apostate from Islam deserving — at least according to Islamic Law — the death penalty. The scriptural basis for Shaltūt's discussion is found, again, in Sūrah 5: "Whosoever does not judge by what God sent down. . . ." Many pious Muslims, so Shaykh Shaltūt writes, teach that such a judge and, he adds, *those who ordered the said judge to apply this non-Muslim law,* are in fact apostates from Islam. In this way, not only the judge (about whom Shaltūt had been asked for an expert legal opinion) but also those who appointed him, that is, the members of the government, are scorched by the fire of the apostasy debate which the extremists have kindled. Shaykh Shaltūt makes it obvious that he regards the government's responsibility as greater than the responsibility of the government's appointee, the judge. From Shaltūt's words, no matter how carefully they were chosen, it is possible to infer that in his days both the judges and the rulers were widely, if perhaps not openly, accused of apostasy from Islam.

In his answer to the question of whether the Egyptian judges have to be regarded as apostates, Shaykh Shaltūt makes an academic division between two kinds of Islamic rulings. Some Islamic sentences, he writes, are directly based on the Qur'ān, or on the Sunnah, or on both of them. A second category is based on legal interpretation of these holy texts. Shaltūt now teaches that an Islamic judgment may differ from all the established Muslim schools of law and yet be based on Qur'ān and Sunnah. In such cases, Shaltūt concludes, the judge need not be considered to be an apostate. It is indeed difficult to imagine that if such a case should occur it would provoke a debate in which the participants would accuse each other of apostasy. When, however, a regulation is based on Qur'ān and Sunnah, so Shaltūt warns his readers, it may happen that a judge (and the government that appointed him) believe that another regulation is better, but by following this belief and by pronouncing a verdict in accordance with it the judge indeed has become an apostate. It is not difficult at all to imagine cases where the situation last described applies: a simple case of theft not punished with amputation of a hand will do.

If a judge, Shaykh Shaltūt continues, lives in a non-Islamic country, or in a country that has no power to determine its own system of law *(maghlūb ᶜalā amrihi fi-'l-ḥukm wa-'l-tashrīᶜ),* he may be forced to pronounce sentences that are un-Islamic. Here Shaltūt comes very close to the activists of the late seventies and the early eighties who teach that Egypt's un-Islamic legal system was imposed upon Egypt by foreign powers, and has hence to be removed and replaced by Muslim laws. The case of such a judge, Shaltūt explains, has to be equated with the case of someone who drinks wine without, however, forsaking the belief that drinking wine is forbidden. Such a judge, Shaltūt admits, is a sinner, but not an apostate. Whenever such a judge sees the possibility to apply Muslim law, he should do so, but if he finds himself unable to realize this aspiration "out of fear for himself or his group *(jamāᶜah),"* Islam permits him to leave things as they are, as long as his heart prefers God's laws. The difference with the theories of the *Farīḍah* is, of course, substantial: the *Farīḍah* orders such a judge to fight and go to battle, alone if necessary. The religious framework in which the problem originates is, however, strikingly similar.

Shaltūt concludes that Qur'ān 5.44 ("Whosoever does not judge by what God has sent down") is only aimed at those who have the power to decide on their own system of law and who know the laws of God but reject these because they prefer man-made laws. This conclusion may be meant to exculpate the judges of the Nasser Era, but it can easily be read as a recrimination of the Nasser government which was after all responsible for the system of law prevailing in its territory. No matter how much Shaltūt supported the Nasser government and is said to have collaborated with it, it is only one step from this fatwā of his to the *takfīr* of the government which became the shibboleth of the militant activists of the seventies and the eighties.

If one wants to read between the lines, a similar phenomenon is found in Shaltūt's fatwā on the Hijrah.[12] Here he writes: "Many of the first Muslims . . . saw that they were obliged to leave their country, *even when it was Islamic,*[13] when heresies and abominations started to spread in it and they found themselves unable to fulfill their religious duties in it. . . ." Especially the phrase "even when it was Islamic" creates problems in interpretation. Also it is difficult to imagine that Shaltūt wanted to accuse the first generation of Muslims — which is generally regarded as having been of exemplary piety — of spreading heresies and abominations. He instead seems to have had his own times in mind when he wrote this line since no possible meaning suggests itself for this passage when taken literally. Certainly after Shukrī Muṣṭafā's *Hijrah* group it is difficult not to hear in Shaltūt's words an echo of the way in which some of the militants exhorted their followers to leave their only nominally Muslim states, even when these states called themselves Islamic, because in such a state a Muslim could not properly fulfill his religious duties. The conclusion of Shaltūt's fatwā is an open question: "Where are we Muslims today?" Do we find ourselves in a Muslim country where Islam is being implemented or in a pagan un-Islamic state that has to be fought the way the Prophet himself fought pagan Mecca? The militants of the *Farīḍah* asked themselves whether Sadat's Egypt could still be called an Islamic country or whether it was a country at war with the real Muslims. Discussing such questions, they could certainly claim only to be answering questions raised by earlier Muslim leaders who were never accused of extremism, like Shaykh Maḥmūd Shaltūt, the theologian of the Nasser Era.

In another fatwā collection, the collection of fatwās published by Shaykh ᶜAbd al-Ḥalīm Maḥmūd in 1981/82, one meets not only veiled allusions to theories like those expounded in the *Farīḍah* but also an almost open discussion of such theories. The *Farīḍah* teaches that under certain circumstances *jihād* can be an individual duty. Shaykh ᶜAbd al-Ḥalīm also writes[14] that "to go to war for God's cause, *al-jihād fī sabīl Allāh,* is at present a duty *(farḍ)* for the Muslims individually *(afrādan),* and it is a duty for all Islamic states,[15] and whoever is slow or lax in this is a sinner." He then goes on by cataloguing the sins a Muslim might commit. Yet the list of sins that follows significantly omits the traditional sin of *takfīr,* and hence fails to condemn the zealots who accused Sadat and his like of apostasy from Islam.

The list does, however, contain — next to murder, wine, lying, atheism, fornication, theft, and slander — the sin of creating "dissension," *fitnah.* Shaykh ᶜAbd al-Ḥalīm's text does not specify what exactly is meant by *fitnah* in this context, but his text does refer to Qur'ān 2.190: "Fight in the way of God those who fight you. . . . Slay them wherever ye come upon them. . . . *Fitnah* is worse than slaughter." The same verse is quoted in the *Farīḍah*. The word *fitnah* in modern Arabic is usually understood as tampering in some way or another with the welfare of the community to the point of provoking civil war, and, of course, the Shaykh's words can be understood as a condemnation of those whose militancy endangers public order. However, the militants themselves might easily understand these words as a condemnation of the ruler who goes against the will of God by ruling according to other laws than those of Islam, thus creating a just cause for revolt. Again it is the lack of an unambiguous condemnation of the militants that gives such a passage (to which no censor could possibly object) an ominous ring.

The militant interpretation of the Shaykh's (deliberately?) ambiguous words might find support in the fatwā that immediately follows. In this fatwā the Shaykh answers the question of how to view a Muslim state that is not ruled by the Qur'ān, and how to view the people who obey "that government." This calls for two remarks. First, the expression "to be ruled by the Qur'ān" is vaguer and less precise than the militant formulas which usually talk of being ruled by *Islamic Law* (instead of being ruled by the *Qur'ān*). The militant Muslims demand total and complete application of the Sharīᶜah both in public and private life, they do not ask for application "of the Qur'ān." Second, the demonstrative pronoun in "that government" is odd since the Shaykh's text did not previously mention a government to which this demonstrative might refer. Was the Shaykh's text revised (or censored?) and was the demonstrative inadvertently left in the text? Is it possible that the Shaykh refers to any other government than his own, that is, the government of President Sadat? However this may be, the answer to the question of whether the rulers and the ruled are apostates should be—at least according to the militant—that such a government, such a state, or such a society is un-Islamic and has hence to be fought. As a matter of course, this militant answer is not given or rejected by the Shaykh.

Shaykh ᶜAbd al-Halīm's answer begins with the observation

that according to him there is not any true Muslim "whether such a Muslim is from the citizenry or from the men of authority, *min al-sha^cb am min rijāl al-ḥukm*" who refuses to be ruled by Islam. "There is no doubt," so the Shaykh continues, by this very formula indicating that a controversial opinion follows, "that whosoever does not want to be ruled by the Qur'ān is not a Muslim." No reader of these words can fail to be reminded of the central thesis of the militant Muslims which says that whosoever does not rule by the laws of Islam is no longer a Muslim. There can be little doubt that many militant Muslims will read these lines by Shaykh ^cAbd al-Ḥalīm as simply a confirmation of their own extremist views. Whether Shaykh ^cAbd al-Ḥalīm Maḥmūd, Rector of al-Azhar University, intended his words to be understood in this way is hardly relevant.

The Shaykh's answer then continues by repeating the familiar argument that in the past colonialism prevented Muslim nations from following their own inclinations as far as legislation is concerned. Again we read that many Muslims, "and amongst them many men of authority" (i.e., rulers), call for "taking as an eternal constitution the rules which religion supplies," and, we are assured, "governments have started to prepare themselves to go in this direction." All these formulas are much vaguer than the clear-cut demands of the fundamentalists, but one may ask whether a militant reader really cares whether the Shaykh writes "rules which religion supplies" or "the specific rules of the Sharī^cah." Almost every line in this fatwā may be given a militant interpretation by those who are set on doing so.

At the end of the fatwā the Shaykh expresses his hope that God will make these aspirations for Islamic rule come true, and that it will all serve *li-i^cādat al-islām wa-'l-muslimīn,* to bring back Islam *and the Muslims* (italics added). It is, to a certain extent, clear what the text means with "the return of Islam" (cf. the translation of the *Farīḍah,* §94), but what can possibly be meant with "the return of the Muslims"? Must God bring them back *as rulers* since the present rulers of the Islamic world cannot be regarded as real Muslims? The text of the fatwā as printed in the Shaykh's collection gives no indication as to how to understand this odd expression, "the return (. . .) of the Muslims." The way it stands now it produces little meaning. Is the text a revised version of an original that too clearly implied that the present-day rulers of the Muslim world are — as the *Farīḍah* believes — apostates from Islam? Or did the original version — if it existed — say that the Muslims and Islam should regain their position of superiority as such?

If we assume that this fatwā opines, be it in a veiled way, that the militant Muslims are right in believing that to rule according to other laws than the laws of Islam is a sin so enormous that those who perpetrate it do actually cease to be Muslims, we can now expect a discussion on the question of which sins are so great that to commit one of them turns a Muslim into an apostate. It is perhaps not too surprising that the discussion on this question does follow. If the perpetrator of a sin from this category of great sins *(kabā'ir)* does not repent, so we read, "the Qur'ān will evict him, and he will have left the borderlines *(ḥudūd)* of Islam by following the footsteps of Satan." An inquisitive outsider who reads these lines may wonder what exactly is meant by "the Qur'ān will evict him," but again a militant reader may understand these words as simply a paraphrase of "he will be ousted by the community" or "he will have become an apostate."

One feels forced to conclude that the writings of these two Azhar Rectors, Shaykh Shaltūt and Shaykh ᶜAbd al-Ḥalīm Maḥmūd, foreshadow the views expressed in the *Farīḍah,* even though these two Rectors, in fact, may have had quite different practical views and were, for instance, quite willing to cooperate with the government.

An illuminating example of this cooperation between al-Azhar and the government has already been reported by Dr. Derek Hopwood.[16] In May 1979 the Azhar scholars declared that the conclusion of a peace treaty with Israel was not contrary to Islamic Law.[17] This meant that the Azhar establishment supported the government in a delicate controversy. In May of the next year a referendum was held in which the government proposed to make the Sharīᶜah the principal source *(al-maṣdar al-ra'īsī)* of Egypt's legislation.[18] The actual content of Egypt's law was, at this moment, left unchanged, but the adoption by referendum of the phrase "principal source" created a permanent source of tension between aspirations and reality, the effects of which may outlive the Egyptian-

Israeli peace by generations. It can, of course, not be established beyond reasonable doubt that this referendum was a reward that the government granted the Azhar establishment in exchange for its support for peace with Israel. Cases like this are, too often, judged on suspicions only.

In the aftermath of the al-Azhar declarations of May 1979, a "dialogue" was held in Ismailiyya between President Sadat and Egyptian religious leaders *(qiyādāt dīnīyah),* the text of which was printed in the Azhar journal[19] of September 1979. Both the contents of the President's speech and the fact that it was printed in the Azhar journal reflect the cordial relations that existed at that time between the religious and the political establishment. The President discussed the question of whether "what is nowadays called *jamāᶜāt*" is really dangerous. He cites a few examples of bizarre behavior by members of the *jamāᶜāt.* A son, for instance, was reported to have refused to accept pocket-money from his father since the father in his turn received his money from the state, the *dawlat al-ḥarām,* the state that this son regarded as contrary to the laws of Islam, therefore as evil and wrong.

Another story that the President tells concerns a man who walked in the streets of Minya with his daughter. Fanatics attacked him and, when the man told them that the girl was his daughter, not his illicit girlfriend, they demanded to see a birth certificate. Another of Sadat's stories is about a boy, also from Minya, who was arrested in Cairo carrying 800 Egyptian pounds and "pamphlets against public order and the State. . . ." Never, so Sadat upholds, should the interests of the public and the interests of Egypt be entrusted to the likes of these people, because there should be "no religion in politics and no politics in religion."[20] "If someone wants to be politically active, well, there are political parties . . . please, let him exercise his full rights . . . but if someone wants to exploit religion to attack the state . . ."—the end of this phrase has to be supplied by the imagination (or the memory) of the public.

Then a lively exchange between the President and ᶜUmar Al-Tilimsānī, the octogenarian spokesman of the Muslim Brothers, follows. The point that the two gentlemen discuss is whether or not there has been an attempt to form an anti-Sadat coalition in which both the Brothers and the Communists would have participated. (The existence of such a proposed coalition would morally disqualify the Brothers since the Communists are atheists, so the reader is probably asked to understand.) After Al-Tilimsānī, other leaders deliver short and polite speeches on behalf of the National Party and on behalf of the Ṣūfī movement, and a certain Muḥammad ᶜAwaḍayn on behalf of the young. The latter brings up the question "about which so many have spoken that it is indeed possible to say that all sides agree on it: a government according to what God has sent down, *al-ḥukm bi-mā anzala Allāh. . . .*"

Then, on behalf of a benevolent society, a certain Muḥammad ᶜAbd al-Maqṣūd offers fifteen copies of the Qur'ān to the President as a present for him and his family. The next speaker is again ᶜUmar al-Tilimsānī, this time in his capacity as editor-in-chief of the monthly *Al-Daᶜwah*. His words sound innocent enough, but his public may have held its breath when Al-Tilimsānī exclaimed: "O ye who call for *jihād!* You will find all of us behind you!"[21] Were these words really addressed to Sadat? Or to someone else who at that time was yet unknown?

The last speaker was ᶜAbd al-Raḥmān al-Bannā,[22] the tame brother of the late Ḥasan al-Bannā, the founder of the Muslim Brothers who was assassinated in 1949. In his short speech ᶜAbd al-Raḥmān assures those present that his late brother had "called for the ways of his Lord with wisdom and sermons," that is, with peaceful means and not with violence. Young people especially must know this, ᶜAbd al-Raḥmān emphasizes. He is, however, not the only one with a special interest in what the young think, know, believe, and will do. Most of the speakers at this session are very much concerned with beliefs that the young hold mistakenly and that have to be corrected.

Of course, most of the militant activist Muslims are young, but it is certain that this meeting asked also those militants who were not young to give their loyalty to the traditional, established Muslim religious organizations, perhaps even to the State and the Sadat government. It is remarkable how little was said at this meeting by Azhar functionaries, although both the Shaykh al-Azhar, Dr. ᶜAbd al-Raḥmān Bīṣār, and the Muftī of Egypt, Shaykh Jādd al-Ḥaqq ᶜAlī Jādd al-Ḥaqq, seem to have been present. Perhaps the Azhar functionaries thought it would be enough to print a detailed report of the meeting in their journal. However this may be, their silent presence must also have authorized and sanctioned the proceedings considerably.

As the text of his speech makes clear, President Sadat believed at this point in time that God wanted him to rule Egypt[23] but he certainly was not struck by megalomania. He seems to have been reasonably informed about what people in the streets said to each other when they murmured about their government, as his use of the expression *dawlat al-ḥarām,* literally, "the state of impropriety," indicates. He also realized the dangers that emanated from the militant Islamic opposition. His own words and the contents of the speeches addressed to him suggest that the (unspoken) aim of the meeting was to bring together all those groups for which there would be no place in a "real" Islamic state whose structure would be in accordance with theories like those expounded in the *Farīḍah:* including political parties, Ṣūfī organizations, benevolent societies, and magazines that limit themselves to missionary activities. The list of the activities of those present at this meeting corresponds strikingly to the list of Islamic activities that the *Farīḍah* declares to be meaningless and of no relevance to the cause of Islam. If the presidential palace had composed the list of invitations for this meeting with the help of the text of the *Farīḍah,* the result would not have been different from what it now became.

On the eve of the assassination of President Sadat, the dangers that the zealotry of the young, *al-shabāb,* presented to the stability of Egypt had moved a little into the background, as the pages of the Azhar journal indicate. In the summer of 1981 only a few articles were printed that might be understood as being polemical against militant Islam. One article on the character of the office of Muftī[24] might be understood as being obliquely aimed at the Muftīs of the *jamā^cāt* who gave fatwās that were indeed "completely different from what people were used to."[25] In the same way, an article in the issue dated October 1981 (but published a little earlier) discusses "leadership" *(qiyādah),* and contains phrases that might be interpreted as critical of the leaders of the *jamā^cāt.*[26] The interdenominational tensions between Copts and Muslims and the government's drastic actions which had attempted to curb these tensions seemed, however, to have become much more important. What had happened?

In the summer of 1981 interdenominational trouble suddenly surfaced in a densely populated area of Cairo, the Al-Zāwiyah al-Ḥamrā quarter. The general outbursts of popular discontent that followed this modest and local beginning have since become known as "the events of Al-Zāwiyah al-Ḥamrā" since the trouble seems to have been started by a small-scale conflict between neighbors in this particular part of Cairo. In order to restore peace and order, the government took measures to prepare for the arrest of a large group of Muslim, Coptic, Marxist, and independent "leaders of opinion." This wave of arrests actually took place on (or a little before) September 5, 1981. Since the conflicts had a nasty sectarian odor, the danger of "another Lebanon" had made people's fears for further deterioration of the Egyptian atmosphere extremely acute. In the eyes of many, even the most drastic measures were justified if they would prevent the "Lebanonization" of Egypt.

It is needless to say that such emotions did not remain without an echo in the Azhar journal. The monthly editorial of the last issue of the Azhar journal that appeared before the assassination of President Sadat[27] gravely tells about pre-Islamic tribal wars in which the pagan Arabs sacrificed themselves for "nothing of value except the delusion that the dignity of their tribe had been injured, or that the honor of the tribe had been violated, and often this was not even real."[28] "The ancient Arabs had no way *(manhaj)* to control their human relations, and were unable to transcend their narrow tribal loyalties."

When Islam came, the editorial goes on to say, this changed: people could give their loyalty to a well-organized, nontribal community, yes, even to humanity as a whole. The formulas used in this editorial may be vague, but they definitely suggest that such a well-organized community is well organized because it follows the Sharīᶜah, and that the community should be structured in such a way as to comprise (Christian) minorities. "The loyalty to which Islam inspires its adherents is not an ethnic *(ᶜunṣurī)* loyalty that creates enmity and envy toward non-Muslims. It is a human loyalty in which Muslims cooperate with non-Muslims . . . under the shadow of the ways of the Lord, *fī ẓilāl al-manhaj al-rabbānī*." This last circumlocution will no doubt be appreciated by the connoisseur, even if the militant readers of such a phrase simply understand it to mean "in a state in which Muslim law is applied."

Similarly, even an article on "the philosophy of the *Hijrah*" (the Prophet's "emigration" from Mecca to Medina in 622 AD) shows how the author of this article is much more occupied with the interdenominational conflict (usually called *al-fitnah al-ṭā'ifīyah)* than with the problems of the extremists who preach a *hijrah* away from contemporary, pagan, un-Islamic Egypt. The author of this article can, for instance, write: "*Hijrah* today means to move away from *fitnah*, internal conflict, and to move away from bad ideas toward positive and constructive thinking."[29]

The shock of the assassination put attention back to where it seemed to belong: the intricate and interrelated problems of Islamic legislation, apostasy by not ruling according to what God sent down, Holy War, terrorism, and public order. Yet the Azhar journal's reaction to the assassination is rather tepid. The journal presents no formal announcement of the assassination, no photograph of the murdered President, no official condolences (as, for instance, found in the Ṣūfī journal).[30] It mentions the assassination only obliquely, on the second page: extremism, so the reader is assured, "reached its limits in what had happened in the Holy Mosque in Mecca; and in the assassination of President Sadat in Egypt." On its first page the journal promises "to throw light on some problems of the contemporary Islamic world . . . the journal will continue its scholarly activities. . . ." In other words, the editors of the Azhar journal prefer to keep a certain distance between themselves and the turbulent recent developments. The journal's readership will not be confronted with direct commentaries on what happened, nor with violent reactions to the theories of Sadat's murderers: equanimity seems to be the order of the day at al-Azhar.

Both the events in Mecca and the assassination of Sadat, so the editorial on the second page of the journal upholds,[31] spring from the same basic religious confusion. This confusion creates problems that can be solved by two sets of measures,[32] the editorial continues. The first set will comprise the clarification of all these accusations of apostasy from Islam. "Also it must be borne in mind that certain people believe that the modern Islamic societies cannot be regarded as Islamic since they deviate from being ruled and governed according to what God sent down. To flee from such societies became, in the understanding of some, a religious duty. Yes, even to fight such societies and to attempt to destroy them became, according to such people, a holy *jihād*." The Azhar journal here summarizes important tenets of the militant Muslims. In view of the spectacular success of these militants in murdering the Egyptian head-of-state, the editorial's comment is rather stoic: "Therefore, a calm *(hādi')* dialogue with those who believe in such [militant] ideas has become a necessity" — dialogue with the assassins and their sympathizers, and a calm dialogue at that, instead of punishment? Only a real stoic will regard such a "calm dialogue" as the proper reaction to murder.

The writer of the editorial, however, goes even further. We should not disregard, he writes, the laudable motives, *al-dawāfi^c al-ḥamīdah,* of the young who so eagerly long for an Islamic society, *al-mujtama^c al-islāmī.* Although, he goes on to explain, the imperialists and colonialists have long ago left Egypt, their ideas and ideology still dominate the Islamic world. Of this the editor wants to give one example: the streets of Cairo are, according to him, full of immoral posters *(afīshāt)* for cinema and theatre. This, the reader has to realize, is extremely harmful to the young and to society as such.

The writer of the editorial then reminds the reader that in the Soviet Union educational programs effectively manage to influence the thinking of the young, and adds that he deplores that, "except for al-Azhar, the Egyptian educational institutions do not fulfill their duty" in this respect.[33] If, as the editorial seems to imply, social tensions have influenced the young and if the sympathy that the young generally feel for modern militancy is a result of social wrongs, would it really be true that the removal of posters from the streets of Cairo will set things right? Might it not rather be the uncontrollable population explosion, or the lack of jobs, houses, and opportunities that determine the social climate in which Islamic militancy finds a sympathetic ear? Western-secular and Egyptian-Islamic thinking diverge when they want to answer such questions.

However this may be, the Azhar journal also contains the press review section *Qālat al-ṣuḥuf.* In this section an elaborate quotation from the Cairo daily *Al-Akhbār*[34] comprises the expected condemnations of the assassination, and of terrorism in general. Yet the same press review section also offers a selection from an article that had appeared (obviously before the assassination) in the monthly *Al-Hilāl*. It is a selection from an article that praises action in the widest sense of the word.[35] Does this include the action of murdering President Sadat? It is very difficult not to get the impression that the editors of the Azhar journal were secretly not very displeased by the disappearance of President Sadat. How many of their readers shared their feelings? How many Egyptians felt similarly? Whatever the answer, the pages of the first issue of the Azhar journal to appear after the assassination of President Sadat seem to take for granted a wide sympathy — especially among "the young" — for the beliefs and the acts of the assassins.

The requisite "calm dialogue," the Azhar journal goes on to explain,[36] will be organized by a top-level committee of which the Shaykh al-Azhar, Shaykh Dr. Muḥammad ᶜAbd al-Raḥmān Bīṣār, will be the president. The name of the new committee will be *lajnah li-'l-mafāhīm al-islāmīyah,* Committee for Islamic Concepts, an appellation that somehow breathes an authentic Orwellian feeling. Among its outstanding members we find Dr. Ḥusaynī Hāshim, Shaykh Muṣṭafā al-Ṭayr, and many others. The committee's task is formulated[37] as "correction and elucidation of the interpretations of certain Traditions which certain persons have attempted to exploit by incorrect explanations," and aimed at the young in the universities.

It is clear from a short notice on the same page of the Azhar journal that not only the young in the universities have to be cured from possible sympathy for the assassins. Another committee, so we read, will concern itself with the religious organizations in the widest sense of the word. (Other sources also give the impression that at this point in time there was some confusion as to the line of demarcation between "recognized" benevolent Muslim organizations and "extremist" *jamāᶜāt.*)[38] This new "Committee for Support *(daᶜm)* of the Religious Organizations," the Azhar journal announces, will make sure that people who are active in these benevolent societies will not get confused by the outbreak of discord in their ranks. In order to reach this aim, a unified program for religious propaganda, *manhaj muwaḥḥad li-'l-daᶜwah,* will be prepared for these organizations. (In this context, no mention is made of the Ṣūfī organizations since these have their own jurisdiction.) The effect of the proposed measures is difficult to ascertain, and the degree to which these plans were realized is not clear. It is, however, evident that these two committees formed part of an organized attempt to check the rise of militant extremism.

Not only the Azhar journal called for a "calm dialogue." This call was also heard elsewhere, be it with a slightly different sense. The government weekly *Māyū,* in its issue of November 16, 1981, also asked for a calm dialogue, but one on the question, "Where are the codes of Islamic Law?" *("Ayn qawānīn al-sharīᶜah al-islāmīyah?").* According to *Māyū* it was this question that needed to be discussed calmly. The author of this article, a certain Muḥammad Rashwān, argued that no matter how urgently many people wanted to see Egypt governed by Islamic laws, much time, effort, and study were still needed to reach the point where all legal codes in Egypt would be brought in conformity with the laws of Islam. Also, a prolonged period of transition was, according to Muḥammad Rashwān, an unavoidable necessity.

According to this article in *Māyū,* the official slogan of the day seemed to be: as far as the application of Islamic Law in Egypt is concerned, a calm dialogue, much study, a gradual adaptation, and a careful transition will be needed. There could, of course, be no question of open Azhar resistance to such an official policy. In the Azhar journal of December 1981, the editorial is devoted to an Azhar reaction on Muḥammad Rashwān's article.[39] The Azhar scholars, we read, fully agree with practically everything that Muḥammad Rashwān had written. Islamic Law certainly had to be adapted to modern needs, but, according to the Azhar scholars, such adaptations could be of form only. As they saw it, if previous generations had been hesitating between two solutions to any one legal question, this did not give modern Muslims the liberty to opt for a third solution. Also, they added, modernization could never mean that a ruling about which past generations had been in agreement could be changed. No matter how tame this may all sound, it does imply that the death penalty for certain crimes (e.g., apostasy and certain forms of adultery) and the controversial amputation of the hand for theft would have to become integral parts of Egypt's (projected) system of Islamic Law. The position that the Azhar editorial takes on this point is, perhaps, as is so often the case, best characterized as "calm pressure."

The last pages of the December 1981 issue of the Azhar journal finally offer the expected official condolences. "Yesterday," we read, although no specific date is given, "President Mubārak received the Rector of al-Azhar University," and then a long list of the Azhar dignitaries who accompanied the Rector follows, mentioning their names, titles, and functions in full. After the meeting, the journal continues, a certain Dr. Al-Najjār, President of al-Azhar, made a public statement, saying that the members "of the Council" had offered their condolences to President Mubārak, expressing their grief *(asaf)* about the hostile action *(ᶜudwān)* against President Sadat. President Mubārak, so he continued, enjoyed the full support of al-Azhar.

Concerning "the ideas of al-Azhar about the role of the young in the coming phase of Egypt's development," Dr. Al-Najjār said that in order "to make the real principles of Islam clear to all concerned, articles in the press and programs on radio and television" would not be sufficient. Only repeated meetings *(liqā'āt)* and discussions with the young could produce results. Azhar scholars would, he assured his public, participate in these meetings and do everything possible to obtain the required results.[40]

In the same statement Dr. Al-Najjār admitted that Azhar scholars had been accused of negligence in fulfilling these tasks, but such accusations, according to him, were groundless. Men of religion, he explained, have many tasks, and under all circumstances: on television, in the pulpit, in general meetings, even in every house where they happened to sit, they would encourage what was laudable and discourage everything that was not—these are, again, words that are possibly ambiguous.[41]

The Azhar journal reported that Egypt's Muftī, Shaykh Jādd al-Ḥaqq ᶜAlī Jādd al-Ḥaqq, was among the Azhar delegation which paid its respects to President Mubārak in order to offer official condolences at the occasion of the death of President Sadat. It is to this Shaykh Jādd al-Ḥaqq that we owe a completely unambiguous, detailed, and authoritative Azhar answer to the theories that were put forward in the *Farīḍah*.

The fatwā in which Sheikh Jādd al-Ḥaqq presents his refutation of the *Farīḍah* is dated January 3, 1982. It is 25 pages long, and it consists of an introduction followed by ten numbered sections which each discuss a specific theme. It is not an exercise in abstractions. The conclusion of the introduction is direct and to the point: there are no sins — apart from not believing in the One and Only God — by which a Muslim may become an apostate.[42] This is demonstrated by Qur'ān 4.116: "God will not forgive the association of anything with Himself, though he forgives anything short of that. . . ." Several Traditions that make the same point are added. According to the Muftī it is, hence, forbidden to call a fellow Muslim an apostate. Next to the Traditions, Qur'ān 4.94 is quoted in order to demonstrate this point: "Do not say to one who gives you the peace greeting (which is customary amongst Muslims), 'Thou art not a believer.'" The implied conclusion is that the assassination of Sadat for his alleged apostasy was a senseless and foolish crime.

The first section of the Muftī's answer concerns *jihād*. According to the Muftī, the meaning of the word *jihād* in the Qur'ān and in the Tradition is not limited to *qitāl*, fighting, not legally and not by the lexicon. If true, this invalidates much of the *Farīḍah*'s contents. Yet the argument may not convince the author of the *Farīḍah* and his combatants since their concerns are not at all philological. To them, the Qur'anic injunction "Fighting is prescribed for you" (Qur'ān 2.216) is probably sufficient scriptural proof for the orthodoxy of their beliefs.

The second section wants to correct the militant interpretation of Qur'ān 5.48: "Whosoever does not rule *(yaḥkum)* by what God sent down, they are the unbelievers." The Muftī argues that from the context of this verse it is obvious that the phrase "what God sent down" refers to the Torah, and not to the specific prescripts of the Muslim Sharīᶜah, and that the verse addresses the Jews in Medina in the days of the Prophet, not the present-day modern rulers in the capitals of the Arab world. Since the same Qur'ān verse also makes "Rabbis and scriptural scholars" the grammatical subject of the verb "to rule" *(yaḥkum)*, most Western scholars will agree with the Muftī.

The third section discusses the question of whether Egypt may be called an Islamic country. The view of the *Farīḍah* that it is not is ridiculed by the Muftī, for example: "The prayer ceremonies are executed, mosques are opened everywhere, religious taxes are paid, people make the pilgrimage to Mecca, and the rule of Islam *(ḥukm al-Islām)* is widespread except in certain matters like the Islamic punishments, usury, and other things that are contained in the laws of the country, but this does not make the country, the people, the rulers, and the ruled apostates, since we believe that God's rule *(ḥukm Allāh)* is better." The Muftī does, however, make it abundantly clear that according to him Muslims should not acquiesce in these imperfections, but should—according to their capacities *(quwwah)*—work for the improvement of even the smallest detail.

The fourth section discusses the legality of tyrannicide. The Shaykh presents several Traditions which make it clear that religion does not sanctify, let alone prescribe, the rising against a ruler who does perform the prayer ceremonies. The Muftī discusses the Qur'ān quotations that the *Farīḍah* uses to prove its point in this respect, and he places these quotations in their Qur'anic context. In their context these verses, again, do not lend support to the extremist views, and this the Muftī qualifies as "to believe in part of the Qur'ān and to consider other parts of it as lies." This is the battle-cry of the *Farīḍah* itself which it aimed at Muslims who did not agree with the militant views of the *Farīḍah*. The *Farīḍah* used this aphorism when it talked about the refusal of some "lax" Muslims to add *jihād* to the list of "pillars" *(arkān)* of Islam, together with praying, fasting, religious taxes, and pilgrimage. It is, of course, taken directly from Qur'ān 2.85 which runs, in Bell's translation: "Do ye believe in part of the Book and disbelieve in part?" The way in which these Qur'anic words are used here by the Muftī in order to propagate a contextual Qur'ān exegesis is extremely interesting.

The fifth section discusses the so-called *āyat al-sayf*, the verse of the sword (Qur'ān 9.5): "Slay the polytheists wherever ye find them, seize them, beset them, lie in ambush for them everywhere." According to the *Farīḍah*, this verse "abrogated 104 other verses in 48 different suras." The Muftī again uses the context of the verse to invalidate the extremist interpretation. He does not have to go into the slippery domain of the *naskh* theories ("abrogation" is the usual translation of *naskh*) since the verse of the sword ends as follows: "if they [the polytheists] repent and establish the Prayer and pay the Zakāt, then set them free; God is forgiving, compassionate." There may be a note of despair in the Muftī's words when he writes: "How can anyone legalize, on the basis of the verse of the sword (Qur'ān 9.5), the murder of a Muslim who prays, pays religious taxes, and recites the Qur'ān?" Also, the Muftī points out, the verse is addressed to pagan Arabs who lived in the Arabian peninsula in the days of the Prophet and who had at that point in time no treaty with the Prophet. Can such a verse be applied so generally as to include a justification of the assassination of contemporary heads-of-state? Most certainly not.

The sixth section discusses the *Farīḍah*'s equation of the Mongols *(Al-Tatār)* with the ruling classes of Egypt. The Muftī not only recalls the indeed proverbial destruction that the Mongols brought upon Transoxiana (Bukhara and Samarkand) but also points specifically to the contents of Ibn al-Athīr's chronicle on the year 617 AH (March 1220 – February 1221 AD), and then asks his readers, "*Hal hunāka wajhun li-'l-muqāranah bayna ulā'ika . . . wa-bayna Miṣr, ḥukkāmihā wa-shaᶜbihā?*"—"Is it really meaningful to compare between these savage destructive Mongols on the one hand, and the rulers and the inhabitants of Egypt on the other?"

The seventh section discusses the way in which the *Farīḍah* makes use of Ibn Taymīyah's fatwās. The Muftī quotes part of a *jihād* fatwā by Ibn Taymīyah:

> We [Ibn Taymīyah] saw the camp of those Mongols and noticed that they do not perform prayer ceremonies, we saw no muezzin in their camp, nor an *imām* to lead the prayer. . . .[43]

Again, so the Muftī points out, we have to think of Qur'ān 2.85, "Do ye believe in part of the Book and disbelieve in part?"—because if the *Farīḍah* had quoted this small but significant fragment as well, it would have been evident to every reader that these comparisons between the Egyptians and the Mongols are simply misleading. Did not the Egyptian army shout the Islamic battle-cry *Allāhu Akbar* (God is Great) when they fought the war of Ramaḍān in October 1973? Does not the Egyptian army pray and fast? Does the army not have *ᶜulamā'* who lead the men in the prayer ceremonies? Doesn't every camp have a mosque? "How can anyone compare those Mongols with the Egyptian army, *Ayn hā'ūlā' al-Tatār min jaysh Miṣr?*"

In the eighth section the Muftī wants to prove that the *Farīḍah* is not a religious document but simply a political pamphlet. In order to demonstrate this, the Muftī concentrates on four points, the first of which is the *Farīḍah*'s discussion of the Caliphate, and the pledge of obedience *(al-bayᶜah)* due to the Leader, the *amīr*. Political authority, the Muftī begins, is based on *shūrā*, literally "mutual consultation." This the Muftī illustrates with several Qur'ān verses, for example, the well-known Qur'ān 42.36: "Their [public] affairs [must be made] a matter of counsel *[shūrā]* among them." The Muftī does not fail to stipulate that legislation *(tashrīᶜ)* and matters concerning the revelation *(waḥy)* are, of course, outside the scope of this *shūrā*. The nation *(ummah)*, the Muftī continues, selects its own ruler *(ḥākim)* by whatever variety of *shūrā* is made convenient by the circumstances, such as direct elections. "No authoritative texts determine a way to select a ruler . . . since this differs in different times and places."

The title of the ruler (caliph or otherwise) is equally determined by accidental influences, so the Muftī maintains. A political entity *(kiyān siyāsī)*, however, must have a ruler, and the selection of this ruler by elections, for example, came in the place of the Pledge of Loyalty *(al-bayᶜah)* that was customary in the days of the Prophet, known from the handbooks of Islamic Law, and discussed in the *Farīḍah*. These ancient pledges of loyalty also included the pledge to fight, but this was simply a means to protect the political entity and its religion, not an aim in itself. At the time of the Prophet there was nothing comparable to the modern obligatory conscription into the national army, and the system of pledging loyalty to the Prophet must be seen as the early equivalent of the modern conscription system.

Consequently, so the Muftī continues, to fight (as a member of one of the *jamāᶜāt*) outside the official army of the State is the equivalent of not observing the traditional pledge of loyalty from the days of the Prophet. Hence, someone who yet goes out to war against this State and its army—as the members of the *jamāᶜāt* have done — is actually fighting God and his Apostle, since logic compels us to conclude that the modern state and its conscript army are the rightful continuation of an institution set up by the Prophet himself. Qur'ān 5.33 has something to say on those who fight God and his Apostle, so the Muftī reminds his readers:

> *The recompense of those who make war on God and His Messenger*
> *and exert themselves to cause corruption in the land*
> *is that they should be killed.*

This verse is also used as the Qur'anic proof for the fixed *ḥadd* punishment for highway robbery, and, if one can go along with the Muftī's arguments and his logic, it ends the discussion and even justifies the death penalty handed out to Sadat's assassins.

The romanticism with which the *jamāʿāt* call their leaders *khalīfah*, Caliph, or *amīr*, Commander, is also the subject of a short discussion by the Muftī. The Muftī wants his readers to understand that the first Caliph, Abū Bakr (d. 634 AD), was of course literally the *khalīfah* or "successor" of the Prophet, but, so he continues, the Caliphs after him were usually called *amīr*, or commander, of the faithful. "This was simply a technical term, and we [today] must call our ruler 'President of the Republic' or whatever other term which has become usual." The early Caliphs claimed no special rights or privileges on the basis of their titles, the Muftī adds, obviously referring to the claims of absolute obedience that the *khalīfah*s and the *amīr*s of the modern *jamāʿāt* are reported to make on their followers.

The second point in this section concerns Islam and *ʿilm*, "knowledge" or "science." The Muftī produces ample evidence from Qur'ān and Tradition which proves that the "quest for knowledge" *(ṭalab al-ʿilm)* is the equivalent of *jihād*, or at least part of *jihād*. The *Farīḍah*'s attack on, and disregard for, science and knowledge is in reality, so the Muftī writes, a "call for illiteracy and primitivism in the name of Islam, which will encourage young people to forget about their studies, both at schools and at the universities." Both the *ʿulūm al-dīn* and the *ʿulūm al-dunyā*, the holy and the profane sciences, are endangered by such an attitude, the Muftī remarks. The occupation of Egypt by Napoleon and the Azhar attitude to it were referred to in the *Farīḍah*, and on this topic the Muftī asks: "Did Napoleon not eventually leave Egypt? Did the Azhar scholars not play an active role in the leadership of the movement of resistance against Imperialism?" The Muftī phrased his rhetorical question carefully, and he may convince some of the members of his public. He adds, moreover, that some forms of *jihād* are senseless, out of place, do not endanger the enemy against which it is directed, and will only result in the murdering of compatriots.

The third point of this section discusses how much cooperation with non-Muslims Islam allows. Examples from Islamic history (e.g., the Coptic bureaucrats who served the Muslim rulers of Egypt) demonstrate, according to the Muftī, that such cooperation is completely legal. The fourth point is partly a repetition of an earlier topic: to serve in the Egyptian army is to fulfill the duty that in the days of the Prophet was fulfilled by giving the Prophet the Pledge of Loyalty. Both this pledge and the service in the Egyptian army are ways of carrying out the duty of protecting *(ḥimāyah)* women and children. Once the states of the Muslims became well organized and stable, a proper army took over the tasks the execution of which was formerly guaranteed by the Pledge of Loyalty.

In the ninth section the Muftī attempts to find precedents in the history of Islam for the *Farīḍah*'s way of thinking. It is not surprising that the Muftī sees strong similarities with the *khawārij,* or "Khārijīs" as they are called in many Western languages. The *Encyclopaedia of Islam* says of the Khārijīs, "the earliest of the religious sects of Islam," that they "never had any true unity of military and political action," but that they yet, "at the same time, regarded other non-Khārijī Muslims as apostates who had to be killed for their apostasy." The Muftī quotes a short passage from Al-Baghdādī's (d. 1037) *Kitāb al-Farq bayn al-Firaq,*[44] in which Al-Baghdādī points out that the Khārijīs regarded many, if not most, Companions of the Prophet as apostates — a ridiculous opinion in the eyes of the Muftī's modern readers who are now by implication asked to regard the modern accusations of apostasy as equally ridiculous. *"Akfarū kull Muslim irtakaba dhanban,"* "They regarded every Muslim who ever committed a sin as *kāfir,* an unbeliever," and hence, since born a Muslim, an apostate who has to be killed for his apostasy, so the Muftī warns his readers. Only those readers who have never committed a sin will not feel threatened.

The tenth and last section discusses the question *"Hal al-jihād farīḍah ghā'ibah?"*—"Is *jihād* really a nonfulfilled duty?" Qur'ān and Sunnah, so the Muftī teaches, command Muslims to resist the enemies of Islam, but they certainly do not order attacks on other Muslims, or on non-Muslim compatriots. Jews and Christians must have freedom of cult and belief, the Muftī insists. They have the same rights as Muslim citizens, he continues. The character of *jihād,* so we must understand, has now changed radically, because the defense of country and religion is nowadays the duty of the regular army, and this army carries out the collective duty of *jihād* on behalf of all citizens. "To conquer oneself and Satan" is equally part of the Muslim duty of *jihād,* the Muftī adds, while calling other Muslims apostates is not. Whatever the people of the *Farīḍah* and their sympathizers might say, *jihād* is, according to the Muftī, not a forgotten or absent duty at all.

The Muftī's response to the *Farīḍah* distinguishes itself by not being ambiguous. Muslim readers of the Muftī's response will no doubt not fail to notice that the Muftī bases his response on verses from the Qur'ān and on Traditions. The way in which the Muftī insists on an exegesis of the Qur'ān that takes the context into account is especially interesting. Without the Muftī's fatwā on the *Farīḍah* it would be difficult not to believe that militant Islam is becoming mainstream Islam.

NOTES

[*Majallat al-Azhar* is abbreviated as *MA;* anno hegirae as AH.]

1. On the attempts to take away the diploma of a certain Muḥammad Abū Zayd who had published a controversial Qur'ān commentary in 1349 AH: see my *The Interpretation . . .*, pp. 87–88, and the Azhar Journal *Nūr al-Islām,* ii, 163–206 and 249–281 (Cairo, 1350 AH).
2. A discussion on the formal qualifications of a Muslim scholar and his right to interpret the Qur'ān is summarized in my "Polemics on Mustafa Mahmūd's Koran Exegesis," *Proceedings of the Ninth Con-*

gress of the Union Européenne des Arabisants et Islamisants, ed. R. PETERS, Leiden, 1981, p. 110.

3. ᶜABD AL-ḤALĪM MAḤMŪD, *Fatāwā al-Imām ᶜAbd al-Ḥalīm Maḥmūd,* 2 vols., Cairo (Dār al-Maᶜārif), 1981 & 1982, 528 & 528 pp., vol. ii, p. 465. See also A.C. ECCEL, *Egypt, Islam and Social Change: Al-Azhar in Conflict and Accommodation,* Berlin (Klaus Schwarz), 1984.
4. JAMĀL AL-GHAYṬĀNĪ, *Muṣṭafā Amīn Yatadhakkar,* Cairo (Madbūlī), 1983, tells how Saᶜd Zaghlūl in the days he was prime minister kept his Azhar dress ready and in good order in his dressing room (p. 104).
5. *MA,* 56/7, April 1984/Rajab 1404, p. 1196.
6. ḤASANAYN MUḤAMMAD MAKHLŪF, *Fatāwā Sharᶜīyah wa-Buḥūth Islāmīyah,* Cairo (Muṣṭafā al-Bābī al-Ḥalabī), 2 vols., both second editions, 1965, 392 and 212 pp.
7. ḤASANAYN MUḤ. MAKHLŪF, *Fatāwā,* i, 182.
8. Ibid., i, 246.
9. Ibid., i, 81.
10. AL-IMĀM AL-AKBAR MAḤMŪD SHALTŪT, *Al-Fatāwā, Dirāsah li-mushkilāt al-Muslim fī Ḥayātihi al-Yawmīyah al-ᶜĀmmah,* Cairo (Dār al-Qalam), Third Ed., 1966, 464 pp.
11. MAḤMŪD SHALTŪT, *Fatāwā,* p. 44.
12. Ibid., p. 434.
13. Italics added.
14. ᶜABD AL-ḤALĪM MAḤMŪD, *Fatāwā,* ii, 224.
15. Syntax and grammar strongly suggest that "and it is a duty for all Islamic states" is a later addition to the Shaykh's text.
16. DEREK HOPWOOD, *Egypt, Politics and Society 1945–1981,* London, 1982, p. 119.
17. *Al-Ahrām,* May 10, 1979, *"al-muᶜāhadah fī ḥudūd al-ḥukm al-islāmī."*
18. *Al-Ahrām,* May 24, 1980, referendum result: 98.96% votes "yes."
19. *MA,* 51/8, September 1979/Shawwāl 1399, p. 1980.
20. Ibid., p. 1995.
21. Ibid., p. 2005. The real thoughts ᶜUmar al-Tilimsānī must have had at this occasion can be inferred from his *Ayyām maᶜa al-Sādāt,* Cairo (Dār al-Iᶜtiṣām), 1984.
22. See, e.g., my *The Interpretation . . . ,* pp. 80–81.
23. *MA,* 51/8, September 1979, p. 1999.

24. *MA*, 53/11, September 1981, p. 1954.
25. Ibid., p. 1958b.
26. *MA*, 53/12, October 1981, p. 2139.
27. *MA*, 54/1, November 1981/Muḥarram 1402, mentions on p. 170 a meeting that took place on September 15, 1981; *MA*, 54/2, November 1981/Ṣafar 1402, mentions the assassination on its first page (p. 180).
28. *MA*, 54/1, November 1981/Muḥarram 1402, p. 6.
29. Ibid., p. 104.
30. *Majallat al-Taṣawwuf al-Islāmī*, xxxii, 3, and xxxiii, 62.
31. *MA*, 54/2, November 1981/Ṣafar 1402, p. 180.
32. The writer of the editorial, Dr. ^{c}Abd al-Mu^{c}ṭī Muḥammad Bayūmī, does not, however, mention the second set of measures.
33. Ibid., p. 182.
34. Ibid., p. 296.
35. Ibid., p. 297.
36. Ibid., p. 303.
37. Ibid., p. 304.
38. ṢALĀḤ MUNTAṢIR, *Ḥiwār ma^{c}a al-Shaykh al-Sha^{c}rāwī*, Cairo (Dār al-Ma^{c}ārif, Kitābuka 142), 1982, p. 5.
39. *MA*, 54/3, December 1981/Rabī^{c} al-Awwal 1402, pp. 324 ff.
40. Ibid., p. 481.
41. Ibid., p. 482.
42. JĀDD AL-ḤAQQ ^{c}ALĪ JĀDD AL-ḤAQQ et al., *Al-Fatāwā al-Islāmīyah*, 10/31, Cairo, 1983, p. 3733 (see Chapter 1, note 8).
43. The Muftī here refers to *Majmū^{c} Fatāwā Ibn Taymīyah*, xxviii, 520.
44. C. BROCKELMANN, *Geschichte der Arabischen Literatur*, Leiden, 1943, S I 666.

CHAPTER 3

The Ṣūfī Reaction

THE WORD "SUFISM" is used to indicate a wide and diverse number of Islamic religious activities and experiences. The diversity of these should, however, not obscure the fact that Sufism is first of all the Islamic form of mysticism.

Systems of mysticism, in all ages and all parts of the world, are characterized by certain identical beliefs. These have been analyzed with clarity by the British philosopher Bertrand Russell in a well-known essay first published in 1914, "Mysticism and Logic." This essay[1] enumerates four characteristics that are common to all forms of mysticism. The first characteristic is the belief in insight as against discursive analytic knowledge.

The negative side of this aspect of mysticism is, according to Russell, the doubt concerning common knowledge which has to prepare the way for the reception of what seems a higher wisdom. (The autobiography of Al-Ghazālī supplies a famous illustration of this point.) Closely connected with this mystical insight is the belief in a reality hidden behind the world of appearance.

The second characteristic, according to Russell's famous essay, is the mystic's belief in the unity and indivisibility of all reality. The third mark of the mystic's perception of reality, so the essay continues, is the denial of the reality of time. The last of the essential doctrines of mysticism, as expounded in Russell's essay, is the belief that all evil is mere appearance, an illusion produced by the analytic intellect. This attitude, Russell writes, is a direct outcome of the nature of the mystical experience: with its sense of unity is associated a feeling of infinite peace.

The different systems of mysticism that one may come across have, however, more in common than these metaphysical beliefs. In the world of appearances there are remarkable similarities between them as well. The concept of a road or a path which the mystic has to follow in order to achieve his aims plays a great role. The mystic has to follow this path under the guidance of a Teacher or Guru, whose personal influence on the mystic may be considerable. This personal influence of the Guru and his successors may produce an amount of social cohesion unheard of in so-called primitive societies. Totalitarian governments, always eager to win the hearts and minds of their subjects, may see this social cohesion as being in competition with their own monopoly on popularity and power.

Mysticism usually produces literature. Having seen the unseeable, a mystic wants to express the inexpressible. This results in poetical descriptions of the mystic's visions and ecstasies, or in prose descriptions of the successive stages of the path that must be followed.

The mystic's uncertainty concerning good and evil has two practical results. The first is a political aloofness and social quietism, which is not unwelcome to modern governments. Second, the uncertainty concerning good and evil may, of course, make the mystic indifferent toward the value of the actions prescribed or forbidden by the code of (religious) law to which he is nominally subject. Also, the mystic's desire to observe his religious rituals may weaken once higher insights have begun to dominate his spiritual life.

This supposed indifference explains the suspicion with which official representatives of official religion look at mysticism, and the frequent reassurances on this point which the mystics feel obliged to utter.

When these generalities concerning mysticism are taken into account, Egyptian Sufism becomes — in spite of its complexity — a less confusing phenomenon.

The best possible public source of information on the contemporary Egyptian Ṣūfī movement is the monthly journal that the Ṣūfīs have published since the spring of 1979. The journal is called *Majallat al-Taṣawwuf al-Islāmī,* "The Journal of Islamic Mysticism." On the one hand, it is imaginable that not everything the Ṣūfīs do or think is spelled out in this journal; on the other hand, sometimes things may be published in this journal that many Ṣūfīs do not deem to be very important or totally true. Yet this monthly is an excellent and rich source.

The *Majallat al-Taṣawwuf al-Islāmī* is beautifully executed and has an attractive and professional appearance. Its conspicuous frontispieces were no doubt designed to compete with the covers of the fundamentalist monthlies *Al-Daᶜwah* and *Al-Iᶜtiṣām,* which at that time also abounded in the Cairo newsstands. The official publisher of the journal is *Al-Majlis al-Ṣūfī al-Aᶜlā,* the Ṣūfī High Council, which is formed out of the larger *Mashyakhat al-Ṭuruq al-Ṣūfīyah,* "General Committee of Leaders of the Ṣūfī Brotherhoods."

The journal calls itself a continuation of *Majallat al-Islām wa-'l-Taṣawwuf,* "The Journal of Islam and Mysticism," a similar journal which started in June 1958 and which continued to appear for almost four years. Even some of the contributors are the same, for example, Dr. Abū-'l-Wafā al-Taftazānī who wrote an article in the second issue of the *Majallat al-Islām wa-'l-Taṣawwuf* in 1958 as well as one in the first number of *Majallat al-Taṣawwuf al-Islāmī* in May 1979.

Another contributor to both the old and the new Ṣūfī journal is Anwar al-Sadat. Both in 1958 and in 1979 an article in which the government congratulates the Ṣūfī movement on the establishment of its journal is signed by him. With the exception of one line the two articles are identical. The difference is found in a paragraph devoted to the necessity of cleansing Sufism from "superstitions." The 1958 version of the article assures the reader that the Ṣūfī leadership "has started to purify the *mawlid* festivities from excessive dancing and music making, and has furthermore got rid of the swindlers and frauds who attended such ceremonies, with the help of the revolutionary government and its devoted Ministers."

In the 1979 version of the same article the political phraseology has changed. No mention is made of the revolutionary government, or its devoted ministers. Also the phrase "the Ṣūfī leadership has started to purify," which so aptly expresses feelings of postrevolutionary optimism, has disappeared, and now we only read that the Ṣūfī leadership "may have entered" upon the true road to the purification of Sufism. It is difficult to escape the conclusion that this change in an otherwise unchanged article was prompted by the awareness that the character of the Ṣūfī festivals known as *mawlids* had changed very little, if at all, between 1958 and 1979.

In its first issue (May 1979), the journal announces the "general rules to which the journal will adhere." These are five in number: (1) The journal will not enter into any Islamic denominational dispute. (2) The journal will attempt to give publicity to a reformatory view *(wajhah iṣlāḥīyah)* of Islamic mysticism, and will further a Sufism that is in agreement with Qur'ān and Sunnah. (3) The journal will inform its readers on the prescripts of Islamic Law, instruct them in the Islamic creed, and help them to understand the Islamic way of life. (4) The journal intends to publish information not only on the activities of the Ṣūfīs, but also on general Islamic activities, including important conferences. (5) The journal will give news on Egyptian society and tell its readers about developments in other Arab or Islamic countries.

This is the official program of the journal, as formulated in the first editorial. Elsewhere we read supplementary, less official statements. We are told, for instance, that one of the aims of the journal will be to educate and refine *(tathqīf)* the less cultured members of the Brotherhoods, or that the publication of the journal serves to defend the Ṣūfīs and Islam against malicious misrepresentation. Every now and then we meet articles that were written in defense of the purity of Sufism, like the article *Laysū Ṣūfīyīn*, "They Are Not Ṣūfīs," in the November 1979 issue.

Each issue opens with a sermon-like article written by Shaykh Muḥammad Maḥmūd al-Saṭūḥī, the Chairman of the Central Committee of the Ṣūfī movement. Each issue ends with several pages that contain news from within the Egyptian Ṣūfī movement. In the same way as its predecessor from the late fifties, the journal publishes the appointments of local and regional functionaries of the recognized Brotherhoods and their branches. It should be kept in mind that there are 67 recognized Ṣūfī fraternities, which all have their local branches. The journal also announces the dates and places of the all-important *mawlid* festivals held in commemoration of Muslim Saints and the founders of Ṣūfī fraternities. It is clearly the news from within the Brotherhoods that is the reason for the existence of the journal.

The journal's first issue gives a summary of the essentials of the Egyptian Law of 1976 concerning the Brotherhoods, the *Qānūn al-Ṭuruq al-Ṣūfīyah*. From this summary the mode of cooperation between the government and the Ṣūfī movement can be inferred. According to this law, the Central Committee of the Brotherhoods will consist of fifteen members: ten chosen by direct elections out of the general assembly of the Brotherhoods, and five appointed by the different branches of the government. It is this committee of fifteen that must approve the foundation of a new Brotherhood, and has then to forward a proposal for its recognition to the Ministry of the Interior. Not all Brotherhoods that existed at the time of the promulgation of the new law were recognized, the journal adds. In particular, the splitting up of a Brotherhood into two new organizations is made subject to regulations which make detachments from the main body of well-controlled Brotherhoods practically impossible.

The government apparatus and the official Ṣūfī movement hence hold each other in a mutual embrace. In spite — or because? — of these close ties the journal of the Ṣūfī movement pays little attention to the political controversies that divide the Egyptian public. Unlike the fundamentalist activist monthlies *Al-Daᶜwah* and *Al-Iᶜtiṣām* of this period, the Ṣūfī monthly hardly mentions Khomeinī's Iran or Begin's Israel. The Soviet invasion of Afghanistan, a subject that was not controversial in Egypt at that time, is, however, frequently discussed.[2]

In one of the articles in the journal's first issue,[3] Shaykh Al-Saṭūḥī tells of an attempt to involve the Ṣūfī orders in an election campaign: the former Prime Minister Mamdūḥ Sālim had offered to leave 30 districts to the organized Ṣūfī movement. In these districts the Ṣūfīs would put up the candidates, who then would receive official support. "We answered, however, that we, men of mysticism, could not participate under our own names in a political struggle and in elections, and this for one reason only: the unity of the great Ṣūfī family . . . thus we are able to spread our message among everybody regardless of the political differences people might have."

The journal and the Ṣūfī movement as such are, however, not totally uninterested in politics. One may encounter vague references to "economic crises" that need study, and "social problems" that threaten the Muslim family, "perhaps even Islamic society as a whole." It is perhaps surprising that the same article pleads for the introduction of censorship on television and in the press. State ceremonies in commemoration of historic national events are duly reported. The readers of the journal also receive guidance on how to vote in the referenda which the government organizes in these years. It is not probable that the quietism that is characteristic of true mysticism has ever become endangered by these gentle extramural activities.

Each issue of the journal of the Ṣūfī movement has a section devoted to questions that are supposedly asked by the readers. Qualified Azhar consultants give their decisions on the matters raised by the questioners. The responses are signed by the *Lajnat al-Fatwā bi-'l-Azhar al-Sharīf,* the official committee of al-Azhar University which has the task to supply such answers to questions on points of Muslim Law in the widest sense of the word.

A question-and-answer section in any journal anywhere in the world usually not only reflects the sphere of interest of the journal's public but also, perhaps even more, the interests of the editors of the journal. This is particularly true of the questions asked and answered in the first issue of a new journal since it is difficult to imagine how the public could have written to a journal before its creation.

The question-and-answer section of the first issue of the Ṣūfī journal (May 1979) discusses six questions: (1) Is hashish forbidden in Islamic Law? The jurisconsults quote Ibn Taymīyah, Ibn al-Qayyim, and other authorities, and give a positive answer.

Everything that intoxicates is forbidden, they conclude, irrespective of whether people eat or drink it. (2) Certain doctors, so the next question runs, carry out an operation to transplant the hymen for girls who lost their virginity because of *zinā*, "fornication." Is this operation allowed or forbidden? The jurisconsults give a short answer. Such transplantations, they argue, are carried out in order to deceive. A doctor is hence forbidden to carry it out, and a girl is not allowed to submit herself to it. (3) The existence of a valid marriage contract which fulfills all legal requirements means that the marriage involved is legal and valid. Must such a marriage contract nevertheless be registered? The answer of the experts is clear: the marriage itself is legal and valid, but as long as it is not registered, no court of law may hear claims concerning alimony or inheritance that are based on such an unregistered marriage. The registration itself they regard as allowed *(jā'iz)*.

This is again a subject as sensitive as drugs and virginity. God's law does not prescribe the registration of marriage contracts, many pious Muslims argue. It is only the State that prescribes such formalities. Does the State have the authority to annul a contract that is valid according to the Law of God? Certainly not, but the State will not assist in enforcing rights and claims that spring from such an unregistered—but valid—marriage.

Two financial questions then follow: (4) After a divorce, so we read, a husband received a cash settlement the amount of which was meant to be the equivalent of the price of a piece of property which he had once presented to his bride as a wedding gift. The amount, however, was now 25 percent higher than the cash value at which the property had been estimated at the time of the conclusion of the marriage. Is this 25 percent a form of interest and hence forbidden according to Islamic Law? The jurisconsultants can put the mind of the questioner at ease. He may accept his money, the 25 percent included.

The second financial question concerns the different forms of "investment certificates" current in Egypt at the time: (5) Is the profit that these certificates offer forbidden or not? The jurisconsultants are of the opinion that Islamic Law only forbids those certificates that offer a definite percentage decided upon in advance. When no percentage is fixed beforehand, Islamic Law, according to the experts, does not forbid the investment certificates.

The last question concerns clitorodectomy: (6) "What is the judgment of Islam on the circumcision of girls?," the plain question runs. The answer is short. The jurisconsults quote a saying ascribed to the Prophet *(ikhfiḍī wa-lā tanhakī)*, "carry out the female circumcision but not to excess." The relative obscurity of the terminology used in this Prophetic saying makes it necessary for the editors to point out that this saying contains not only a divine command to circumcize girls, but also the injunction not to "exaggerate" in its execution.

An unusually perceptive modern Western poet once summarized the *Weltanschauung* of his contemporaries in the catch phrase "sex and drugs and rock-and-roll." Up to a point, the editors of the Ṣūfī journal have the same, perhaps universal, interests. In their case, however, these interests are controlled by the prescripts of Islamic Law as expounded and interpreted by the official and qualified Azhar jurisconsults. The contents of the question-and-answer sections in the successive issues of the Ṣūfī journal illustrate this abundantly.

The photograph printed above these sections also potently symbolizes the submission to Azhar authority. On this photograph we see two men dressed in the traditional garb of an Azhar scholar. They are obviously being questioned by two middle-aged women who have covered their heads and dressed in a way which suggests complete observance of the Islamic concepts of female modesty. They sit in an otherwise empty office room, with bare furniture, and books in the background. The books symbolize ancient scholarship and learning. In the foreground we see a telephone — suggesting the presence of the twentieth century and its overwhelming technical possibilities — all put at the service of Islam. Somehow the photograph breathes an atmosphere of true Islamic solidity.

There can be very little reason to accuse the people on this photograph of the sin of *al-istiqlāl ᶜani-'l-Sharīᶜah,*[4] "to make oneself independent of the revealed law," no matter how frequently this accusation has been made against mystics, not only in the history of Islam, but also in the history of other religions that are dominated by a revelation and a revealed law.

Many other points could be selected in order to demonstrate how far the views of the editors of the Egyptian Ṣūfī movement agree with the views of Muslims in general. One of these is particularly important: the application of Islamic Law in public life, the shibboleth of the activists. In several articles in the journal the most — if one may use the expression — conservative attitude possible is argued in connection with the *taṭbīq al-Sharīᶜah,* the application of God's Law, and one writer even explicitly states[5] that any attack on those who call for a strict and total application of the laws of Islam is in reality an attack on the Holy Law itself.

The well-known verses from Sūrah 5 are also brought forward in support of a position that is very close indeed to that of the activists: "Judge between them by what God sent down," and "Whoever does not judge by what God sent down — they are the unbelievers." It is, then, not surprising to see that attempts at a more liberal interpretation of the Qur'ān and Islamic Law like those advocated by Justice Muḥammad Saᶜīd al-ᶜAshmāwī are denounced by the Ṣūfī journal as "rebellion against Islam in the name of Islam, *al-khurūj ᶜalā-'l-Islām bi-'sm al-Islām.*"[6]

In spite of these activist and Azhar influences, the basic mystical attitudes of the editors of the journal show themselves frequently in its pages. One writer, for instance, argues in the November 1979 issue that

> in the shadow of Islam, *fī ẓill al-Islām,* there is no struggle between man and himself, neither between man and society, nor between man and the universe, since perfect harmony is one of the fruits of Islam . . . the Creator of all is one, His will is one . . . there are no sharp boundaries, *ḥudūd fāṣilah,* between religion, *dīn,* and world, *dunyā,* or between the world and the hereafter, or between mind and body, or between material and spiritual, all these are enclosed in one order, *yashmuluhum niẓām wāḥid,* an order that is constant, *thābit,* and lasting, *mustaqirr,* and of great brilliance. One will not find in the Custom of God any change, *lan tajid li-Sunnat Allāh tabdīlan.*[7]

These last words are a quotation from the Qur'ān, and the use made of it here, where it has to support the mystic's feeling that change, division, and opposition are illusions only since all is one, is certainly typical of mysticism. Others, such as Dr. Zakī Najīb Maḥmūd, have on the contrary argued that the essence of Islam is its dualism, *thanawīyah,* between man and God, heaven and earth, and so on.[8]

Once more, it is noteworthy how in this article, in spite of its true mystical character, a slogan that sounds like a battle-cry which is used by the activists crept in: *Al-Islām Dīn wa-Dunyā.* In its own context this slogan is usually translated as "Islam is a religion and a world order." Many Egyptian Muslims will yet associate this motto with the Muslim Brothers. It is surprising how skillfully it is woven into the list of apparent oppositions. The article makes perfectly clear that, to a good Muslim, these oppositions are not real. By denying the reality of the opposition between *dīn* (religion) and *dunyā* (world), the Muslim mystic obeys the innate tendencies of mysticism but—at least in the Egyptian political context—he also happens to take up a political position close to that of the activists. This, in its turn, is not in accordance with the political aloofness which one expects of a mystic. Nevertheless it will be difficult for an Egyptian reader of this article not to conclude that its author sympathizes with the Muslim Brothers, or that their slogan *Al-Islām Dīn wa-Dawlah,* "Islam is a religion and a state", can also be subscribed to by a Ṣūfī.

Nevertheless, the tendency to believe in unity and to refuse to admit opposition or division anywhere is abundantly present on the pages of the Egyptian Ṣūfī monthly. Next to it, great importance is attached to the absence of indignation or protest. The Stoics used to employ the term *ataraxis* to refer to this state of equanimity. According to many, it is desirable to be free of passion, neither loving nor disliking. In an interesting article in the journal,[9] Dr. Abū-'l-Wafā al-Taftazānī talks about the Ṣūfī views on the same concepts, and links these with Qur'ān 57.23: "That you may not feel sad at what you have missed, or be uplifted with joy at what has come to you."

In another article[10] Dr. Abū-'l-Wafā makes a link between the concept of equanimity and Qur'ān 13.28: "Those who believe, their hearts are at peace in the *dhikr* of God." The Arabic word *dhikr* is one of the words that are difficult to translate without losing some of their connotations. *Dhikr* denotes a group of meanings which includes "remembering" and "invoking," especially of God's name, and this particularly in the Ṣūfī *dhikr* festivals where certain words or phrases are repeatedly and incessantly "mentioned," often to the accompaniment of music and dancing. According to Dr. Abū-'l-Wafā, so the Ṣūfī reader of the journal has to conclude, the *dhikr* festivities of the Ṣūfī Brotherhoods are mentioned in the Qur'ān and the aim of these festivities, so it appears, is to bring peace to the hearts of the believers.

Dr. Abū-'l-Wafā al-Taftazānī, who is professor of Islamic philosophy at the University of Cairo and who succeeded Shaykh Al-Saṭūḥī as the Chairman of the Ṣūfī movement at the latter's death in February 1983, has published an impressive series of articles in the monthly in which he demonstrates how the essential beliefs of mysticism can be traced to the Qur'ān, in verses where many would have failed to see the mystical implications.

Also, the specific practices and characteristics of Islamic mysticism get attention, but these are, as a matter of fact, well known to the readers of the journal and need little explanation. The *dhikr* festivals are, of course, connected with passages from the Qur'ān in which the verb from which *dhikr* is derived occurs, as in Qur'ān 33.41: "O you who have believed, call God frequently to mind," and 4.104: "Remember God, standing or sitting or lying on your side."

A pilgrimage to the tomb of a Saint is not approved of by orthodox Islam. Yet it is a frequent Ṣūfī practice. On this sensitive and at times controversial subject the journal[11] tells its readers that the meetings held at the tombs of saints are not a heretical practice that has slipped into Islam, a so-called *bid^c^ah*. Such visits and meetings, the journal explains, are allowed on the condition that they are only "a simple visit to the dead in their grave. . . . However, such a visit would be forbidden if during the visit things are committed that are against Islam; the visit, moreover, should not necessitate a period of residence at the tomb."

This last addition is clarified by a saying ascribed to the Prophet which concludes the journal's discussion of visits to the tombs of Saints: "Do not break camp but for three things: the Mosque of Mecca, the Mosque of Jerusalem, or my mosque here." The implicit historical context[12] of this saying makes its authenticity suspect. During the lifetime of the Prophet there were no situations in which it could have been a relevant admonition: Jerusalem was conquered by the Muslims in 637, five years after the Prophet's death. The purpose of the saying is to make pilgrimages to Jerusalem and Medina as permissable as the pilgrimage to Mecca. The Ṣūfī journal wants to use this saying to support the view that visits to tombs — when they do not entail a period of residence at the tomb — are allowed.

The journal's view that "a simple visit" is allowed when nothing forbidden accompanies the visit seems very much a tautology. Yet the public of the Ṣūfī monthly cannot have failed to understand its meaning. Is it possible to find out what kinds of "forbidden things" are referred to without, however, taking recourse to the reports of Western travelers, the observations by Western scholars, or the Islamic orthodox polemics against Sufism? Do the pages of the Ṣūfī journal itself supply information on these forbidden abuses — if they may be so called?

Sadat's above-mentioned contribution to the Ṣūfī journal lists a number of objections against the religious practices in use among the Ṣūfīs. He divides his objections into five groups: (1) Certain Ṣūfī leaders exploit their position financially. (2) Some men are regarded as holy because of their long beards and wild hair cuts, or because of the strange rites they perform, their amulets, their wooden swords, and their overall dirtiness. (3) A third group of Ṣūfīs amuse the common crowds with meaningless games and try to attract them with pseudomiracles. They swallow glass, eat fire, consume live snakes, walk on swords, beat on drums, make loud music, and dance with "hysterical movements," *ḥarakāt histirīyah*. It does not seem that Sadat's catalogue of amusement park attractions offered during the *mawlid* festivals omits anything important.

In the context of "forbidden things" which accompany the visits to the tombs of Muslim Saints, the last two objections that Sadat's article enumerates probably have little importance: (4) Some Ṣūfīs mix philosophical speculation with religion, and (5) other Ṣūfīs confuse Sufism with asceticism or even monasticism.

The frivolous festivities that surround religious celebrations have always attracted criticism from men of religion. This already was the case in Christian pre-Islamic Egypt. Wilhelm Riedel, in his introduction to *The Canons of Athanasius,* wrote:

> We can learn [from several fourth century sources] of the annually recurrent festivals of the martyrs which took place in chapels dedicated especially to them. From [one source] we moreover gather that such celebrations were by many denounced, clearly on the account of the abuses to which they frequently gave occasion. Such festivals took place usually at night and appear to have acquired the character of public holidays with which secular entertainments were combined; hence attendance at them is forbidden to monks and nuns.

The denunciations of the profane character and atmosphere of the festivities that accompanied the commemoration of Ṣūfī Saints at their graves and tombs hence sprouts from an old and venerable tradition. The injunction not to make a period of residence at the tomb necessary, as the Ṣūfī journal brings forward, would certainly preclude what many would regard as real fun.

The *mawlid* festivals, and Sufism in general, enjoy much popularity with the great mass of the people. Some think that, by definition, *hoi polloi* are never well educated, and never have refined tastes. They are, so one has to conclude, rarely rational. These matters are touched upon in an interview that we read in the October 1979 issue of the Ṣūfī journal.[14] In this interview a certain Dr. Ibrāhīm Madkūr, a well-known literary critic who is president of the Arab Language Academy of Cairo, tells his questioners (among other interesting things) that the Ṣūfī leaders have great influence on the masses (*ᶜāmmat al-nās,* the common crowd), and that according to him this influence is no doubt salutary, but, so he adds, "Maybe some of them mix their teachings with irrationalities based on ignorance, which is not in keeping with the spirit of the age, *rūḥ al-ᶜaṣr.*"

The editors of the Ṣūfī journal, it seems, have to defend themselves on two fronts. Not only do they have to convince a critical orthodox Muslim reader of their journal that their Sufism does not go beyond the boundaries set by Qur'ān and Sunnah, they also have to persuade the world that their particular brand of Sufism is in accordance with the "spirit of the age." It is perhaps in the light of this defensive attitude that we must look at the succession of Shaykh Al-Saṭūḥī as Chairman of the Ṣūfī movement's Central Committee in early 1983. The new chairman carries the title of doctor, which implies a Western-style higher education. In the eyes of many, such an education is more in accordance with the spirit of the age than the traditional Islamic system of higher education which supplies even to its most successful students nothing more than the honorific title of shaykh.

It is not impossible to imagine a certain amount of controversy on the character of the "spirit of the age." It is, however, certain that this much-invoked spirit looks askance at mysticism in general and at Sufism in particular. An Egyptian representative of the spirit of the age, Muḥammad Fahmī ᶜAbd al-Laṭīf, wrote in 1979 that "stupidity and ignorance have shown delusions and irrationalities in the emotional constitution of this people to the effect that these delusions and irrationalities have become transmuted into a firm system of beliefs to which this people *(hādhā al-shaᶜb)* religiously cling, both in its social and in its religious life."

These harsh words, to which little could possibly be added, are taken from the 1979 preface of a book that was first published in 1948.[15] In the intervening 30 years, so the writer claims, he has not had to go back on one single opinion expressed in the first edition. The book contains an unfriendly study of the Ṣūfī Saint Aḥmad al-Badawī, whose tomb is venerated at Tanta. The book not only condemns the veneration of this particular Saint and its alleged abuses, but it condemns the whole Ṣūfī movement.

The writer holds the Ṣūfīs responsible for all ills that have befallen Egypt and the Egyptians, the occupation by Napoleon and the invasion by the British not excluded. His basic accusation against the Ṣūfīs and their leaders can be summarized as *al-istighrāq fi-'l-tawakkul,*[16] literally "immersion in trust of God," excessive reliance on God's protection and the omission of sensible human precautions against threatening disasters. Whatever happened in Egypt, he writes, "the Ṣūfī leaders always stood passively at the side, *yaqifūna dā'iman fī nāḥiyah al-salbīyah,* and their influence was not worth mentioning, *lā najid lahum atharan yudhkar.*"[17]

According to Muḥammad Fahmī ᶜAbd al-Laṭīf, the attitude of the Egyptian Ṣūfī leaders contrasts unfavorably to the attitude of the "sons of al-Azhar." Azhar students and graduates, so he assures his readers, have always played an active role in Egyptian social and political life. The Libyan Sanusīyah Brotherhood is also mentioned and praised for its resistance to Italian imperialism, although (so we read) by its very nature the Sanusīyah also was originally nothing more than a Ṣūfī fraternity. Yet, their struggle against the Italians is said to have been one of the most radiant examples of *jihād,* war against unbelievers, in the history of Islam.[18]

Muḥammad Fahmī ᶜAbd al-Laṭīf gives an elaborate and extremely negative picture of the Ṣūfī movement, its practices which he calls abuses, and its emphasis on equanimity which he calls fatalism. One of the negative labels that Muḥammad Fahmī ᶜAbd al-Laṭīf uses deserves, however, to be more closely looked at. The way the Brotherhoods are organized and regulated gave rise to a system that Muḥammad Fahmī ᶜAbd al-Laṭīf feels he has to expose as *niẓām kahanūtī,* a priestly order, a hierarchy.[19]

Even in the context of an attack on Sufism, such a remark brings to mind the fact that Islam may not know, or even permit the establishment of, church-like organizations, complete with popes or councils. Nevertheless, Muslims sometimes feel the need to give an organizational and institutional framework to religious activities connected with pastoral counseling. It is this need that the Ṣūfī Brotherhoods want to provide. The charismatic teacher of the mystic's path has great personal influence. It is quite natural that this influence causes the establishment of groups of followers, and hence the rise of church-like organizations, complete with (possibly corrupt) hierarchies.

The tensions that held Egypt in their grip on the eve of the assassination of President Sadat inevitably found their reflections on the pages of the Ṣūfī monthly. One of the most outspoken contributors to the monthly, a certain Fu'ād al-Sayyid, wrote an editorial in the September 1981 issue under the title "Where now is this tolerance *(samāḥah)* among the Muslims?" The article contains several references to the "war" *(ḥarb)* that, according to this author, was at that time breaking out and in whose center radical activist Muslims were to be found, going to battle against the Copts and against their own government.

The end of the article sounds truly prophetic. There looms a danger, we read, that young people will fall prey to self-assured, biased fanatics who will exploit the youth's ignorance of the fundamentals of their religion, and who will persuade them of the truth of their (the fanatics') way of thinking *(tayyār)*. Thus might a legitimate defense of the creed be turned into something different: full-scale war against the adherents of their own religion who have refused to join them under the banners of the so-called "organizations," the *jamāᶜāt*.

The article opens by arguing that it is precisely the tolerance, religious tolerance, of the Muslims that made the majority of the Egyptians convert to Islam. Islam, we are told, once conquered the world, "and not by superior technology or advanced weapons" (as the Western powers once did) but by convincing the people with whom it came into contact of its superior values, of which tolerance, *samāḥah,* is one. This is the reason, so we read, why so many "sons of this country," *abnā' hādhihi al-bilād,* became Muslim by conviction, not by force.

The author then continues by describing how Islam grew and how Islamic society flourished because it was united under one banner, the banner of Islam. Especially today, he stresses, the Islamic world has all the potentials for prosperity: freedom from foreign occupation, vast mineral resources, possession of strategic localities which control world traffic, and so forth. Why then is there no Islamic unity? The answer to this question is divided into two parts: there are outside factors, and there are internal factors. Only one outside factor is mentioned: some Islamic countries collaborate with imperialist powers whose policy it has been and still is to prevent the danger of Islamic unity since, so this author believes, this unity would make the pursuit of their imperialist policies impossible.

The internal factors that are now mentioned are considerably less abstract. The author says to have met, in mosque sermons and newspaper articles, with painful attacks that are being made on the Ṣūfī organizations and on "other Islamic institutions." The attackers, he writes, believe that these organizations and institutions compete with them for the religious leadership. The "other Islamic institutions" remain mysteriously unnamed in the articles by

Fu'ād al-Sayyid. There can, however, be no doubt that next to the Ṣūfī High Council it is al-Azhar—the most important Islamic institution in Egypt, if not in the world—which must have been the subject of these attacks. In the *Farīḍah* al-Azhar is singled out and mentioned by name, and other extremist lay preachers have certainly said similar things.

If no attacks on al-Azhar were being made at the time, it would be difficult to understand the article that the Ṣūfī monthly published in the October 1981 issue[20] about controversies between the government and al-Azhar. The examples of controversies that the article gives are, however, not very recent. They are all older than 30 years and date from before the Nasser-Naguib Revolution of 1952. The article as it stands, in spite of its opposite intention, is an indication that the general public is losing—or has lost—its belief in the independence of the Azhar from the Egyptian government. The problem is, of course, which institutions will replace al-Azhar as the most trusted religious authority should al-Azhar indeed lose this role: the Muslim Brotherhood, the *jamāᶜāt,* or the Ṣūfī leadership?

According to Fu'ād al-Sayyid, there is a war going on against Sufism (and against these "other institutions") in which certain people spread empty accusations against the Ṣūfīs and ascribe actions to them that are contrary to the principles of the Islamic religion. They utter these accusations, he continues, in order to win new members for their own organizations, the *jamāᶜāt*. This war that Muslims are launching against their fellow Muslims, so the author believes, is against Qur'ān and Tradition.

"If we are to treat non-Muslims according to the tolerant principles of Islam, should we not be obliged to treat each other as brothers as well and dispute in only the best possible way?" and "Is there not one *rashīd* (rightly guided) among them who is able to warn them of the dangerous consequences of this conflict which is flaring up?" The use of the word *rashīd* in the last rhetorical question deserves special attention. The leaders of the *jamāᶜāt* organizations call themselves *khalīfah,* caliph, and, according to Islamic history, the first four great Caliphs had carried the title of *rāshid,* rightly guided. The Caliphs Abū Bakr, ᶜUmar, ᶜUthmān and ᶜAlī (632–661) are traditionally known as *al-khulafā' al-rāshidūn*. By using the epithet *rashīd* the author manages to make it perfectly clear whom he is addressing—without, however, giving these modern self-styled caliphs the satisfaction of addressing them as caliph, since this might in some eyes imply a form of recognition of their caliphal title.

In the next issue, also dated October 1981, Fu'ād al-Sayyid continues in the same vein, using the same terminology as in the previous issue. He warns the reader of "the danger of the ranks of the religious organizations being infiltrated with destructive ideas under the guise of religion," and he attacks the claims to absolute authority heard from these modern caliphs: "(Young people) accept orders from them without having the right to object, or the right to refuse to carry out their orders." Once more, he warns against sermons heard from the pulpits in the mosques in which Sufism and "other Islamic institutions" are being attacked.

The Egyptian nation, he writes, is becoming hopelessly divided, and this will not only be a division between Muslims on one side and their brothers, the Copts *(ikhwānuhum al-aqbāṭ),* on the other, but it will be a division among the Muslims themselves as well. He sees no hope that this development can be stopped by "sermons, friendly advice or tears about what is happening." The example of Lebanon is mentioned, a once prosperous country that is being ruined by sectarian fighting.

Fu'ād al-Sayyid finally mentions a project he has heard about: new preachers for the mosques would be trained, and would then form a "new enlightened element," "capable of protecting the participants in the mosque services, and especially the young" against being infiltrated with extremist ideas. The mosque sermons, so he emphasizes, are at present boring and uninteresting, but they could be an excellent means of "educating" the masses.

Somehow the implication of this article by Fu'ād al-Sayyid seems to be that mosque sermons are either colored by extremism and hence dangerous but not boring, or they are official, too long, dull, and boring. Quoting an untranslatable proverb, he makes it clear that, according to him, only might can put things right. In his discussions on the modern mosque sermons, Fu'ād al-Sayyid does not say that more sermons, or better sermons, or even the best sermons imaginable, will only make Egypt's situation more critical since the more attention the general public devotes to its religious passions, the greater the danger becomes that (religious) violence will erupt. It is, however, not impossible to understand his articles in this way.

The first issue of the Ṣūfī monthly that appeared after the assassination of President Sadat had printed on its multicolored frontispiece a verse done in calligraphy from the Qur'ān:

If you do not help him
Yet God has helped him
When the unbelievers expelled him with only one companion
The two of them were in the cave
And he said to his companion
Grieve not, surely God is with us.[21]

In its own Qur'anic context this verse refers to the Meccan unbelievers who had expelled the Prophet Muḥammad who was at that time accompanied only by his later successor as leader of the community, Abū Bakr, the first Caliph after Muḥammad's death in 632 AD.

In the context of the frontispiece of the Ṣūfī journal of November 1981, however, many readers will have understood the verse differently: "If you do not help him" might be seen as an oblique reference to the inactivity and powerlessness of the President's bodyguard, and the "expulsion" can easily be understood as the assassination. The "cave" is a fitting description, indeed, of the fatal parade-ground where the assassination took place. Would it even be possible to understand the last words "to his companion" as farewell words addressed by the murdered President to his successor?

The customary sections of the monthly are this time preceded by a page devoted to the required official condolences. A photograph of Sadat and Mubārak that seems to have been taken less than an hour before the assassination is printed over more than half of the page. The accompanying text tells how the Ṣūfī High Council held an emergency meeting after the news of the death of President Sadat became known, and how a delegation from its midst was sent to the Republican Palace to offer its condolences on behalf of the Egyptian Ṣūfī movement. The wording of the condolences is given in full. In these condolence paragraphs Sadat is called *al-ra'īs al-mu'min,* the believing President, a honorific title customary in those days, and the assassination is referred to as *istishhād,* martyrdom.

The last lines of this page are devoted to Mubārak's candidacy for the Presidency of the Republic. The Ṣūfī High Council, so the text runs, has decided to support this candidacy and calls upon the leaders of the Ṣūfī Brotherhoods and upon all agents *(wukalā')* of the Ṣūfī High Council in the provinces to go to the polling boxes and vote in favor of Husnī Mubārak. It appears from these condolences, and from this call to vote, that the Ṣūfī High Council fully cooperated with the transition arrangements that had to be made, and closely followed the official government policies.

The next section of this issue of the Ṣūfī monthly is an "Open Letter" to the new President, Husnī Mubārak. This open letter is written by Fu'ād al-Sayyid who — of course — recalls how often he warned against "destructive elements" that had infiltrated the ranks of the religious organizations. Also, he wants his readers to remember how he had criticized the unconditional obedience that the leaders of these organizations required from their followers. These followers are again and again referred to as *shabāb,* "youth." Because of the youthful age of those who are misled by men exploiting their religious fervor, he feels entitled to call (again) for strict censorship on radio, television, and in the press since young people, so he writes, get bewildered by what they hear, see, and read.

The editors of the journal reprint, now for the third time, Sadat's article on Sufism that had also appeared in 1958 and 1979. The 1958 title of the article, *Al-Jihād al-Akbar,* is, however, understandably left out. The word *jihād* has so often been used by Sadat's enemies that it would be in bad taste to print it above this article which serves to commemorate the murdered President. The article itself has not been changed, and it dutifully argues that the highest form of *jihād ("al-jihād al-akbar")* is the struggle for the purification of man's own soul.

The December 1981 issue of the Ṣūfī monthly again contains reactions to the assassination of Sadat. Under the title "Hypocrisy is the greatest evil of our society" *(Al-Nifāq āfat mujtamaᶜnā),* Fu'ād al-Sayyid writes that there is "nothing more dangerous for a society than the spread in it of the evil of hypocrisy *(nifāq),* because hypocrisy is like a veil that protects the eyes from the light of realities. . . . A society in which hypocrisy prevails is a society of darkness and error, in which the gap between the ruler and the ruled becomes wider and wider." In spite of the references to the occurrence of *nifāq* in the Qur'ān, it is not the Qur'anic context of *nifāq* that we have to think of in this article, but the modern context of this word, in the way in which it is used by Dr. Ibrāhīm ᶜAbduh, for instance, in his *Rasā'il min Nifāqistān,* "Letters from (a country called) Hypocrisia."[22]

In this fascinating book Dr. Ibrāhīm ᶜAbduh argued that the flattery and hypocrisy with which the Egyptians surround their rulers since time immemorial inevitably destroys the realistic world outlook these rulers had before they came to power. After the assassination of Sadat, Dr. Ibrāhīm ᶜAbduh published a new small volume of essays, *Wa-min al-Nifāqi mā Qatal,* "There is something in hypocrisy that kills," in which he collected examples of the (according to him) gruesome flattery in which Sadat was enclosed in his later years. The reference that Fu'ād al-Sayyid makes to the gap between the rulers and the ruled indicates that he, too, has been thinking along the same lines.[23]

According to Fu'ād al-Sayyid, the only defense against personality cult is faith in God since faith in the Creator will make people see their rulers and their governments in a realistic perspective. He writes that the State with all its power and al-Azhar with all its scholarly facilities will have to cooperate in order to give people a proper understanding of their faith and to protect them from false teachings. The mass media have to be made subservient to these aims, he pleads again. The conclusion of his reflections on the subject is, however, slightly ambiguous. We should, he urges, rethink the problems concerning the regulations of Islamic law and their application in our Islamic society. Does he want this rethinking to result in total application of these rules, or in adaptation of the rules to modern demands and frailties? The reader of this article can only guess.

It is again the Muftī of the Republic, Shaykh Jādd al-Ḥaqq ᶜAlī Jādd al-Ḥaqq, who has to supply direct reaction to the assassination and the self-justification of the extremist radicals who committed the murder. In the December 1981 issue of the Ṣūfī journal the Muftī is interviewed by a certain Muḥsin Fahmī who asks the questions the average Ṣūfī reader can be supposed to want to see answered. The way in which the Muftī in this interview talks about the young, *al-shabāb,* sounds slightly condescending, but nobody can deny that some of the murderers of Sadat were young, and that support for their theories is first of all to be found with young people. The first question that Muḥsin Fahmī poses must have occupied—and probably still occupies—many minds: Why is violent Islamic activism so increasingly attractive to young men? The way in which Muḥsin Fahmī formulates the question is, however, infinitely more circumspect: "Which causes push young people to deviations?"

The dignity of the Muftī office precludes a simple answer like "I wish I knew." Instead, the Muftī answers that modern schools and universities apparently do not create "a generation that knows its obligations toward its Lord and the affairs of its country." The Muftī also makes mention of foreign influences and false teachings that are spread by the mass media. Then he adds that within the family itself proper religious education is bound to fail because, even if the head of the family, *rabb al-usrah,* attempts to educate his family in the appropriate way, his efforts will be frustrated by the mass media "which reach him in the depth of his house."[24]

The Muftī cannot have meant that the contents of the Egyptian television programs educate the viewers to support Islamic activism by propagandizing overtly or, perhaps, covertly, for the use of violence in the name of Islam. It is precisely the lack of attention paid by the media to things Islamic that the activists complain about. Does the Muftī agree with them on this point? Is it possible that the Muftī means to say that the Egyptian television is not Islamic enough? One is forced to conclude that he can only have meant to say that, by showing so many foreign serials ("Dallas" and its likes) in which Islam plays no role at all, and local soap operas in which Egyptian heroes, too, attach so little value to Islamic ideals, the media confuse the pious and create a world from which "young people" might want to escape. One of the few escapes open to them if they do not want to forget that they are

Muslims is to become better Muslims. This escape may easily lead them to "deviations," *inḥirāf,* and push them to extremism. The Muftī's remarks on such things as foreign influences, false teachings, and deficient educational systems do not, however, fully explain the rise of Islamic activism in general, or the assassination of Sadat in particular.

The second question is not a question but rather a statement to which the Muftī is presumably asked to react. "Some believe," we read, "that the nonapplication in our society of the law of Islam, *ᶜadam al-taṭbīq al-kāmil li-'l-sharīᶜah al-islāmīyah,* is one of the important causes of extremism." The Muftī's reaction starts by affirming the necessity of the application of Islamic Law in the State of Islam, *dawlat al-Islām,* since Islam is not only a creed *(ᶜaqīdah)* or system of devotions *(ᶜibādāt)* but also a detailed system of law.

Many an activist must be bewildered by such a statement. If this is true, what could possibly be wrong with enforcing the truth? The Muftī, however, continues by saying that, after more than a century of nonapplication (for which, according to him, the Ottoman Turks and the European powers are responsible), it is not easy to go back to a phase of total application. Preparations for such a return should, however, be made, but the technical difficulties, he warns, are considerable.

The third point with which the Muftī is confronted concerns the interpretation of the verse from the Qur'ān, "Whosoever does not judge by what God sent down, they are the unbelievers."[25] The interviewer says that the young who have lately deviated from the true course have offered several interpretations of this verse. He asks if the Muftī could throw light on this matter. Since in the *Farīḍah* this verse and its interpretation play a large role, there can be no doubt that the Arabic term *al-shabāb al-munḥarif* ("deviating adolescents") is indeed—both here and elsewhere—a euphemism for Sadat's assassins.

The Muftī gives a scholarly reply which is partly a repetition of his fatwā discussed above. These "Whosoever does not judge" verses were all revealed, so he explains, at the end of passages that talked about the Torah or the Gospel. They are hence addressing Jews and Christians, so the Muftī argues. Are they also applicable to Muslims? The Muftī teaches that in Qur'ān 107.4 we read: "So woe to those that pray." Can we draw conclusions from this single verse without taking into consideration the whole of the Qur'ān? Does this verse really justify the condemnation of everybody who prays? That would certainly be absurd, so the Muftī concludes, and he adds that similar caution has to be applied when interpreting "Whosoever does not rule by what God sent down, they are the unbelievers."

If, so the Muftī maintains, we take all relevant material from Qur'ān and Tradition into consideration, we are forced to conclude that the "Whosoever does not rule" verses certainly do not mean that every Muslim who ever deviated from one of the rulings of Islamic Law has become an apostate by this very deviation. The accepted teachings of Islam, the Muftī explains, is that whosoever has trespassed the laws of Islam, for instance, because of laxity or necessitating circumstances, does not by this fact stop being a Muslim, as this single verse "Whosoever does not rule" would seem to suggest.

It is evident that the Muftī here supposes his public to be roughly familiar with the arguments of the militant activists. These have contended that not only Sadat but all rulers over Islamic countries are in reality apostates from Islam and hence deserve the death penalty that Islam prescribes for apostasy, since they rule by their own laws and not by the laws of God. It is not probable that he assumes his public to have read the text of the *Farīḍah*. It is, however, plausible that the arguments that the *Farīḍah* present in a written form are supposed to be circulating orally among the general public. If this is right, it suggests once more that the text of the *Farīḍah* represents a widespread mentality that has not been exterminated with the execution of the author of the *Farīḍah* and the actual assassins of Sadat.

The Muftī ends his arguments by saying that in the present age we want to return to the rule by the laws of Islam, since we must follow the true road. Again, possible extremists among the readers of the Ṣūfī monthly would be left with an unanswered question: Is it allowed to use force to reach this noble aim, the rule of Islam? This is, however, not the final question with which the interviewer confronts the Muftī. He asks a question which, according to many, is not much less embarrassing: What does the Muftī think of the role of the *rijāl al-dīn,* the men of religion, in the current process of Islamic developments in Egypt? Have they done their duty in the recent period?

The Muftī answers that it cannot be denied that many blame the *ᶜulamā'* for what had happened (a rather circumspect euphemism for the assassination of Sadat and the national tensions that preceded and followed it). According to him, this is not reasonable. The influence of the *ᶜulamā',* so the Muftī specifies, is extremely limited. They do not have the means at their disposal that are necessary to make people understand Islam properly; only the mass media have the capabilities for doing so successfully. (If the Muftī is right, the general public cannot have properly understood Islam before the rise of television.) The Muftī now takes the opportunity to plead for larger influence of the *ᶜulamā'* on the programming of the television and on the university curricula, since, according to him, this is a way to put things right. Seminars and camps are among the means which the Muftī enumerates as useful for young Muslims in getting to know their religion, "not only its creed and devotions, but also the way of behavior it prescribes, both within the family and within society."

In the monthly "seminar" *(nadwah)* section of the journal, a long discussion on belief is offered to the interested reader. The participants in this seminar agree that Muslims must not accuse each other of apostasy, and they draw parallels with early Islamic history, especially referring to (again) the wars with the Khārijīs. The Muslim activists, however, are only superficially interested in metaphysical beliefs and creeds — to them the laws of Islam and their application in public life are the center of their ambitions.

In this seminar Dr. Abū al-Wafā al-Taftazānī explains that faith without ethical consequences is like an empty building, and that it should be visible from a person's words and deeds that he is a Mohammedan. (The word *muḥammadī* is, exceptionally, used, and not the more normal word *muslim,* probably to emphasize the need for obedience to the specific prescripts given to the followers of Muḥammad, a collection of prescripts that is historically known as the Sharīᶜah, and not obedience to vague, timeless, edifying generalities.) Dr. Abū al-Wafā implicitly refers to the *Farīḍah* and its author when he stresses that only qualified and recognized Islamic scholars have the right to form new opinions and impose these authoritatively on the Muslim public in the name of their religion. (The author of the *Farīḍah* — even by his own account — certainly was no recognized, traditional Islamic scholar.) Dr. Abū al-Wafā also turns against one of the tenets of the *Farīḍah* when he emphasizes the need for *ᶜilm*, scholarship, and careful study. He does have the courage to mention the question of whether Islam may be spread through force and violence by saying that in Egypt Islam did not spread through force, as the survival of the Coptic language for several centuries after the Arab Muslim invasion of 636 AD demonstrates, according to Dr. Abū al-Wafā al-Taftazānī.

The monthly information section of the journal once more mentions the official condolences offered by the Ṣūfī High Council at the Republican Palace, and warns the local leaders and organizers of the Ṣūfī movement to be careful and see to it that "certain persons who are not from the Ṣūfī Brotherhoods" do not infiltrate their meetings and organizations. Then the usual list of appointments, decisions, and arbitrations follows. It almost seems as if everyday life has again taken its normal course.

NOTES

[*Majallat al-Taṣawwuf al-Islāmī* is abbreviated as *MTI*.]

1. This essay has been reprinted several times, e.g., B. RUSSELL, *Mysticism and Logic*, London (Allen & Unwin), 1963, pp. 9–30.
2. E.g., *MTI*, x, 14.
3. *MTI*, i, 40.
4. *MTI*, vii, 31.
5. *MTI*, iii, 32.
6. Qur'ān 5.44 is quoted, e.g., *MTI*, vi, 19. The response to Judge Al-ᶜAshmāwī: *MTI*, vi, 52. Cf. *Al-Akhbār*, July 15 and 19, 1979.
7. *MTI*, vii, 50; Qur'ān 35.43 and 48.23.
8. Cf. my "The Philosophical Development of Zakī Nagīb Mahmūd (b. 1905)," *Bibliotheca Orientalis*, xxxiv, 5/6, (1977), pp. 298–300; and

ZAKĪ NAJĪB MAḤMŪD, *Tajdīd al-Fikr al-ᶜArabī*, Beirut (Dār al-Shurūq), 1981, p. 257.

9. *MTI*, i, 24.
10. *MTI*, ii, 14–15.
11. *MTI*, vi, 60.
12. See, however, M.J. KISTER, "'You shall only set out for three Mosques': a study of an early tradition," in *Muséon*, lxxxii (1969), 173–196.
13. W. RIEDEL and W.E. CRUM, eds., *The Canons of Athanasius*, London, 1904, Repr. Amsterdam (Philo Press), 1973, p. xix.
14. *MTI*, ix, 19.
15. MUḤAMMAD FAHMĪ ᶜABD AL-LAṬĪF, *Al-Sayyid al-Badawī wa-Dawlat al-Darāwīsh fī Miṣr*, Cairo (Al-Markaz al-ᶜArabī li-'l-Ṣiḥāfah), 1979, 192 pp., Manshūrāt Samīr Abū Dāwūd.
16. Ibid., p. 151.
17. Ibid, p. 161.
18. Ibid., and cf. EDWARD MORTIMER, *Faith and Power, the Politics of Islam*, London, 1982, pp. 73–76.
19. MUḤ. FAHMĪ ᶜABD AL-LAṬĪF, *Al-Sayyid al-Badawī*, p. 175.
20. *MTI*, xxxi, 22.
21. Qur'ān 9.40, in a translation adapted from R. Bell and A.J. Arberry.
22. See my "Ibrahim Abduh (b. 1913)," *Bibliotheca Orientalis*, xxxvii, 3/4, (1980), pp. 128–132; and IBRĀHĪM ᶜABDUH, *Wa-Min al-Nifāqi Mā Qatal*, Cairo (Mu'assasat Sijill al-ᶜArab), 1982, 144 pp.
23. Similarly MUṢṬAFĀ AMĪN, *Min Wāḥidah li-ᶜAsharah*, Cairo (Al-Maktab al-Miṣrī al-Ḥadīth), 1977, p. 367: *aṣbaḥ (al-ḥākim) sajīn al-munāfaqah*.
24. *MTI*, xxxiii, 22.
25. Qur'ān 5.44.

CHAPTER 4

Shaykh ᶜAbd al-Ḥamīd Kishk

On September 4, 1981, the first page of Egypt's national newspaper *Al-Ahrām* reported that the authorities had withdrawn the "permission to appear" from not only three Islamic fundamentalist journals (*Al-Daᶜwah, Al-Iᶜtiṣām,* and *Al-Mukhtār al-Islāmī*), but also from their alleged Christian counterparts, the journals *Al-Waṭanī* and *Al-Kirāz*. These journals were accused, and declared guilty, of inciting people to religious civil war *(fitnah ṭā'ifīyah)*. At the same time, so *Al-Ahrām* reported, a group of persons had been arrested on the same charges, namely, inciting religious civil war and destroying national unity. A few days later, *Al-Ahrām* published an official list of 1,536 names of those who had been put under precautionary arrest *(taḥaffuẓ)*. Practically all shades of public opinion at that time extant in Egypt were represented in this list (the real number of people arrested in those days may have been bigger than the official 1,536). At the same time, measures were taken against the head of the Coptic Orthodox (i.e., monophysite) Church, Pope Shenūda III. In practice, these measures amounted to banishment to a faraway monastery, and suspension of his day-to-day authority over the affairs of his Church.

In anticipation of the publication of a complete official list of the detainees, the first page of *Al-Ahrām* of September 4 already mentions a small number of prominent Egyptians who at that moment were in prison. In this small group we come across the name of a certain Shaykh Kishk, in full Shaykh ᶜAbd al-Ḥamīd ᶜAbd al-ᶜAzīz Muḥammad Kishk, preacher of the *ᶜAyn al-Ḥayāh* Mosque in the *Miṣr wa-'l-Sūdān* street in the Cairene quarter known as *Ḥadā'iq al-Qubbah.*

As far as it can be ascertained, this was the first time that Shaykh Kishk was ever mentioned by name in *Al-Ahrām,* or any other official Egyptian newspaper, journal, or magazine. In spite of this press silence, the Shaykh had managed to become extremely well known and popular. His books and sermons — the latter delivered with great virtuosity — have always met either with excited assent or with worried disapproval. Some observers have called Shaykh Kishk an Egyptian Khomeinī, but the resemblance between Kishk and Khomeinī is superficial at best. Both have their sermons and speeches registered on cassette tapes and distributed by their followers, but this means little more than that both — unlike many others — have groups of supporters and adherents.

Khomeinī is a theologian and theoretician who once wrote that the masses in the Islamic countries will trust as their rulers only those who present themselves as "men of religion," *rijāl al-dīn* ("professional theologians," as one is tempted to translate). Khomeinī, at least in the Egyptian Arabic version of his book on "the rule of the legists," *wilāyat al-faqīh,* advocates a strict form of Islamic theocracy.[1]

In Shaykh Kishk's printed books we find, however, little or no theoretical reflection on the question of where power really belongs, and who should rule. Yet it is quite possible that certain remarks that the Shaykh makes are understood by the militants as support for their views, for example, when the Shaykh exclaims that the best *jihād* is "a word of justice" *(kalimat ᶜadl)* aimed at an unjust ruler (see the translation of the *Farīḍah,* §51). Words, however, are obviously not the same as bullets.[2]

Shaykh Kishk's political views (as far as they can be found in his books) sometimes resemble some form of anarchism, as, for instance, when he writes with great nostalgia about the days when there were no policemen to stop people to ask for their driver's license, or frontier guards who ask for passports and entry or exit visas: those were the days when the Muslims conquered the world, Shaykh Kishk remembers.[3] Yet anarchism is too strong and too Western a word to describe Shaykh Kishk's attitude. Shaykh Kishk obviously shares the dislike for rulers and government officials so common in the Middle East and elsewhere. This attitude was perhaps best put into words by Saᶜd Zaghlūl (d. 1927, prime minister of Egypt from January to November 1924), who once remarked that citizens tend to look at their rulers the same way a bird looks at the hunter.

The Egyptian theologian and politician Dr. ᶜAbd al-Munᶜim Aḥmad Nimr[4] writes in a book published in 1980 that Islam is both a religion and a state, *al-islām dīn wa-dawlah*. This formula is, of course, the well-known slogan and battle-cry of the Organization of the Muslim Brothers. To make a distinction between Islam as a religion and Islam as a social and political system, so Dr. Nimr upholds, is simply un-Islamic. The very idea of this separation between *dīn* and *dawlah*, Dr. Nimr maintains, is imported from the West, *fikrah mustawradah min al-gharb*.[5] It follows implicitly from Dr. Nimr's words that those who are using and advocating the *dīn wa-dawlah* slogan—that is, the fundamentalists in all their variegations—are thinking in Western terms since a traditional Muslim who has remained untainted by the modern West neither would nor could see the point of this *dīn wa-dawlah* slogan: in its obviousness it would be meaningless to him.

Within this context Shaykh Kishk seems to be very much a traditional Muslim to whom the Western way of looking at State, Religion, and Society is not self-evident in the way in which it is self-evident to modern fundamentalists, militant or not. Shaykh Kishk would, of course, never disagree with words like those written by Dr. Nimr who argues that we should judge and rule "according to the book of God, both in our public and our private affairs," and, indeed, he does say and write similar things, but somehow the tone is different: Islamic Law should replace man-made laws, so he writes, and "Qur'ān commentaries, the volumes of Tradition on the life of the Prophet Muḥammad, and the texts from the Islamic heritage" should be translated into foreign languages in order to put Islam back into the forefront of human civilization. To further this aim, we read, the authorities and the *ᶜulamā'* should cooperate closely, and so on.[6] Islamic Law, so the Shaykh assures his readers, is not regional but international, always logical, always just.[7]

It is difficult to deny that the emphasis in Shaykh Kishk's thinking falls on personal and private piety, not on something as transitory as worldly power. The essence of Islam, according to Shaykh Kishk, is the Qur'ān, the communal prayer on Fridays, and the participation in the pilgrimage to Mecca.[8] Piety, according to the Shaykh who here quotes a saying ascribed to ᶜAlī ibn Abū Ṭālib, is to fear the Lord, to act according to the Revelation, to be satisfied with little, and to be prepared for the Final Journey.[9] Life is of no importance, so the Shaykh teaches, in comparison with death: one of the books of Shaykh Kishk derives its title from the mystic Ḥasan al-Baṣrī (d. 728) and runs: "Fast and Abstain from the World, but Eat and Drink from Death!"[10]

According to Shaykh Kishk, it is good to meditate on death and dying since this prevents us from enjoying the world.[11] The highest reality, so we read, is death which will come no matter how long human life is extended.[12] Shaykh Kishk's fascination[13] with death is evident from his description of dozens of deathbed scenes, and it sometimes strikes a Western observer as slightly morbid. He urges his public, for instance, to imagine how, having died, they will be washed and buried, and how on their very pillows their widows will make love to other men.[14] It is implausible that such preoccupations go together with political activism.

In the summer of 1981 the number of books that had appeared in "The Library of Shaykh Kishk," *Maktabat al-Shaykh Kishk,* had reached 31. From number 15 onward, these books contain a short sketch of the life of Shaykh Kishk at the end of the book.[15] These sketches are all identical. According to these semiofficial biographies, Shaykh ᶜAbd al-Ḥamīd ᶜAbd al-ᶜAzīz Muḥammad Kishk was born in Shabrakhīt, a village not far from Damanhūr (a town in the Egyptian Delta), in 1933. He knew the Qur'ān by heart at the age of 12. After he had received his primary school certificate in Alexandria, "God blessed him with blindness, and although he sought treatment for two years, he thanks God for the loss of his sight, since God compensated for this loss by giving him insight." He studied at al-Azhar University, and worked for some time as preacher and *imām* in mosques, in the service of the ministry of *Awqāf.* Since 1964 he has preached in the *ᶜAyn al-Ḥayāh* Mosque, in the *Miṣr wa-'l-Sūdān* street in Cairo.

His books were dictated,[16] and although they are widely distributed through all bookstands in Cairo, his fame and reputation are based first of all on the vigor of his sermons. These are registered on cassette tapes, which carry a number and a date. For instance, the sermon of December 12, 1980, carries the number 394, and the sermon of June 23, 1978, carries the number 274. In December 1980 approximately 90 tapes were available in Cairo, all containing sermons of approximately 90 minutes. From a careful analysis of the numbers and dates of these tapes, it might be possible to find out on which Fridays Shaykh Kishk did not preach a Friday sermon, for instance, because of his health, or because of a sojourn in prison.

Shaykh Kishk's national fame seems to have started around 1966 when he was thrown into prison by Nasser's police. Rumors have it that he was put behind bars every now and then during the reign of Sadat, even before September 1981. The reason for these periods of imprisonment, many Copts say, are connected with his attacks on Christianity. Perhaps, however, his attacks on the government and its representatives also have something to do with it. In the summer of 1980 a persistent rumor spread that Shaykh Kishk had seen Jesus Christ in a dream, and that this apparition had influenced him greatly. Some people said that it even made him consider conversion to Christianity. On the one hand, it is improbable that these reports originate in the circle of Shaykh Kishk himself since they weaken his prestige considerably: a Muslim who wanted to convert to Christianity would find himself in serious social, if not legal, difficulties. Such rumors, on the otherhand, may be based on a misunderstanding of the importance that Shaykh Kishk attaches to the Return of Jesus at the end of time.[17] This tenet of Islam is little known to non-Muslims.

In his many books and sermons, Skaykh Kishk, of course, discusses doubt and unbelief. According to him, doubt and unbelief are caused by a disease of the mind.[18] Unbelief, so he teaches, is a form of egoism: man wants to put himself on the throne of God.[19] The Shaykh writes that it is the universe itself that "tells of the unity of the Almighty."[20] Even scientists, Shaykh Kishk maintains, admit the occurrence of phenomena that can only be understood and explained if we accept the interference of the Almighty.[21] Those who do not fear God are obliged to fear everything else, we are assured.[22] It follows that those who do fear the Lord can live without fear of worldly disaster and are absolved from taking sensible precautions against it.[23]

The Qur'ān, according to Shaykh Kishk, contains ample proof that it is not man-made but divine. When Qur'ān 24.40, which tells about the "darkness on a roaring sea," was read to "the English sailor Mr. Brown," Shaykh Kishk tells, the former was at once convinced of the superhuman character of the Qur'ān, and converted to Islam. The information that this verse contains on the marine sciences, *ᶜulūm al-biḥār,* is proof, so we must understand, that the Qur'ān is God's word since these things could never have been known to Muḥammad who was not a sailor himself.[24] Shaykh Kishk, like most modern Muslims, believes that the special miraculous character of the Qur'ān, in Arabic called *iᶜjāz,* is found in the correspondence between the Qur'anic description of the universe and the "realities" that modern science has discovered.[25] He shares, however, the traditional viewpoint that the Qur'ān's linguistic eloquence is also a proof of its divine origin.[26]

Shaykh Kishk warns those who "carry the Qur'ān" and make it their profession to recite it at public and private occasions. These Qur'ān reciters should realize their responsibility, he writes, and should not, in order to please the public, make a purely artistic musical performance out of their recitations.[27] Here Shaykh Kishk must know what he is talking about: many of his enemies accuse him of making his own Friday sermons into pieces of perfect vocal and verbal art which delight his public because of their artistic beauty, and not because of the religious message they contain.

The Qur'ān, Shaykh Kiskh teaches, needs interpretation, and this interpretation was first given by Muḥammad, in whom we must believe.[28] His example must be followed[29] since it was written "that thou (i.e., Muḥammad) mayest make clear to the people what has been sent down to them."[30] Since the Prophet has said that everything he says is true,[31] we should study and read the Traditions on his life. Shaykh Kishk quotes extensively from these Traditions. Many of the pages he writes consist of little more than long quotations from the recognized collections of Traditions.

Shaykh Kishk calls Muḥammad "the greatest teacher of humanity,"[32] and although Shaykh Kiskh, as all orthodox Muslims, no doubt believes to the letter that the Prophet could neither read nor write, he adds that the alleged illiteracy of Muḥammad means that Muḥammad had no teacher, *lam yakhtalif ilā ustādh,* and did not go to a university,[33] thus summarizing and popularizing the feelings that according to most Western scholars underlie the ancient tradition of Muḥammad's supposed illiteracy.

Although Shaykh Kishk is very much preoccupied with the end of the world, eschatology, and death, he also makes statements about this world. His remarks on how we should imagine a proper Islamic society are, of course, of great interest. Do these remarks betray sympathy for the ideas and acts of the extremists of the *Farīḍah?* Do these remarks betray sympathy for Khomeinī? A proper Islamic society, so Shaykh Kishk tells us,[34] has to be based on (1) mutual love and friendship, (2) the firm establishment of the custom to command one's fellow human beings to do what is appropriate according to Islamic Law, *al-amr bi-'l-maᶜrūf,* and (3) the establishment of the custom to forbid people to do what is detestable according to Islam, *al-nahy ᶜani-'l-munkar.*

The first point is not at all political, and the second and third need not be political, but in a politically tense atmosphere they could easily be understood to be veiled demands for the introduction of a theocracy. Again, it is possible that some of the Shaykh's public understand such words as a call for a theocracy in Egypt, whereas the Shaykh himself has no specific, concrete political aspirations or ambitions. If this were so, the political interpretation of the Shaykh's sermons could contribute to the way in which his sermons appeal to his public (there are certainly many who love to hear such words), whereas those who interpret the Shaykh's words as "purely religious" do not get worried upon hearing from their Shaykh political statements about utopias which only interest them superficially or, more probably, do not interest them at all.

The list of prerequisites of the Islamic society (not State) continues with (4) the performance of the prescribed ritual prayers, (5) the alms tax called *zakāt*, and (6) obedience to God and His Apostle, and this "is a principle which contains everything that Muḥammad proclaimed on the authority of his Lord." These last words could, again, easily be understood as a demand for a strict and total application of Islamic Law, especially by those who wish to hear these demands.

Shaykh Kishk derives these six points from Qur'ān 9.71:

The believers . . . are friends one of the other,
they urge to what is reputable,
and restrain from what is disreputable
and observe the Prayer,
and pay the Zakāt,
and obey God and His messenger.

It is evident that the second and third points of this list especially, "urging to what is reputable and restraining from what is disreputable," although truly Islamic, may not be good manners, and, even if not intended politically, could easily be regarded as meddlesome interference that causes controversy and embarrassment —two things governments would like to avoid.

It is the specific duty of the *ᶜulamā'*, the class of religious scholars, to do this urging and restraining, Shaykh Kishk expounds.[36] Again, it is perfectly possible to read in such a statement an echo of Khomeinī's *wilāyat al-faqīh*, the rule of the legists. On the other hand, one can not deny that counseling the believers is one of the duties of the *ᶜulamā'*, and it is imaginable that Shaykh Kishk's words are politically harmless.

In particular, Western readers of Shaykh Kishk's books will doubt whether he really has political aims in mind when he writes about the just and Islamic society. For instance, the most serious social evil, according to Shaykh Kishk, is not poverty, ignorance, superstition, corruption, or lack of organization—as many a Westerner would say—but adultery, *zinā*.[37] "The dissemination of this crime," Shaykh Kiskh writes, "has caused the decay and disappearance of the Greek, Roman, and Persian empires."[38] "Adultery," he quotes with approval from the writings of a medical doctor, "eats away at the bones of humanity the same way the woodworm eats away at the wood."[39] It is difficult not to conclude that Shaykh Kishk is first of all interested in the private life and the personal piety of the believers, and only secondarily in what Westerners would regard as matters of public interest: polity, constitution *(dustūr),* public and private law—subjects so close to the hearts of the militant Muslims, whether their militancy is limited to reading the fundamentalist journals *Al-Daᶜwah* and *Al-Iᶜtiṣām* or whether they support extremists like those of the *Farīḍah.*

The feeling of having been humiliated and offended by the West is widespread in the Arab and Islamic world. Shaykh Kishk, as a matter of course, shares such feelings, and writes: "If only we had honored the Book of God[40] nobody would ever have humiliated us, and the banner of Islam would be all over the world!"[41] Shaykh Kishk's view of the West is not unambiguous. He calls Western civilization a *fata morgana*[42] which is responsible for much bloodshed and two world wars in less than a quarter of a century.[43] Shaykh Kishk holds the West responsible for the cruelties of slavery, which is a Western invention, so he upholds.[44] Racial discrimination in South Africa and the United States have not escaped the Shaykh's notice. Yet, in spite of all these things, he more than once calls the United States "the greatest nation as far as civilization is concerned in our present age," *aᶜẓam al-umam ḥaḍāratan fī ᶜaṣrinā hādhā.*[45]

Shaykh Kishk believes that the West is full of enemies of Islam who will not rest until they have caused discord within the Muslim community and until they have made the pious forsake their religion:[46] "They will not cease to fight you until they turn you from your religion, if they are able."[47] Especially noteworthy among these enemies are the orientalists *(mustashriqūn),* who "concentrate their efforts on the problem of the divine inspiration of Muḥammad *(al-waḥy)* since this is the first basis of Islam."[48] Although many Western scholars have actually devoted much of their effort to worthy subjects such as editing ancient Arabic poetry or indexing the canonical collections of the sayings of

Muḥammad, there may be some truth in Shaykh Kishk's accusations if we look at the examples he adduces: Westerners have indeed, be it long ago, alleged that Muḥammad was an epileptic, or, a "Roman priest who became angry because he was elected neither cardinal nor Pope."[49]

Yet, the West and Western science are not all bad. Shaykh Kishk tells us how Western scientists and cosmonauts have testified to their belief in God[50] and how someone like the former American President Richard Nixon has, according to Shaykh Kishk,[51] admitted that the West is spiritually poor and is going through a spiritual crisis: materialism is retreating, Shaykh Kishk reassures us. It is important to realize that Shaykh Kishk's feelings on this subject are widely shared in Egypt. They are also commonplace among liberal and Westernized Egyptians. "Western civilisation is ultramaterialistic and, many claim, spiritually poor," the *Egyptian Gazette*, a Cairene English-language daily, informed its readers on January 8, 1981; the anonymous editor continues by mentioning the West's decadence and its "social and moral decay."

Shaykh Kishk, needless to say, rejects "materialism"[52] and compares its adherents to "bats who keep their eyes closed and are unable to observe visually the corporate bodies which we observe in the light of the sun."[53] Materialism and unbelief, Shaykh Kishk teaches, are also felt to be wrong in the West itself: 80 percent of all ill persons in the larger American cities are suffering, so Shaykh Kishk writes, from nervous diseases that are directly caused by their unbelief in the One God.[54] Those in the West who argue that psychotherapy is taking over, or has taken over, the functions of pastoral counseling by churchmen cannot but admit that Shaykh Kishk is partly right on this point.

Probably even worse than the West and its orientalists, *mustashriqūn*, are the Westernizers within the Islamic world itself, the *mustaghribūn*, so Shaykh Kishk maintains. These *mustaghribūn* study "Freud and Sartre, are only interested in women, *qiblatuhum nisā'uhum*, and they know nothing of Islam except its name."[55] Such people, Shaykh Kishk warns, want to undermine Islam by limiting themselves to the Qur'ān without regard for the canonical Traditions from the Prophet and the established traditions of Islam as such.[56] This, again, must be understood as an attack on those Muslims who hesitate to identify the whole of Islamic Law in all its details with the command of God.

It is only to be expected that Shaykh Kishk praises the wisdom of Islam, which permits polygamy, a system that Shaykh Kishk much prefers to the Western system of surrounding oneself with "hundreds of illicit girlfriends."[57] It is not known on what sources Shaykh Kishk bases such a statement. It may well be that his use of the word "hundreds" is hyperbolic.

Shaykh Kishk blames the West—perhaps not unjustly—for the existence of Zionism and the State of Israel, which, so he quotes from Theodor Herzl, is nothing more than an extension of Western civilization and a dam against Arab barbarism.[58]

Shaykh Kishk regards the consumption of pork as one of the most heinous sins a Muslim could possibly commit. It is, of course, true that Muslims abhor the thought of eating pork since they generally believe that pork causes diseases, contains harmful parasites and viruses, and causes rabies and brain fever. Rarely is the objection raised that if this were true the inhabitants of Muslim countries would on the average be much healthier than the pork-eating inhabitants of the West.[59] Shaykh Kishk mentions one argument against eating pork which is seldom found in writing but which one does sometimes hear in conversations: pork meat is forbidden because of the "shameless sexual behavior" of pigs.[60] Eating pork might in some mysterious way, so we are probably asked to believe, influence the behavior of those who eat it and make them lose their feelings of decency and shame.

Shaykh Kishk is no exception to the rule that religious dignitaries, both in Islam and Christianity, have always felt free to give their co-religionists ample advice on matters pertaining to love in its physical aspects. Shaykh Kishk talks at length about the depravities of the modern world, and he warns the Muslim youth strongly of its dangers. As so often with this kind of pastoral guidance, lay people wonder whether or not in this way ideas are being put into otherwise innocent minds. Especially when Shaykh Kishk enumerates which films are being shown in Cairo that go against basic Muslim morality, it is not certain whether all members of his public use this information in the way the Shaykh wants them to.

Be that as it may, Shaykh Kishk makes a few bold remarks on sex. The crime of masturbation, he writes, has terrible consequences: it causes, for instance, complete lethargy, and he who practices it will be unable to walk much because of the ensuing feebleness of his legs. He will lose his sight, and he will age prematurely. Cure, so the Shaykh promises, is to be found in marriage, or in reading the Qur'ān, praying, fasting, and physical exercise.[61]

Intercourse during menstruation is forbidden by Qur'ān 2.222: "Withdraw from women in menstruation, and come not near them until they are clean." Yet this prohibition does not seem to suffice: Shaykh Kishk adds that sexual abstention during menstruation is "a period of rest for the male, necessary no matter how potent he is."[62] The female side is also taken into consideration: intercourse during menstruation is "the most important cause of infection of the vagina."[63] Something similar seems to be the case with homosexual intercourse: this "crime" damages the pituitary gland, *al-ghuddah al-nukhāmīyah*,[64] and makes it impossible to keep the procreative apparatus, *al-jihāz al-tanāsulī*, free of microbes.[65] The agonies of those stricken by syphilis or gonorrhoea are painted in frightening detail: sufferers from these ailments "cannot move or think—it makes them worthless members of society."[66] According to Sheikh Kishk, the number of people in the West who suffer from syphilis and gonorrhoea is extremely high. He mentions percentages of more than 75 percent. In his long digression on these two maladies Shaykh Kishk does not mention the possibilities of remedy, even writing: "Doctors are at a loss *(ḥāra)* how to treat these ailments, they defy any cure. . . ."[67] (This must all sound much less funny since the rise of the Acquired Immune Deficiency Syndrome, generally known as AIDS, than it did before. It would not be difficult to find similar or worse assertions, not only with Western colleagues of Shaykh Kishk, but also with Western scientists and medical men who feel that they have the duty to discourage promiscuity.)

Shaykh Kishk mentions the Jews both in his books and sermons. When doing so, he does not, of course, share the sensitivities that exist in Europe. European history, especially in the late thirties and the early forties of this century, has made European antisemitism a subject that falls into a category of its own. Arabs do not share this sensitivity since they have no responsibility for the Holocaust. It is, then, not in the light of the attempts at genocide made in Europe that we must read Shaykh Kishk's remarks on the Jews.

In the West, some newspaper publicity has been given to the allegation that Shaykh Kishk characterized the Jews as "snakes and scorpions" in one of his sermons. In one of his books these "snakes and scorpions" are also mentioned, but in a slightly different and a little less sinister context. After the Battle of Badr in 624 AD,[68] so Shaykh Kishk tells us, "the hearts of the Jews of Medina were filled with the snakes of hatred and the scorpions of hostility."[69] This is not the same as saying that the Jews, as such, are to be equated with snakes and scorpions, although one must leave room for the possibility that the Shaykh's public would not make such a fine distinction. The printed passage in which these words occur is difficult to date, but it is certainly to be dated before December 1979,[70] and it could well have been written in the aftermath of President Sadat's historic visit to Jerusalem and the Camp David agreement.

Shaykh Kishk's (disguised) intention in this passage is perhaps to emphasize that treaties like the treaty between Muḥammad and the Jews in Medina, or the treaty between Sadat and Begin, have no real value: the Jews will try to attack the Muslims and Islam anyhow, treaty or no treaty. Does not the Qur'ān itself say: "If thou [Muḥammad] fearest treachery at all from any people [the Jews of Medina] cast back to them [thy convenant] equally"?[71] It is clear that the Egyptian government would not like such insinuations and suggestions, especially not when made through pious quotations from the Qur'ān and the canonical collections of Traditions.

Shaykh Kishk, furthermore, bravely participates in what has been called the War of Quotes which is going on in the Middle East. On both sides, it is believed that somewhere there will turn up a quotation or a historic document that, once known to the world, will solve the Middle East problem by the force of its sheer conviction.[72] Shaykh Kishk himself, however, supplies the other side with what many would regard as ammunition when he makes statements like, "the Jews are Jews in all times and places."[73] Although such a statement is, formally, a tautology, many will hear an echo of antisemitism in it.

It is, moreover, Shaykh Kishk's conviction that God punishes the Jews for their — according to the Qur'ān, only attempted[74] — murder of Jesus, for the killing of John the Baptist, and other Prophets. Their only salvation, so he teaches, would be to believe in Muḥammad, the Apostle of God.[75]

In the sermon of December 12, 1980, Shaykh Kishk attacks one of his competitors for the favor of the Egyptian public, Shaykh Al-Shaᶜrāwī.[76] This attack is interesting since it throws some light on the way in which Shaykh Kishk thinks about Judaism and Christianity, and it provides an insight into the general climate of some of the inter-Islamic debates.

The Egyptian monthly *Al-Daᶜwah,* the Muslim Brotherhood journal, in its issue of January 1978 (no. 20) reports on how one of its journalists failed to get an interview with Shaykh Al-Shaᶜrāwī, who at that moment occupied the post of Minister of *Awqāf.* Shaykh Al-Shaᶜrāwī refused to be interviewed, saying — at least according to *Al-Daᶜwah* (p. 50) — that he would rather cooperate with the People of the Book than with the Muslim Brothers and their monthly *Al-Daᶜwah;* in Arabic: *"Ufaḍḍil al-taᶜāmul maᶜa Ahl al-Kitāb ᶜala 'l-taᶜāmul maᶜa 'l-Ikhwān al-Muslimīn wa-Majallat al-Daᶜwah!"*

Even in the one-sided account of *Al-Daᶜwah,* it is obvious that the objections of Shaykh Al-Shaᶜrāwī first of all (and, perhaps, exclusively) concern the journalistic methods of *Al-Daᶜwah,* methods that are, according to some, related to those brought to perfection by the German *Bildzeitung.* This could have been the end of the affair, but it is not. Like good wine, such stories should be allowed to ripen. Almost three years later, in his sermon of December 12, 1980, Shaykh Kishk decries how "an Islamic scholar, once Minister of Religious Affairs" declared to *Al-Daᶜwah* that he would rather cooperate with Jews and Christians than with the Muslim Brothers; in Arabic: *"Ufaḍḍil al-taᶜāmul maᶜa 'l-Yahūd wa-'l-Naṣārā ᶜala 'l-taᶜāmul maᶜa 'l-Ikhwān al-Muslimīn!"* No mention is made of the context of the refused interview, and "People of the Book," a good Qur'anic expression, has been sharpened into "Jews and Christians."

In this sermon, Shaykh Al-Shaᶜrāwī is not mentioned by name, but the public will no doubt have understood. With a voice broken in anger and sadness Shaykh Kishk bitterly complains about this scandalous and unnatural preference of Shaykh Al-Shaᶜrāwī. "Christians," Shaykh Kishk grumbles, "have deified a man. Cooperate with such people rather than with the Muslim Brothers? The Jews have arrogantly killed, or attempted to kill, Prophets and Apostles — cooperate with such people rather than with the followers of the Martyr Ḥasan al-Bannā?"[77]

Shaykh Kishk often talks and writes about Jesus Christ, but when he does so he does not talk about Christianity but about Islam. To Shaykh Kishk and to Muslims in general, Jesus is in no way a rival of Muḥammad, but the figure about whom the Qur'ān has said: "The Messiah, Jesus, son of Mary, is only the messenger of God, and His Word which He cast upon Mary, and a spirit from Him."[78] Moreover, the return of Jesus at the end of time is a traditional Muslim tenet, connected with several verses from the Qur'ān.[79]

Christians have another view of Jesus. Many of them believe "that Jesus Christ is one, true God and true man, possessing the divine as well as the human natures, united in Him without confusion, and without division," and that "Christ's body . . . was incorruptible, not of itself liable to death, but liable only as and when He willed."[80] To the Muslims, and to Shaykh Kishk, this is sheer blasphemy. Shaykh Kishk, in his sermon, expresses his surprise at the fact that God's mercy is so great that he provides with the means of subsistence even people who believe that God has an equal, *nidd*, and a son, *walad*.[81] "How can they [the Christians] claim that one of God's creatures is equal to him in divinity and greatness?"[82]

In his sermon of December 12, 1980, Shaykh Kishk goes further and lets his eloquence run away with him: Jesus, so Shaykh Kishk starts his attack, ate and drank, and he even slept, but does the Qur'ān not say: "God — there is no god but He, the Living, the Eternal; slumber affects Him not nor sleep"?[83] When Jesus ate and drank, Shaykh Kishk continues, he must have consisted of cells, and these cells must have secreted biological waste —hence Jesus must have used the bathroom, and the Shaykh then thunders: "A God does not use the bathroom!!," *"Al-Ilāh lā yadkhul dawrāt al-miyāh!!"*

In the Egyptian context such a remark hurts more than it possibly could in the West, where few people will bat an eyelid at the announcement that God himself has died, or that the resurrection of Jesus Christ is not a historical event.

Yet Christianity has some influence on Shaykh Kishk. It is possible to trace at least five quotations from, or direct allusions to, the text of the New Testament in his books. One of the most interesting as far as the subject matter is concerned is a parallel to Matthew 22:36 (and corresponding passages): "Which is the great commandment in the Law?—Thou shalt love thy God with all thy heart. . . ." Shaykh Kishk writes: "The believer's creed must be compressed into: loving God . . . ," *ᶜaqīdat al-mu'min yajib an yatarakkaz fī maḥabbat Allāh.* It is true that these two passages continue differently, yet the correspondence is striking, even if Shaykh Kishk's wording would be influenced by Sufism, which also puts great emphasis on the love for God.[84]

It is not plausible, though admittedly possible, that such an emphasis on love goes together with political ambitions, revolutionary schemes, and participation in the struggle for wordly power. Also, the emphasis that Shaykh Kishk gives to esoteric speculation on eschatology, the return of Jesus at the end of time, *barzakh*[85] (the state in which the dead await resurrection), the *karāmāt al-awliyā'*[86] (the miracles of the Ṣūfī Saints) and the metaphysics of the soul[87] point to the same apolitical direction.

Yet Shaykh Kishk's social criticisms may be thought to imply political consequences. In his sermon of December 12, 1980, he does not only attack the Jews, the Christians, lax Muslims, and an ex-rector of al-Azhar University but also a football captain and a businessman who presented his wife with an expensive coat. Would those in power really care about such criticisms? In the early twenties Saᶜd Zaghlūl[88] is reported to have said, be it in a slightly different context, that a government is not bothered by sermons: *al-ḥukūmah quwwah lā taṣil ilayh(ā) al-khuṭab.* The case of Shaykh

Kishk, however, demonstrates that this is no longer completely true in the seventies and eighties since the Egyptian government obviously was concerned, otherwise they would not at times have put the Shaykh behind bars.

There are, moreover, two small but clear indications that the Egyptian government tried to reach a compromise with Shaykh Kishk in the period following the assassination of Sadat. On Sunday, November 8, 1981, a month after the assassination, a new issue of the Cairo magazine *October* appeared (no. 263). In this issue, a certain Aḥmad Muṣṭafā interviewed a small number of prominent Muslim detainees who had now been in prison for two months.[89] He asked them for their reactions on the news of the death of President Sadat, and their views on the Muslim extremists. A prisoner cannot express his opinions with complete frankness and there is all reason to distrust the answers that journalist Aḥmad Muṣṭafā ascribes to them. Yet the extreme ambiguity and evasiveness of some of the answers may convince those who read these interviews of the overall reliability of Aḥmad Muṣṭafā's reports.

The first prominent prisoner is ᶜUmar al-Tilimsānī,[90] in spite of his great age still the semiofficial spokesman for the Muslim Brothers. Asked about the assassination, Al-Tilimsānī answers that it deeply saddened him, first because of the consequences that such actions have, and second because of the fact that Islam disapproves totally *(yunkir kull al-inkār)* of assassinations. The "consequences that such actions have" may refer to anything, but it might certainly refer to the impending execution of the assassins. Of course Islam disapproves of assassinations, but Islam does not disapprove of the death penalty pronounced by a regular court. Nevertheless, Al-Tilimsānī goes on by saying that, if he could have prevented the assassination, he would have done so.

Al-Tilimsānī reminds his interviewer that he has always been "one of the elements that called for tranquillity," *min al-ᶜanāṣir allatī tadᶜū ila-'l-hudū'*. He mentions how in March 1972 he had already publicly supported certain conciliatory measures taken by Sadat with regard to the Muslim Brothers. Asked about his opinions on the *jamāᶜāt*, he laughs (so the reporter says) and answers: "What do you think about their considering me a *kāfir*, an infidel?"

With this oblique allusion to ideas like those expressed in *Al-Farīḍah al-Ghā'ibah,* the section devoted to ᶜUmar al-Tilimsānī ends. (The *Farīḍah* actually did not call ᶜUmar al-Tilimsānī an infidel, but it did argue that activities like publishing an edifying journal like *Al-Daᶜwah,* of which ᶜUmar al-Tilimsānī was the editor-in-chief, do not contribute to the [according to the *Farīḍah*] necessary establishment of an Islamic State).[91]

Shaykh Kishk is the second prominent Muslim who is interviewed by Aḥmad Muṣṭafā. On the photograph that accompanies the text of the interview the Shaykh looks considerably slimmer than before his arrest. This will have convinced those who knew him that the photograph printed here was indeed taken recently, and in prison. Implicitly the photograph conveys the message that the Shaykh is alive and in good health. (In the last days of October 1981 the rumor spread in Cairo that the Shaykh had died in prison.) On the photograph the Shaykh is all smiles, and the text of the interview emphasizes his joviality, friendliness, and jocularity.

"Before I asked my first question," Aḥmad Muṣṭafā writes, "I reminded the Shaykh of one of his sermons in which he had attacked me for a frank journalistic report on marriage ceremonies in the United States where I lived for seven years." The Shaykh, so he goes on, laughed and joked about this for a long time. Under the surface of all his jocose writing, the message may be hidden that Aḥmad Muṣṭafā does not want his readers, and a possible censor, to forget that he became estranged from his country by this long absence, and that, if he inadvertently lets through unacceptable ambiguities by Shaykh Kishk, he cannot be blamed for it. Who would be able to recognize hidden allusions to obscure domestic affairs or ancient Islamic history, after seven years out in the big world?

Shaykh Kishk's answers to Aḥmad Muṣṭafā's questions do not look very controversial. Without effort the Shaykh strings together a number of pious phrases. Murder, he says, is a big sin and Islam forbids the shedding of innocent blood. Islam, he teaches, has never tried to solve problems by the use of force, because force is destructive. "Did not the Muslims get involved in civil war only after the murder of Caliph ᶜUthmān? Since then war and murder have spread all over . . . the Muslims still suffer from this shedding of innocent blood."

This reference to the murder of Caliph ᶜUthmān in 656 AD may have helped those readers of the *October* magazine who knew their Islamic history to remember that, after ᶜUthmān's murder and the civil wars that followed it, the worldly Umayyad dynasty (Caliphs in Damascus, 661–750) came to power.[92] Their reign, so pious Muslims traditionally believe, was un-Islamic. One Caliph from this family even became especially known for his love of wine. The rulers who came to power in the aftermath of the murder of ᶜUthmān can be seen as the first examples of the *ḥākim ẓālim*, the "Unjust Ruler" whom Muslims must resist. After the murder of Caliph ᶜUthmān, so many believe, religious authority and worldly power have started to become separated. Fundamentalists believe that this separation is wrong. President Sadat, however, was an ardent supporter of such a separation, as his slogan *lā siyāsah fi-'l-dīn wa-lā dīn fi-'l-siyāsah* ("no politics in religion and no religion in politics") demonstrates. Does Shaykh Kishk manage to express that, according to him, a ruler like Sadat would never have come to power in the Islamic world if the murder of ᶜUthmān had not prevented Islam from remaining a true theocracy?

The next question that the Shaykh has to answer is whether force may be used to further the cause of Islam. Here the Shaykh answers that Islam spreads by itself and does not need the use of force. At the end of his answer to this question, he tells a story about a contemporary of the Prophet, a certain Usāmah, who once killed a man who—either out of fear for his imminent fate or because he really had converted to Islam on the spot—professed to be a Muslim. The Prophet is reported on this occasion to have rebuked Usāmah so severely for having killed a man who called himself a Muslim that Usāmah exclaimed, "I wish I had not yet been a Muslim on the day I killed that man!" This story is, of course, relevant to the assassination of Sadat. It is well known that Sadat, of course, professed to be a Muslim, and to declare him to be an infidel—as his assassins did—and to punish him for his alleged apostasy would have been severely rebuked—but not punished!—by the Prophet. Taken by itself, this is what this story seems to suggest.

The answers to the last two questions are equally hard to explain. What does Shaykh Kishk think of the events of Asyūt in Upper Egypt, where during disturbances—presumably between

Copts and Muslims—77 or more soldiers were killed by the rioters? Here Shaykh Kishk answers that these killings served no purpose. "In this country we should live together like brothers"—now the reader may expect to be told that Copts and Muslims should live together in proverbial brotherhood, but instead of the expected we read that soldiers and civilians should live like brothers. Since the brotherhood theme is so frequently introduced into the discussion in order to preach conciliation between Copts and Muslims, many readers might be at loss: the words they hear sound familiar but the message seems to be different. Are they asked to live like brothers in one country together with their government and its armies? Does Shaykh Kishk want to ignore the Copts in Egypt, or was the Asyūt uprising in reality an uprising of militant fundamentalists that had little or nothing to do with the Copts?

How to cure *(ᶜilāj)* the problems of the young is the last question put to the Shaykh. When we realize again that "the young" *(al-shabāb)* is the most-used euphemism for the Muslim extremists, Shaykh Kishk's answer becomes interesting if not odd: the Prophet, so he replies, once said, "Be good to the young—when God sent me with my mission they were the ones who supported me." Do "the young" have to be regarded as the true partisans of the Prophet? In the context of the aftermath of Sadat's assassination, this sounds ominous indeed.

Yet this interview of November 1981 with the imprisoned Shaykh creates the general impression that the Shaykh and the new government had in some way reached an armistice, or, at the very least, that negotiations to reach an armistice had been opened.

On Saturday morning, January 23, 1982, Shaykh Kishk was (as far as is known) still in prison. Yet the bookstands in Cairo offered that day for the first time a new booklet for sale that was written (or dictated) by the Shaykh. The contents of the small book indicate that it was written after the assassination of Sadat. It had certainly not been prepared before the Shaykh was arrested in the beginning of September 1981. The fact that it was publicly offered for sale at this date (January 23) must therefore mean that it was written, printed, bound, and distributed while the Shaykh himself was still in jail. The booklet comprised 80 pages, and it was presented as number 32 of the "Library of Shaykh Kishk," *Maktabat al-Shaykh Kishk*. It is slightly shorter than the average volume in that series.

It is not farfetched to see an allusion to Sadat's assassination in the Arabic title of the booklet, *Maṣāriᶜ al-Ẓālimīn*. The plural *maṣāriᶜ* is best translated as "the miserable end" or "the violent death," and *ẓālimīn* as "transgressors" or "sinners." *Ẓālim* is, however, also the standard epithet for the Unjust Ruler, *Al-Ḥākim al-Ẓālim*. In a neutral translation the title would become "The Death of the Transgressors," but in the context in which the book appeared this will not do. In Egypt after Sadat's assassination the title can only be understood as "The Fate of Unjust Rulers," like Sadat.

The book has a motto which has been taken from Qur'ān 11.104: "Such is the grip of thy Lord when he takes hold of a town in its wrong-doing; verily His grip is painful, violent." The word "town," *qaryah*, here used in its plural *qurā*, can be understood as a Qur'anic near-equivalent of the modern word "state," and the words "in its wrong-doing," in Arabic *wa-hiya ẓālimah*, again contain a reference to *ẓulm*, "tyranny," "unjust and un-Islamic rule." In the context in which Shaykh Kishk here placed the verse it may well be understood as a reference to the fundamentalist tenet that the modern states in the Islamic world are not Islamic at all, but *ẓālim*, unjust, because they are not ruled by Islamic Law but by man-made laws. In such a context the verse is then taken to prophesy the painful divine punishment that is in store for any state or town which is *ẓālim*, not constituted in accordance with God's laws. The prophecy contained in this verse from the Qur'ān, so we are supposedly asked to understand, was fulfilled by the violent death of the head of a state that was ruled by other laws than the laws of God.

Those who know the Qur'ān by heart will no doubt realize that the verse quoted as a motto to the booklet continues with, "Verily in that is a sign for whoever fears the punishment of the Hereafter." In other words, whoever fears the punishment of the Hereafter has to see in the assassination a sign that "towns" and states have to be ruled by the laws of God, not by the laws of men—certainly not by the laws of men who dare to conclude treaties with the traditional enemies of Islam and who publicly drink champagne to celebrate the conclusion of such treaties.

The preface of the book contains the usual prayers for the Prophet Muḥammad, who receives the usual epithets: *sayyidnā*, "Our Lord," *nabiyyunā*, "Our Prophet," but also *ᶜaẓīmnā*, "the august one." The adjective *ᶜaẓīm*, "great" or "august" is used very frequently in modern Arabic prose for political leaders and heroes. Does it, in its present context, suggest to many readers that for Muslims the only true hero and political leader is their Prophet Muḥammad, and not the sultans and presidents who are glorified by their own courts until they seem to possess almost superhuman qualities?

The Prophet, so the preliminary prayers continue, "preached a message, brought faithfulness, advised his nation, and exterminated *al-ẓulmah*, "darkness." Only the laws of Islam can be meant with "the advice which the Prophet gave to his nation." The extermination of *ẓulmah*, "darkness," is an allusion to the disappearance of paganism from Arabia in the days of Muḥammad. The word "*ẓulmah*" is, however, closely related to "*ẓulm*, "injustice," not only by the internal logic of semantics but also by its linguistic root *ẓ-l-m*, and the word may hence contain, certainly to a sensitive Arab ear, a latent reference to the much discussed *ḥākim ẓālim*, "unjust ruler."

After these opening prayers Shaykh Kishk declares in a short preface that by means of this new book of his he wants to remind man what will happen to his soul when it appears before its Creator, *mā yalqawnahū baᶜd mā taṣil al-rūḥ ilā khāliqihā*. Although this is a frequent theme in the booklets published by Shaykh Kishk there is a distinct possibility that in this context it refers to the divine judgment over Sadat, whose soul had so recently publicly gone up to its Creator.

After the preface the text of Surah 69 follows. The seventh and eighth verses of this Surah may bring back to mind the scenes that immediately followed the assassination of Sadat: "(There) you see the people laid prostrate as if they were the stumps of fallen palm-trees — Now dost thou see any remnant of them?" The ninth verse discusses the Pharaoh, who deified himself: the Qur'anic prototype of an unjust ruler who disregarded the commands of God.

"Pharaoh," of course, is an obvious code name for anyone in authority in Egypt. Then the Surah speaks about Sodom and Gomorrah, the story of Noah, the Final Judgment, Heaven and Hell. The Surah finishes with remarks concerning the nature of Muḥammad's mission and the character of the Qur'ān.

After having heard the verses 40 – 43 from this Surah, so Shaykh Kishk reminds his public, ᶜUmar ibn al-Khaṭṭāb (Caliph, 634 – 644) spontaneously converted to Islam. Starting from verse 43 "(The Qur'ān) is a revelation from the Lord of the worlds," Shaykh Kishk then goes on to say: "Yes, it is the word of God! And only someone whose wits have left him could presume to be God's partner in His word *(kalām)* or in His rule *(ḥukm)*!"

Here we meet again with a possible hidden allusion. Muslims agree that "to be partner in God's word," that is, to produce verses of the Qur'ān that would have to pass as authentic revelation, is unthinkable. According to Shaykh Kishk's exclamation it would not only be unthinkable for a Muslim to claim for himself the apostolic prerogative of speaking in the name of God, but it would be equally unimaginable for a true Muslim to claim the right to give laws, to rule. To give laws and to reveal the Qur'ān are equally the exclusive domain of God and His Apostle. Humans are not admitted to this sacred territory, not even when they are a sultan or president.

There is another indication that there may be more to this exclamation ("Yes, it is the word of God," etc.) than meets the eye. The Arabic expression rendered with "someone whose wits have left him" may be more accurately translated as "someone whose vision became inanimate" — a possible allusion to a rather macabre detail in the news bulletins at the time of Sadat's assassination: it was announced several times that the doctors who officially established the death of the President pronounced him to be dead because his eyes did not respond to light. If this last interpretation of the words of Shaykh Kishk is not too farfetched, his words could be taken to mean: "Only a fool, blinded in death, like the murdered President, would be so arrogant as to want to introduce his own laws next to and above those of God — as foolish an act as trying to add to the Qur'ān a few lines of one's own making."

Even if, in spite of these indications, Kishk's words reported up to now were completely innocent and bore no relation to Sadat's violent death, the last lines of the passage under discussion cannot be understood but as a reference to the lack of popular mourning after the death of Sadat. In these last lines Shaykh Kishk rhetorically addresses ᶜUmar, the Caliph of the Golden Age of Islam, and exclaims: "O ᶜUmar, O Light of the People of Paradise, how Islam wept at your death, yes, the Qur'ān is the word of God!" When Shaykh Kishk recalls how Islam has wept for ᶜUmar who was assassinated in 644, Kishk's public must have remembered that they did not weep for Sadat when the latter was assassinated in 1981.[93] Whether they did not do so out of fear for the new régime or because of the possible unpopularity of the murdered President is in this case unessential.

The booklet *Maṣāriᶜ al-Ẓālimīn,* as most writings by Shaykh Kishk, consists largely of quotations from the Qur'ān, the Tradition, and the writings of Muslim scholars from the past. This makes good sense: a possible censor would feel extremely foolish if he had to suppress a quotation from the Qur'ān, a Prophetic saying, or a passage written by a long forgotten or prestigious thirteenth century scholar. Yet the combination of quotations often succeeds in suggesting what the author wishes to convey.

The last chapters of this small book talk in detail about the burning question raised by the Muslim extremists: which acts or beliefs constitute the sin and crime of *kufr,* unbelief. The importance of the question is obvious. If Sadat did not commit those acts, or did not hold those beliefs, he had not become an apostate, and the arguments behind the self-justification of his assassins are false.

The Shaykh's compilation of "signs of unbelief" contains many expected elements, for instance, the belief that Saints are better *(afḍal)* than Prophets (this tenet is directed against extreme Ṣūfīs). Another sign of *kufr* is not to believe in all the Prophets (this is directed against Jews and Christians, who reject Muḥammad but accept others as Prophet or Apostle). The belief in the eternity of the world is also, according to Shaykh Kishk, a sign of *kufr* (directed against "materialists," atheists, and Marxists who do not believe in the createdness of this world). Certain acts are also enumerated: to drink alcohol and to eat pork, or not to pray and not to keep the month of Fasting all constitute *kufr.* The last sign that the Shaykh mentions is to call a Muslim an unbeliever, since this, so he writes, amounts to calling Islam itself unbelief. These words seem to imply that Shaykh Kishk accuses Sadat's murderers, who called the Muslim Sadat an unbeliever, of apostasy and unbelief.

No matter how hard one looks for ambiguities or allusions within these passages and in the way in which Shaykh Kishk puts them together, there can really be only one conclusion. Personal piety is central to Shaykh Kishk's thinking, and he is not — like the extremist fundamentalists — exclusively and constantly preoccupied with the Islamic State and its legislation. The great "sign of unbelief," and hence of apostasy, to which the author of the *Farīḍah* gives all priority, namely, to rule by other laws than God's laws, is not mentioned or alluded to in this part of the Shaykh's reflections. This can be explained by more than censorship alone.

Shaykh Kishk is enough of a virtuoso to be able to suggest views that a censor would deem unacceptable if expressed openly. No matter how much he seems to be an activist from the way he speaks and preaches, the contents of his books and sermons indicate that, according to Shaykh Kishk, personal and private piety simply comes first. A strong argument in favor of this interpretation of Shaykh Kishk's message can be found in the attack that the author of the *Farīḍah* makes on those who do not explicitly disagree with the demands for an Islamic State and an Islamic legislation but who seem to believe that, once those who call themselves Muslims become better Muslims, this problem will lose its importance. If there were no prominent Muslims who actually held this view, there would have been little need for the author of the *Farīḍah* to have written about it.

Shaykh Kishk's uniqueness is found in the disturbing way in which his voice expresses nostalgia for the Kingdom of the Heavens — but it is a Kingdom of the Heavens he longs for, not a Kingdom, or a Republic, of this world.

A few days after the appearance of Kishk's book *Maṣāriᶜ al-Ẓālimīn* on January 23, 1982, the news was announced that Shaykh Kishk had been released from detention. Even the BBC World Service reported his release on January 26. The new Egyptian semiofficial weekly devoted to religious affairs, *Al-Liwā' al-Islāmī*, now began to contain contributions by the Sheikh, for the first time on February 18. One week later, this weekly even printed a large photograph of the Shaykh and his son Muṣṭafā on its first page. The detention and the press boycott were over, the Shaykh seems to have given his blessings to the new régime, and the régime seems to have decided to tolerate his frank criticisms on anything that the Shaykh deems to be un-Islamic. An outsider can only be curious as to how long the marriage that follows such a honeymoon can continue to last.

NOTES

[The *Maktabat al-Shaykh Kishk* (Cairo, Al-Maktab al-Miṣrī al-Ḥadīth) is abbreviated as *MSK*.]

1. RŪḤ ALLĀH AL-KHUMAYNĪ, *Al-Ḥukūmah al-Islāmīyah*, Cairo *(iᶜdād wa-taqdīm dr. Ḥasan Ḥanafī)*, 1979, pp. 23 and 128.
2. *MSK*, xxvii, 93.
3. *MSK*, i, 13.
4. Minister of Religious Affairs *(Wazīr al-Awqāf wa-shu'ūn al-Azhar)*, February 1979–May 1980.
5. DR. ᶜABD AL-MUNᶜIM NIMR, *Tafsīr Sūrat al-Jāthiyah*, Cairo, 1980, p. 81.
6. *MSK*, iii, 135.
7. *MSK*, xvi, 129.
8. *MSK*, xi, 44.
9. The Arabic rhyme words are *Al-Jalīl, Al-Tanzīl, Al-Qalīl, Al-Raḥīl;* the word *tanzīl* may of course refer to the Sharīᶜah as well as to the Qur'ān. Cf. *MSK*, i, 34, and the sermon of December 12, 1980.
10. *MSK*, xxvi, 78.
11. Ibid., 24.
12. Ibid., 5–8.
13. *MSK*, xv, 107; *MSK*, xxiii, 57.
14. Sermon of December 12, 1980.
15. No. 11 also contains this biographical sketch.

16. *MSK*, xxvi, 79; *MSK*, xxvii, 95.
17. *MSK*, xxii, 29 & 55–59; *MSK* xxiii, 11; *MSK*, xxiv, 18; *MSK*, xxv, 71.
18. *MSK*, v, 83–84.
19. *MSK*, viii, 45.
20. *MSK*, ix, 14.
21. Ibid., 19.
22. *MSK*, i, 34.
23. Similarly, Muṣṭafā Maḥmūd, *Al-Qur'ān: Muḥāwalah li-'l-Fahm al-ᶜAṣrī li-'l-Qur'ān* (n.p., n.d. [Cairo, 1970]), p. 187; attacks on this attitude, e.g., in ᶜĀ'ishah ᶜAbd al-Raḥmān Bint al-Shāṭi', *Al-Qur'ān wa-'l-Tafsīr al-ᶜAṣrī*, Cairo, 1970, pp. 96–99.
24. *MSK*, xiii, 74.
25. Ibid., 69.
26. *MSK*, i, 24.
27. *MSK*, iii, 42–60.
28. *MSK*, iv, 84.
29. *MSK*, iii, 49.
30. Qur'ān 16.(46)44.
31. *MSK*, iii, 50.
32. *MSK*, x, 9; *MSK*, xi, 65. In Christianity a similar remark about Jesus would be the shibboleth of what many would call extreme liberalism; in Islam, of course, such a remark does not have this function.
33. *MSK*, x, 54.
34. *MSK*, xiii, 149–151; *MSK*, xxvii, 91; Qur'ān 3.104 and 9.71.
35. Richard Bell's translation.
36. *MSK*, xv, 19.
37. *MSK*, x, 77.
38. Ibid., 102.
39. Ibid., 103.
40. The formula might be understood as "If only we had applied the Sharīᶜah" by those who want to understand it that way.
41. *MSK*, i, 19.
42. *MSK*, xiv, 95.
43. Ibid., 91.
44. *MSK*, iii, 99.
45. Ibid., 113; *MSK*, x, 110: *arqā al-bilād ḥaḍāratan*.

46. *MSK*, viii, 51.
47. Qur'ān 2.217.
48. *MSK*, x, 34.
49. Ibid., 41–42.
50. *MSK*, xiii, 16; *MSK*, xiv, 12.
51. *MSK*, xiv, 10.
52. *MSK*, viii, 46.
53. *MSK*, xv, 107.
54. *MSK*, vii, 36.
55. *MSK*, xiii, 15; *MSK*, xi, 65.
56. *MSK*, iii, 48.
57. *MSK*, xvi, 129–132.
58. *MSK*, ii, 110; *MSK*, xxiv, 136.
59. See, however, DR. ᶜĀṭif Aḥmad, *Naqd al-Fahm al-ᶜAṣrī li-'l-Qur'ān*, Beirut (Dār al-Ṭalīᶜah), 1972, pp. 26–31.
60. *MSK*, viii, 35.
61. *MSK*, x, 98–100.
62. *MSK*, x, 116. This passage, somehow, implies monogamy.
63. *MSK*, viii, 73.
64. *MSK*, x, 94.
65. Ibid., 115.
66. Ibid., 104–110.
67. Ibid., 110 and 116.
68. Cf. A.J. WENSINCK, *Mohammed en de Joden te Medina* (Leiden, 1928), pp. 145–157.
69. *MSK*, xxiv, 135.
70. Ibid., 79.
71. Qur'ān 8.58.
72. E.g., *MSK*, ii, 11 & 118–130.
73. *MSK*, iv, 76.
74. Qur'ān 4.157.
75. *MSK*, iv, 83.
76. See Chapter 5.
77. Ḥasan al-Bannā, the founder of the Muslim Brotherhood, is called a martyr because he was assassinated in 1949.
78. Qur'ān 4.171.

79. *Encyclopaedia of Islam*, second ed., IV, 84, s.v. 'Īsā, "The Return of Jesus," and references.
80. O.F.A. Meinardus, *Christian Egypt: Faith and Life*, Cairo (American University-Cairo), 1970, pp. 200–201.
81. *MSK*, xxiv, 126.
82. *MSK*, v, 116.
83. Qur'ān 2.255.
84. *MSK*, v, 24, cf. Mt 7:15; *MSK*, vi, 18, cf. Mt 26:39; *MSK*, ix, 37, cf. Mt 17:20; *MSK*, xiii, 159; cf. Mt 22:36; *MSK*, xxiv, 70, cf. Mt 5:38.
85. *MSK*, xv, 107; *MSK*, xxiii, 6 & 34; Qur'ān 23.100.
86. *MSK*, xi, 68.
87. *MSK*, xxvi, 31–47.
88. Quoted by Muṣṭafā Amīn, *Min ᶜAsharah li-ᶜIshrīn*, Cairo (Al-Maktab al-Miṣrī al-Ḥadīth), 1981, p. 11.
89. The weekly *Uktūbir*, nr. 263, November 8, 1981.
90. Cf. p. 45 in Chapter 3.
91. Cf. p. 7 in Chapter 1.
92. Cf., however, W. Montgomery Watt, *The Formative Period of Islamic Thought*, Edinburgh, 1973, p. 10–11. It may even be that Shaykh Kishk intends to equate Sadat with ᶜUthmān who also "had failed (. . .) to carry out penalties prescribed by the Qur'ān" (Watt, op. cit., p. 10).
93. The link between the murder of Sadat and the murder of ᶜUmar is also made in Ṣalāḥ Muntaṣir, *Ḥiwār maᶜa al-Shaykh al-Shaᶜrāwī*, p. 49.

CHAPTER 5

Shaykh Al-Sha^c^rāwī

WHEREAS SHAYKH KISHK was boycotted by the Egyptian mass media during the Sadat era, Shaykh Muḥammad Mutawallī Al-Shaᶜrāwī (b. 1911) was seen more often on the Egyptian television screen than Anwar al-Sadat himself. This means that he appeared very often indeed on the Egyptian television screen.

Shaykh Al-Shaᶜrāwī's national fame seems to have had its beginnings in his participation in the weekly religious TV program *Nūr ᶜalā Nūr* ("Light on Light")[1] which was broadcast in Egypt in 1973. These same programs seem to have been shown in Kuwayt and other Arab countries. This, of course, contributed to his local prestige in Egypt.

Shaykh Muḥammad Mutawallī Al-Shaᶜrāwī rose to his great fame from humble beginnings.[2] He was born in the village of Daqādūs, in the Mit Ghamr district, in early April 1911. He was educated in primary and secondary Azhar schools[3] in Zaqaziq and Tanta. In 1936 he received his secondary school certificate at Zaqaziq, and continued his studies in Cairo at al-Azhar University. Here he received his *ᶜālimīyah* degree in 1941, and the *takhaṣṣuṣ* in

1943, from the Arabic Language Faculty. This implies that his Azhar training was more concerned with philology and linguistics than with theology and dogmatics.

Having concluded his Azhar training, he was now a member of the Azhar élite, and qualified for the careers open to Azhar graduates. After appointments as a teacher in Zaqaziq, Tanta, and Alexandria he left for Saudi Arabia in 1950. Here he eventually became professor at the ᶜAbd al-ᶜAzīz University in Mecca. After his return to Egypt he became director of the office of the Rector of al-Azhar in the days of Shaykh Ḥasan Ma'mūn (1894 – 1973) who fulfilled the Rectorate from 1964 to 1970. Thereafter a period of six years in Algeria followed. Again returning to Egypt, Shaykh Al-Shaᶜrāwī worked in the Ministry of *Awqāf* and Azhar Affairs, eventually as the Cabinet Minister for that ministry from November 9, 1976, to October 18, 1978.

Once freed from such administrative responsibilities, his fame rose to unique heights. In the summer of 1980 he appeared, for instance, twice daily on the television screen to deliver a Ramaḍān sermon.[4] People who watched how the Shaykh delivered his daily sermons on their television screens could not but identify him strongly with the trusted and prestigious class of traditional *ᶜulamā'*. Many, one gathers, were deeply impressed when they saw how he manipulated his cloak, which might have been uninfluenced by modern fashions but which had exactly the right shade of simple brown for maximum effect on color television. Few people would have been able to appeal, so seemingly without effort, to those who want to be modern and at the same time to those who want to be traditional.

The way in which the Shaykh speaks, however, is not at all traditional. His Arabic is certainly Azhar Arabic since the variable terminal vowels that the Azhar way of speaking Arabic requires are often audible. Yet the influence of Arabic as colloquially spoken in Egypt is large. Every now and then Shaykh Al-Shaᶜrāwī admonishes his audience in plain and pure Egyptian speech. Even in the printed versions of his talks colloquial words emerge, for example, almost systematically *baᶜdēn* (literally "subsequently, later") instead of the more formal *baᶜd dhālika*. The editors of the texts of Shaykh Al-Shaᶜrāwī have usually made efforts to adapt the Shaykh's texts to the needs of the printed page.[5]

Shaykh Al-Shacrāwī certainly does not want to addṛess an educated élite only. He is not above explaining to his public the meaning of a word like "pronoun."[6] He even looks as if he positively enjoys explaining such things to his public. Although he may sometimes seem pedantic, he also every now and then makes successful efforts to avoid comparatively simple grammatical terms like "article."[7] (Articles play, of course, an important role in the exegetical arguments that are interspersed throughout his sermons.)

In a way which one is tempted to call Socratic, he poses questions to his studio audience, filmed live, and tries to draw out the answers — often, however, replying himself before giving his audience the opportunity to fill in the required antiphon. His vivid and energetic way of delivering his sermons differs considerably from the rather monotonous robot-like or overexcited style in which many Azhar scholars speak in public. Shaykh Al-Shacrāwī's performance charms the television watching public, irrespective of its creed or lack of it. The fame and success of Shaykh Al-Shacrāwī can be said to have been impossible without the opportunities television offers to those who know how to exploit them.

Shaykh Al-Shacrāwī's charisma, so conspicuously present when he performs before the television cameras, is much less obvious in his writings. His enemies call him a clever actor — never a clever writer. Yet, in August (Ramaḍān) 1980, the bookstands in Cairo were offering for sale 35 books by or about Shaykh Al-Shacrāwī, together containing a total of 3,112 pages, all rather recently written. With such an output, repetitions are inevitable. For instance, the text of the booklet *Al-Islām, cAqīdah wa-Manhaj* is found again as pages 9 to 60 of his book *Al-Ṭarīq ila-'Llāh*. Of the latter, pages 113 to 156 are identical to pages 5 to 39 of his book *Al-Islām wa-Ḥarakat al-Ḥayāh*.

Some of the books that had Shaykh Al-Shacrāwī's name or portrait on their cover were, however, not written by the Shaykh himself but were edited versions of speeches he had delivered, or they contained the texts of television programs in which he had participated, or they comprised newspaper interviews with the Shaykh. The booklets that have appeared regularly since January 1981 under the slightly misleading traditional designation of *fa-*

tāwā (expert answers on questions of Islamic Law) are composed by a certain Dr. Al-Sayyid al-Jamīlī, who is well known in Egypt for books on popular medicine in the Egyptian equivalent of what one is tempted to call a *Readers' Digest* style.[8] These fatwā volumes each consist of chapters that begin with a question raised by Dr. Al-Sayyid al-Jamīlī, followed first by a sometimes rather short answer presumably by Shaykh Al-Shaᶜrāwī, and then by a commentary on this answer by Dr. Al-Sayyid.[9]

There is little or no reason to think that the contents of these volumes do not reflect the religious interests of the Egyptian Muslim public. These volumes may, however, not be totally reliable in their reproduction of Shaykh Al-Shaᶜrāwī's ideas. There is, for instance, a subtle difference between his thoughts on what a Westerner would call superstition as expressed in the first fatāwā volume edited by Dr. Al-Sayyid in January 1981, and the wording of a booklet[10] on spirits and miracles published by the Shaykh himself, also in January 1981. Since both books were published at the same time, it is not probable that a difference between the two books can be explained by, for instance, a further development of thought on the subject. The only possible explanation of a difference seems to be that the Shaykh is more subtle than his followers.

The Israeli scholar Professor Hava Lazarus-Yafeh wants to place on record that Shaykh Al-Shaᶜrāwī "makes no attempt to educate [Egyptian] society and raise its level of religiosity, or to purge it from superstitions, fanaticism and fundamentalism."[11] Shaykh Al-Shaᶜrāwī's attitude in this, so she makes her readers understand, contrasts unfavorably with earlier modernist Muslim religious leaders. This harsh judgment by Professor Lazarus-Yafeh is based on these fatāwā volumes, especially on what these volumes have to say about the *jinn*, or spirits, which, according to Egyptian popular belief, co-exist with humanity in this world.

The *jinn*, it is generally believed, do indeed exist, and humans may even subject them and be served by them. The *jinn*, so the Qur'ān[12] revealed, are created from fire. Shaykh Al-Shaᶜrāwī does not contradict these widespread, popular (and partly Qur'anic) beliefs, neither in the *Fatāwā* edited by Dr. Al-Sayyid, nor in the booklet on the subject which is fully his own. He does add a few interesting remarks, however. First he speaks to the skeptic who doubts the existence of supernatural powers. Should such a skeptic not find an example of supernatural powers in the abilities of the *rijāl al-mabāḥith,* the agents of the secret police (both the Gestapo type and the James Bond type)? Do not such agents control powers that awe any skeptic?[13] It is difficult not to suspect Shaykh Al-Shaʿrāwī here of some irony.

More important is an illuminating comparison that the Shaykh makes when he talks to those who do believe in the supernatural. It is indeed possible, so the Shaykh says, to control spirits. However, he continues, like the possession of a gun, the services of the *jinn* are a dangerous gift. How can one be sure that the intentions with which this gift is used will always remain good? Is it possible to guarantee that only good use will be made of spirits or guns? Better to leave them both alone.[14]

In the same breath, Shaykh Al-Shaʿrāwī adds that only evil spirits allow themselves to be held in check by human magic, and that hence any member of the realm of the *jinn* that is ready to serve man must be an evil spirit. Is it possible not to understand such words as a warning not to occupy oneself too much with the so-called supernatural? In the light of these warnings by the Shaykh Al-Shaʿrāwī, it becomes difficult to subscribe to the judgment of Professor Hava Lazarus-Yafeh. Moreover, have other religious leaders, through outright attacks on superstition or otherwise, ever really "raised the level of religiosity of [their] public"?

It is possible to adduce more examples of a similar approach in Shaykh Al-Shaʿrāwī's books. Elsewhere we read that the difference between a real Ṣūfī miracle worker and a fraudulent one is found in the anger that frauds feel when the reality of their miraculous gifts meets with skepticism.[15] A real Ṣūfī ought not to be interested in whether his supernatural energies are doubted or not, so the Shaykh argues. At the end of his booklet on the *jinn,*[16] he literally writes *laysa maṭlūb minka an tuṣaddiqahu,* "you are not required to believe all this," whereas such reservations are absent in the fatāwā volume by the learned doctor Al-Sayyid al-Jamīlī.

Dr. Al-Sayyid al-Jamīlī is no doubt moved by great admiration for Shaykh Al-Shaʿrāwī. This shows itself not only in (perhaps) a slight simplification of the Shaykh's subtle arguments, but also in Dr. Al-Sayyid's wish to see great wisdom, if not genius, in acts and decisions that, in the eye of the skeptic, are simply attentive maneuvering and cool professional competence. Dr. Al-Sayyid tells us, for instance, how a group of Shaykhs once visited Shaykh Al-Shaᶜrāwī at his office when he was the Cabinet Minister for *Awqāf* in order to present a serious complaint:

A group of Christians had illegally taken possession of a piece of land that once had been dedicated as a Muslim religious endowment, a *waqf,* and they wanted to build a church on that land. . . . Now the Shaykhs wanted their colleague, the Cabinet Minister, to give an injunction to hand over this piece of land to them, in order to erect a Mosque on it. . . . Shaykh Al-Shaᶜrāwī did not think long before he found a fitting solution to this problem. . . . He called his First Under-Secretary and instructed him to investigate the matter. . . . He would, so he promised, then take the appropriate measures. . . . This is what justice, power and wisdom are all about. . . .[17]

Not everyone, however, is as easily impressed as Dr. Al-Sayyid. In a column entitled *yawmīyāt,* "diary," in the daily newspaper *Al-Ahrām* on March 31 and April 1, 1982, both times on p. 18 of the paper, the journalist Aḥmad Bahā al-Dīn (who is called a Marxist by some of his enemies) voices some criticism of the Shaykh's verbosity.

The point that Aḥmad Bahā al-Dīn makes is connected with Qur'ān 91.1–2: "By the Night when it veils—by the Day when it shines out in splendor." Talking about this verse the Shaykh had told an eager interviewer from the popular weekly *Al-Muṣawwar* that it had not been good to bring electricity to the countryside. "People now are awake at night and are late to work . . . the night is for resting, the day for working . . . ," and so on. Aḥmad Bahā al-Dīn then concludes his first column with the words, "Which argument shall I choose out of the million arguments against these words? Until tomorrow!"

In his second column Aḥmad Bahā al-Dīn poses four questions: (1) Why is electricity only harmful in the countryside? What about the towns? (2) Does this verse really forbid illumination at night? Did not the Prophet and his Companions make use of such means as candles? (3) Is it not conceivable that people in the countryside spend their nights awake but carrying out meritorious acts like praying, or watching Shaykh Al-Shaᶜrāwī on a television set powered by electricity? Is it reasonable to suppose that the illumined nights will only be used to drink liquids that Islam forbids? (4) Is electricity in the countryside only for pleasure, or does it also supply power to machines and factories? Does this verse from the Qur'ān forbid all that, too?

However, to have ended his first column with a simple "Until tomorrow" was a grave tactical mistake. Ṣalāḥ Muntaṣir quite justifiably points out in *Al-Ahrām* of April 6 that the provision "If God permits," *in shā' Allāh*, has to be added to all pronouncements on the future.[18] Ṣalāḥ Muntaṣir has no need to state explicitly that only an atheist could omit this pious formula—his public knows such things and does not need to be reminded of such elementary truisms.

This attack by Aḥmad Bahā al-Dīn on Shaykh Al-Shaᶜrāwī comes from someone who, to put it mildly, seems *not* to be obsessed by the necessity of founding an Islamic State and applying the entirety of the rules of Islamic Law in public and private life, by force if necessary. However, also those who are in favor of such an Islamic State and the ensuing complete application of the God-given Islamic laws, have at some time taken offense with Shaykh Al-Shaᶜrāwī's thinking.

On Sunday morning, December 25, 1977, a certain Muḥammad ᶜAbd al-Quddūs, a journalist, paid a visit to Shaykh Al-Shaᶜrāwī, who at that time fulfilled the office of Cabinet Minister for *Awqāf.* This Muḥammad ᶜAbd al-Quddūs came to see Shaykh Al-Shaᶜrāwī "with the aim to interview the Shaykh about the rumor that the masses kept repeating that the Shaykh, so successful as a preacher, now failed totally as a Cabinet Minister." The journalist, by his own account, does not seem to have succeeded in putting his, no doubt, friendly questions on this subject to the Shaykh. Cynics might be tempted to conclude from this that it proves the competence of the Minister, and the incompetence of this journalist, who represented *Al-Daᶜwah*, the fundamentalist monthly of the Sadat Era.[19]

The standards of competence that *Al-Daᶜwah* applies are, however, different. Shaykh Al-Shaᶜrāwī's failure as a Cabinet Minister was, according to *Al-Daᶜwah*, reflected by his supporting a law that would forbid the Call to Prayer to be amplified electronically.

"Does the loudspeaker succeed in attracting someone who does not want to pray to the mosque?"—"If the matter were in my hands, I would forbid the nightly Call to Prayer by loudspeaker in the whole Republic," so *Al-Daᶜwah* summarizes the view of Shaykh Al-Shaᶜrāwī.

This controversy over electronic Calls to Prayer is not unimportant. The supporters of a Muslim theocracy are in favor of it—they probably pray anyhow. Others, however, are disturbed by it. They resent the noise, and they resent being awakened in the dark of night by the electronic force of the amplified minaret. It needs little explaining that the value of real estate can be heavily reduced by the establishment of a mosque in the vicinity if this mosque makes use of electronic means to increase the audibility of the Call to Prayer, which is sent out five times every 24 hours.

The Nile island of Zamalek, the traditional diplomatic neighborhood in the middle of Cairo where real estate prices are at their most fevered and where real estate agents expected that their clients would receive more than US$1,000 per square meter in 1980, is mentioned regularly in the discussions on this topic. It is also mentioned in Shaykh Al-Shaᶜrāwī's defense of his own position (as reformulated by *Al-Daᶜwah*), be it in the context of students who need their hours of sleep in the nights before an examination, and not in the, perhaps, more realistic context of well-paid foreign diplomats cancelling their rent contracts.

Yet *Al-Daᶜwah*, having exposed Shaykh Al-Shaᶜrāwī as a nonsupporter of electronic Calls to Prayer, seems to feel that the Shaykh could be an ally and concludes the article with the expression of the pious wish to be united with the Shaykh in the struggle for Islam. In this struggle, so we read, "only the Muslim Brothers did not succumb to tyranny on the day that many began to collaborate, and issued fatwā after fatwā . . ."—a hardly coded reference to the Shaykh's government position and his extensive output of religious literature.

Is the Shaykh's point of view on the publicly audible Call to Prayer by loudspeakers consistent with his other views and actions? When one takes a realistic look at Egypt, or at Zamalek only, it is obvious that a law prohibiting electronically amplified Calls to Prayer could never be enforced. Someone like Shaykh Al-Shaᶜrāwī would hence gain nothing, and only weaken his position, by opposing a prohibition that had no future anyway. Perhaps his lack of enthusiasm for resistence to the prohibition of loudspeakers and the consequent attack by the notoriously antigovernment *Al-Daᶜwah* made his position with the secularists even stronger since it made him look more reliable in their eyes. It is needless to say that, in Zamalek as elsewhere, sleeping students, development aid experts, ambassadors, and *ancien régime* millionaires all continue to be interrupted in their sleep by pious electronic Calls to Prayer.

Shaykh Al-Shaᶜrāwī is a prominent public figure. As such he has been involved in numerous incidents and polemics.[20] All of these deserve study and analysis since they throw an interesting sidelight on Egyptian Islam. Yet one cannot help being curious as to what the Shaykh really thinks and believes on the central question of modern Egyptian Islam: Should there be a theocracy in which the real ruler is not a person but Islamic Law, or not?

In the background of all of Shaykh Al-Shaᶜrāwī's preaching and writing, an implicit optimism and feeling of superiority make themselves felt. Such characteristics are something relatively new. They were hardly there in the theology of the Islamic reformers at the end of the nineteenth century. Military and political developments in the nineteenth century had placed the Muslims in a position that could not but be regarded as inferior to the non-Muslim West.[21] Why had the Muslims suddenly become backward? How had they, as Mr. Edward Mortimer put it, lost their ability to dominate their non-Muslim surroundings? The writings of the Muslim reformers at the turn of the century abundantly reflect this insecurity. A few remarks made by the reformer Muḥammad ᶜAbduh (1850–1905) will serve to illustrate this.

A powerful and influential friend of ᶜAbduh, the Earl of Cromer, who as British Consul-General practically ruled Egypt from 1883 till 1907, called ᶜAbduh in his memoirs an "Agnostic."[22] It is difficult to see on what exactly Cromer based himself when he wrote down this observation.[23] If it is not simply a misunderstanding of conversations with ᶜAbduh — such a misunderstanding is not likely in the case of an administrator of Cromer's stature — it might be connected with ᶜAbduh's views of the

Qur'ān: in many cases ᶜAbduh teaches that we *cannot know* what exactly is meant by the words of the Qur'ān, for example, when the Qur'ān speaks of the Final Day, Judgment, Heaven and Hell. ᶜAbduh teaches that in such cases we should simply leave certain phrases of the Holy Book unexplained.

Modern Egyptian students of ᶜAbduh's writings, such as Dr. Muḥammad Ḥusayn Al-Dhahabī,[24] recognize this position of ᶜAbduh. No matter how much one respects ᶜAbduh's refusal "to add to the Holy Book from one's own," it is obvious that the traditional Qur'ān commentaries that left no questions unanswered and that left nothing unexplained might, on the one hand, be accused of a certain *horror vacui* but are, on the other hand, also more self-confident and secure.

It is ᶜAbduh's carefulness in interpreting cryptic passages in the Qur'ān that may have earned him the designation of "an agnostic." This caution, however, was of no avail when he attempted to explain *sabᶜan shidādan,* "seven (heavens) firm," in Qur'ān 78.12 by a reference to the seven planets known in his days.[25]

Shaykh Al-Shaᶜrāwī, full of confidence, now asks how Muslims should interpret this verse after the discovery, in the decades following ᶜAbduh's death, of additional planets. Other explanations of a rationalist nature once proposed by ᶜAbduh are equally confidently rejected by Shaykh Al-Shaᶜrāwī, even when these interpretations were ultimately derived from the authoritative encyclopedic writings of Al-Ṭabarī (d. 923).[26]

After ᶜAbduh's prudence, the self-confidence of Shaykh Al-Shaᶜrāwī seems only reasonable. Somewhere between ᶜAbduh and Al-Shaᶜrāwī the British occupation of Egypt came to its end. Egypt gradually became a politically independent state. Moreover, Egypt's enemies failed again and again, for instance, in their threefold attack on Suez in 1956. And, many say, did not Egypt even beat her expansionist neighbor Israel in the October war of 1973? Add to all this the liberation of the Sinai, completed in 1981, a century after the abortive ᶜUrābī Revolt and the occupation of Egypt by the British army that followed this revolt, and the reasons for optimism and confidence in the future are clear. The tide has turned upon Egypt. If it is true that the Muslims are backward, they are certainly making up for their supposed backwardness. Who can doubt that they will eventually regain their traditional superiority?[27]

Shaykh Al-Shaᶜrāwī shares these general feelings of optimism; they are the very background of his preaching: All is not well but good times are coming. In the years after the Egyptian revolution of 1919, the Shaykh tells in an interview, "Our ambition was the purification and liberation of Egypt."[28] The history of this period he summarizes as "demonstrations one day, prison and interrogation the next."[29] Yet, out of the chaos of an Egypt ruled by the monarchy and the Free Officers' Revolution of 1952, political independence emerged. The foreign non-Muslim yoke was thrown off.

In interviews, the Shaykh claims to have been active in the leadership of student organizations and to have participated in the organization of demonstrations.[30] Although his statements on these matters are vague, there is no reason not to believe him. It would be difficult indeed to imagine anyone leading a student's life in Egypt without getting involved in demonstrations. If Shaykh Al-Shaᶜrāwī as a student did indeed take part in the leadership of student movements, it is certain that his acute political instinct prevented him from taking risks that would have got him into the kind of trouble that would have made his rise to fame impossible.

Can a similar instinct for avoiding unnecessary risks be observed in another aspect of Shaykh Al-Shaᶜrāwī's work? It is, indeed, surprising that, in spite of his numerous books, articles, and pamphlets, and in spite of his numerous newspaper interviews, Shaykh Al-Shaᶜrāwī seems to have managed to avoid making direct unambiguous statements on the burning question of the decade: "Should a Muslim State, where Muslim Law rules supreme, replace the present-day secular states?" How can a prominent Muslim under such heavy media exposure remain silent or evasive on this topic?

A good example of his evasiveness on this particular subject can be found in the interview in *Al-Ahrām* by Ṣalāḥ Muntaṣir.[31] When the interviewer asks whether the Shaykh has relatives or friends in the extremist societies, *al-jamā^c^āt al-mutaṭarrifah,* the Shaykh answers that all his friends, "and for this I thank God, understand their religion perfectly."

However, in 1975 Shaykh Al-Sha^c^rāwī, whose popularity and fame had at that time not yet reached their peak, wrote a short introduction to a book called *Ḥizb Allāh,* The Party of God, a book of which a certain Wā'il ^c^Uthmān, an engineer by training, was the author.[32] The title of this book, the Party of God, suggests that its author wished to participate in the debate on the return of political parties that was at that time current in Sadat's Egypt. The contents of the book, on the other hand, indicate that this was only partly so. "Islam," the engineer writes, "only recognizes two parties: the Party of God and the Party of Satan." Closely following the day's jargon, yet subtly changing it, he then adds: "Muslims should unite in order to work for the return of the rule of God's party, *^c^awdat sayṭarat ḥizb Allāh.*"

In this way, "Sadat and his clique" are implicitly designated as the Party of Satan. "Many thought I meant the Communist party when I wrote about the Devil's party," Wā'il ^c^Uthmān declares in the preface to the second edition of his book, but this is a misunderstanding, he writes, although, as he has to admit, the communists are an "essential support" of this Party of Satan. It is, as a matter of course, impossible to point out one single phrase or one single paragraph that makes Wā'il ^c^Uthmān's intentions evident. Even combined and translated into English, these quotations will perhaps not convince everybody:

> When you understand the Qur'ān . . . you can judge any Ruler no matter how religious he pretends to be. . . . The Party of Satan is that group of people who pretend to believe in Islam but in reality are Islam's first enemies. . . . How can we identify this group? That is easy! Islam is clear! One simply has to believe in God and His Apostle, and to act according to God's provisions *(al-^c^amal bi-aḥkām Allāh).*[33]

In the book's introduction we come across a definition of Satan's Party:

> Those who stumble along under legal provisions *(aḥkām)* and systems of legislation *(tashrī^c^āt)* which they want to serve as replacements for God's laws *(aḥkām Allāh).*[34]

This definition fits any government that ever issued any law or any code on any subject, the Egyptian government not excluded.

The Apostle, so the engineer continues, founded his own state *(aqāma dawlatahu)* in which the Muslims enjoyed full sovereignty and from which Islam spread all over the world. "O, if only someone could bring me to a country where the rule of the followers *(anṣār)* of God is absolute, then I would go and live there, without fear or worry."[35] What, one may ask, is there then to be feared? "There is a terrible contrast between what a Muslim youth hears and sees in his house, and what he meets outside. I do not think that I need to prove this. As soon as a Muslim young man goes out in the street, he comes upon placards advertising wine *(i^c^lānāt al-khamr)* and immoral movies. . . ." Three lines further down on the same page, the engineer takes back his words about the safety of the house: "When he sits in his house and puts on the television, the disaster is at its greatest: on all channels we hear and see calls to depravity and decadence. . . ."[36]

The engineer acutely observes that he cannot be free as long as he is "subject to man-made laws."[37] He then continues: "Our youth enjoys the freedom of having its hair long *(ḥurrīyat iṭālat al-sha^c^r)* and women enjoy the liberty of showing their bodies . . . we hear from those who create 'fashion' (Ar.: *mōḍa*) and its waves in the Western world, and we find that those people are all Jewish males who play with women any way they want to, and, my God, how happy these women are with the freedom to go naked which these followers of Satan have given to them."[38]

The engineer tells his readers that he arrived at his current views during his stay in Europe: talking to people about Islam, he found himself unable to point to any one state where these laws of Islam, so beneficial to mankind, were being applied.[39] It is noteworthy that this frustration that made him conscious of the crisis of Islam occurred while he lived in the West. It is equally memorable that Wā'il ^c^Uthmān is an engineer and not a *shaykh,* which means that his education, whatever it has been, was essentially Western and not traditionally Islamic. Someone who wanted to argue that Islamic militancy is the product of the meeting of Islam and the modern West can certainly find support for such a view in the writings of Wā'il ^c^Uthmān.

Wā'il ᶜUthmān, being acquainted with the West, tries to seek an explanation for Western progress *(taqaddum)* and the backwardness *(takhalluf)* of the Islamic world. "The West," so we read, "does not believe in Islam, and therefore the people in the West are successful according to their efforts. We, however, we know the Truth but we have forsaken it. God consequently has become angry at us, and has decided that we should remain in a state of backwardness as long as we do not return to Him, and live our lives as our Creator wants us to. . . ." And here again the engineer returns to the ever-exciting subject of women who dare to leave their houses, "who show their nakedness, artfully display their charms, and mix with men in general"—and so on, and so on.

Switching back and forth between his theological reflections and the shamelessness current amongst contemporary females, the engineer finally concludes with a quotation of the well-known verses from Surah 5: "Whosoever does not rule *(yaḥkum)* according to what God has sent down, they are the unbelievers, the evildoers, the sinners."[40] The Arabic words used are *kāfir, ẓālim,* and *fāsiq.*

Many an outsider might be tempted not to take all this talk about long hair, Jewish haute couture designers, and so forth very seriously. This, however, would be a mistake. Wā'il ᶜUthmān had to spend some time in prison for his book, which may be an indication of the earnestness with which the subject matter he wrote about is regarded in Egypt. Wā'il ᶜUthmān's book may lack the intellectual consistency and the iron logic of *Al-Farīḍah al-Ghā'ibah,* but the *Farīḍah* and Wā'il ᶜUthmān agree on several points. They both, for instance, condemn the Sadat régime as un-Islamic, and they both regard the nonapplication of Islamic Law by a Muslim ruler as apostasy from Islam.

There is, however, also a difference between the *Farīḍah* and Wā'il ᶜUthmān. The *Farīḍah,* with grandiose monomania, puts all the emphasis on Islamic laws and Islamic government. The individual or collective behavior of Egypt's population, the things Egyptians take pleasure in and the things they detest, are not debated in the *Farīḍah.* (The most recent event in Egyptian history that the *Farīḍah* explicitly mentions is Napoleon's occupation of Egypt in 1798.)

This preoccupation with legislation is shared by Wā'il ᶜUthmān, but Wā'il ᶜUthmān also takes into account how people really behave and act. Although he probably would like to forbid many things that go on in Egypt today, he at least does not overlook those things — as the author of the *Farīḍah* unhesitatingly does. Wā'il ᶜUthmān, however, discusses in some detail the many social realities that are not easily brought within the realm of Islamic Law but that nevertheless can be quite contrary to what many understand to constitute proper Islamic conduct. It is, of course, exactly the specificness of his criticisms that makes it difficult for an outsider to take him seriously.

Shaykh Al-Shaᶜrāwī cannot be called an outsider, and he took Wā'il ᶜUthmān completely seriously. In 1975 in his preface to Wā'il ᶜUthmān's book, it is fascinating to see how frankly Shaykh Al-Shaᶜrāwī endorses the sometimes remarkable views of Wā'il ᶜUthmān, especially when one realizes that the practical political views of Shaykh Al-Shaᶜrāwī are not particularly clear from the latter's own voluminous writings and elaborate speeches.

In the eulogy with which Shaykh Al-Shaᶜrāwī begins this preface, he quickly comes to the point:

> Glory to God . . . who preserved cells of belief, *khalāyā al-īmān*, which heathendom does not know how to exterminate, and the core of which tyranny does not know to corrupt. . . .

"Cells," *khalāyā*, is no doubt the word that the secret police uses to designate terrorist organizations. "Heathen," *jāhilī*, is the word that modern pious Muslims use to designate the powers that be, even when these powers claim to be Muslim. "Tyranny," *ṭughyān*, is a general term for the government in the jargon of the Muslim activists, and Sadat's enemies often used this word to characterize his régime. The reference to corruption of the core has to be understood as an allusion to the tranquillizing effect that pleasant government jobs might have on the religious conscience. There is little reason not to paraphrase this eulogy as follows: "Glory to God who preserved cells of activists which our pagan government does not know how to exterminate, and the core of which the present régime does not know how to buy off by offering them jobs and salaries." Since the moment Shaykh Al-Shaᶜrāwī wrote this preface in 1975, several assassinations and riots have demonstrated how true this is.

From the sequel to the opening eulogy it is evident that Shaykh Al-Shaᶜrāwī fully agrees with engineer Wā'il ᶜUthmān, whose book he describes as *ᶜabqarī*, a work of genius.[41] The real genius, however, is Shaykh Al-Shaᶜrāwī himself. Wā'il ᶜUthmān published three or four pamphlets at most and was then thrown into prison; Shaykh Al-Shaᶜrāwī has published in the years after 1975 hundreds of books and pamphlets, and was even, for some time, appointed Cabinet Minister for *Awqāf.*

It seems, indeed, odd that such a man would endorse the specific views and social criticisms of Wā'il ᶜUthmān. This cannot be explained by the Shaykh's possible ignorance of the contents of Wā'il ᶜUthmān's book. Wā'il ᶜUthmān was a student leader in the Engineering Faculty of the Cairo University and as such he played an important role in the student unrest in Cairo in the late sixties and the early seventies.[42] This involvement in the student movement must be reason enough for anyone who is not a fool to be cautious when writing laudatory prefaces. It is unimaginable that Shaykh Al-Shaᶜrāwī, who is no fool, would consent to write a preface to a book by a card-carrying, known activist without having carefully read the book.

It seems stranger still that in this preface Shaykh Al-Shaᶜrāwī darkly alludes to the need for forms of Islamic activism that go further than verbal criticism and prayer. It was mentioned above[43] that the author of the *Farīḍah* complains (without, however, mentioning names) that no pious Muslim has ever really served the cause of Islam once he became burdened by ministerial duties and dignities. Also, the fundamentalist monthly *Al-Daᶜwah* severely attacked Shaykh Al-Shaᶜrāwī in the period he was Cabinet Minister for *Awqāf.*[44] It seems, however, that already in this period — or, rather, already before it — the Shaykh's sympathy for the cause of the militant fundamentalists was considerable. Yet sympathy is not the same as collaboration or complicity.

It would be unreasonable to fail to take Shaykh Al-Shaᶜrāwī's theology into account when trying to draw an overall picture of his way of thinking. It is no doubt true that, in descriptions of Islam until recently, too much attention was paid to theology and ideology at the expense of practical politics, religious practice, Muslim Law, and other down-to-earth religious phenomena. This is not sufficient reason, however, now to leave out dogmatics and theology altogether: Muslims are equally justified in feeling misrepresented by any summary of their religious attitudes that in its turn leaves out this aspect.

Natural belief in God's existence is the starting point of Shaykh Al-Shaʿrāwī's theology. People believe in God, according to the Shaykh, because their intellect *(ʿaql)* demonstrates *(dalla)* that He exists: Man's mind inevitably comes to the conclusion that there must be a Higher Power behind the world as we know it.[45] The Shaykh regards this philosophical and theoretical belief as the first step. He realizes, however, that only someone who already believes in God's existence notices that God is the cause of all causes.[46] God created time and place, and hence He Himself is not subject to the limitations that time and place imply.[47] He is Absolute Pure Existence, *Al-Wujūd al-Muṭlaq li-Dhātihi.*[48] By necessity God is not discernible — if He would be, He could not be God, so the Shaykh upholds. Only from what He has created, man can deduce that He must exist. He Himself is hidden.[49]

Whatever philosophical notions such remarks imply, it is evident that Shaykh Al-Shaʿrāwī feels that he has to try to convince his public that God really exists, and this with arguments that are not derived from religion or revelation itself, but from a supposedly innate religiosity. The occurrence of such apologetic remarks on doubt and unbelief in the writings of the Shaykh are a strong indication that religious doubt — which has been so effective a force in the Europe of the Enlightenment — does exist in a similar way in the contemporary Muslim world. In spite of the centrality and universality[50] of religion in Muslim countries, this doubt is important enough to have influence upon Shaykh Al-Shaʿrāwī. The European Enlightenment, however, was not only the product of religious doubt, but also of a multitude of other intellectual and social factors. No one could possibly predict whether or not Muslim religiosity will in the future show an Enlightenment type of development, even if religious doubt becomes a much more widespread phenomenon than it is at present.

Shaykh Al-Shaᶜrāwī acutely observes — as his Western ecclesiastical colleagues have done before him — that modern science is one of the factors that has seduced the modern mind into doubting.[51] Yet, at the same time, modern science is called upon to rescue religion: the Qur'ān, so the Shaykh teaches, either confirms the modern sciences, or at least does not contradict them, and this is seen as a useful support for the cause of Islam.[52] Yet, Shaykh Al-Shaᶜrāwī realizes the danger of putting too much value on the tenet that the Qur'ān anticipates and predicts modern science: he knows that scientific theories change, and asks what one would do if a theory that Qur'ān commentators have miraculously derived from the wording of the Qur'ān later on turns out to be untrue.[53]

In Shaykh Al-Shaᶜrāwī's system, a natural monotheism results from rational observation of the world. This natural belief in the Creator, however, is not sufficient. It has to be supplemented by knowledge of God's commandments. The Shaykh admits that difference of opinion in this matter is a disturbing possibility. It is here that an appeal to an authority beyond the sphere of what is human becomes unavoidable. Although reason makes it extremely plausible that Allāh, "the proper name of He Who exists by necessity," has a Messenger, the decisive argument for this being so must be found in passages in which the Qur'ān assures the believer that it is "verily the speech of a noble messenger,"[54] and in the Qur'anic injunctions to believe in God and His messenger. God, in His Qur'ān, calls upon men to believe in Muḥammad, God's Apostle.[55] Muḥammad's position, so we read, is hence extremely special, *khāṣṣat al-khāṣṣah*.[56]

The heart, Shaykh Al-Shaᶜrāwī teaches, is the physical seat of belief.[57] Belief is the tranquillity of the heart about things that fall outside the scope of human reason.[58] Hence, belief cannot be the subject of permanent debate, the Shaykh explains.[59] Nevertheless, the word "belief" is also used in Shaykh Al-Shaᶜrāwī's pamphlets in a slightly different sense, not to denote an emotional-intellectual state but something more tangible, almost synonomous with law: man ought to act "according to his belief," every human act results from belief that lives in the heart, and it is belief, so we are assured, that regulates human behavior. The essence of belief, we read elsewhere, is devotion. Man must believe, the Shaykh writes repeatedly, in order to know how to live properly. Directly after belief in God, the Shaykh teaches, comes belief in what God told us.[60]

Muslims believe, so the Shaykh writes, in the Angels, the Apostles, the Books, Good and Evil, the Resurrection, and so on, because God said to, *Allāh qāla dhālika*. The *ᶜibādāt*, religious observances or acts of devotion that Muslim Law prescribes, are necessary (so the Shaykh believes) only because God told men so. They have no extrareligious value in this world. As an example, the ritual ablution before prayer is mentioned explicitly. Some modernists have argued that these ablutions are necessary and useful for hygienic reasons and have hence an extrareligious value. This, however, the Shaykh laughs away, and he reminds his audience that, if there is no water present, these ablutions may also be performed with sand or dust. Where, in that case, does modern hygiene come in, he scornfully asks.[61]

The two central points *(qawsayn)* of Islamic belief, the Shaykh teaches, are God and the Last Day.[62] To Western ears such a formula may sound only vaguely edifying—to Muslims, however, it is a sharp reminder of the duty to apply the One and Only Law revealed by their One and Only God. It also makes them remember the Final Judgment which they will face at the end of time: at this Judgment they will have to answer how they have applied this God-given law.

Following traditional tenets, the Shaykh explains that Muḥammad was only the *muballigh*, messenger, of God. Although Muḥammad had no sons, his name is carried on by the Islamic practice of naming children after him.[63] Both the Apostle Muḥammad and his book, the Qur'ān, are fully part of this world, and *ḥissī*, perceptible, by such human faculties as sight and hearing. Yet their being special, their being indeed the messenger of God and the Speech of God respectively, cannot be observed by the human senses: this can only be believed.[64]

Shaykh Al-Shaᶜrāwī's opinions on the Qur'ān are not uncommon. He explains to his public that the Qur'ān came down in stages, *marāḥil*, and not in one piece.[65] The revelation occurred in response to the historical events during Muḥammad's lifetime.[66] The order in which we now find its chapters printed is not the order in which these came down. The Shaykh thinks that the order in which we find the chapters of the Qur'ān is deliberate and meaningful.[67] Every now and then the reader comes upon phrases that seem to imply that the order of the surahs in the Qur'ān has been decided upon by a divine Editor: *rattaba kalāmahu tartīban muṣḥafīyan. . . .*[68]

The Shaykh attaches great importance to the *ibhām* of the Qur'ān, that is, its capability of being understood in more than one way.[69] Also, the meaning the Qur'ān must have had to Muḥammad's contemporaries in Mecca and Medina is given great weight in deciding upon the correct exegesis.[70] (When composing his booklets on Qur'ān interpretation, the Shaykh most probably made use of a concordance since, even when one knows the Qur'ān by heart, it is almost impossible to write with certitude that a certain word or expression "occurs 23 times" in the Qur'ān without resorting to such an index.[71])

The most important of all religious observances *(ᶜibādāt)* — so we are made to understand — is the prayer ceremony, *ṣalāh,* which every Muslim must carry out five times a day. According to Shaykh Al-Shaᶜrāwī, the *ṣalāh* symbolizes all of the five duties of Islam. The confession of belief *(shahādah),* "There is no God but God and Muḥammad is his Apostle," is recited many times during the *ṣalāh*. This confession is traditionally counted to be the first of the "pillars" of Islam.

The prayer ceremony, itself the second pillar, does not only contain the first pillar, the confession, but the other three pillars are also met with: during the ceremony a Muslim abstains from food and drink, even from talking, hence the pillar of fasting is also represented. During the ceremony, a Muslim turns to Mecca and the Kaᶜbah, and in this way the pilgrimage, *ḥajj,* plays its role. The pillar of *zakāt,* almsgiving, or religious taxation, can be found in the circumstance of sacrificing time — time that could be used otherwise.[72]

An outsider might easily object that speculations of this kind are nothing but words. There is, however, the controversy[73] about *jihād,* war against unbelievers: is it or is it not the fifth pillar of Islam? (Those who count *jihād* as the fifth pillar do not count the *shahādah* as a pillar.) Is *jihād* the forgotten duty of Islam, *al-farīḍah al-ghā'ibah?* These pious meditations on the prayer ceremony and the way the Shaykh enumerates the five "pillars" suggest that the Shaykh does not count *jihād* to be the fifth pillar. This would make the Shaykh's position different from that of the more violent Islamic zealots.

Is such a difference only a matter of words, or is it more than just a (possibly even accidental) difference in terminology? One might well ask whether the talks by Shaykh Al-Shaᶜrāwī are not just a warming-up which prepares the listeners for more violent forms of Islamic action. Do the words apply that Professor Jacob M. Landau[74] wrote about Turkish Islamist propaganda: "While all this seemed fairly innocuous . . . anyone . . . immediately understood the real meaning . . ."? Does Shaykh Al-Shaᶜrāwī help in supplying the zealots with "passive — and sometimes active — assistance by an amorphous mass of supporters"?[75] If it is difficult to answer such questions, this in itself might be significant since peaceful intentions do not have to be hidden, whereas it is not wise to express sympathy for a Muslim Brother type of organization that, like the *Farīḍah* group, might be inclined to use force in order to implement Islam.

Nobody can fail to notice that the terminology used by Shaykh Al-Shaᶜrāwī comes close to the terminology found in the writings of Sayyid Quṭb, the leader of the Muslim Brothers who was executed by the Nasser government in 1966. Sayyid Quṭb writes in his famous book *Maᶜālim fi-'l-Ṭarīq,* Signs on the Road, that Islam is not only a "system of belief," *ᶜaqīdah,* which has to be made known to mankind but also a *manhaj,* "way of life," that has to be implemented, and acted upon, in human society.[76] From the phrases that Sayyid Quṭb uses, it is obvious that, according to him, Islam is not only words, discussions, beliefs, and theories, but also — and perhaps in the first place — action and organization. It is especially the word *manhaj,* usually in opposition to *ᶜaqīdah,* which occurs extremely frequently both with Sayyid Quṭb and with Shaykh Al-Shaᶜrāwī.

The way in which Shaykh Al-Shaᶜrāwī uses the term *manhaj* elicits questions. Linguistically, the word *manhaj* simply means "way," and hence it is obviously related, at least semantically, to another word that originally simply means "way": the Arabic word *sharīᶜah,* the usual technical term for Muslim Law. Yet, the word *manhaj* does not have the legalistic connotations of the word *sharīᶜah.* The word *manhaj* sounds sufficiently vague so as not to worry anyone—not even those who feel that if Islamic Law (the *sharīᶜah,* the Islamic *manhaj par excellence)* were fully applied, a complete change of government and polity would be necessary.

It would not be difficult to put together a string of definitions of *manhaj*[77] casually offered by the Shaykh during his sermons and in his pamphlets that, all taken together, would unmistakably establish that in the Shaykh's idiom the word *manhaj* is nothing but a synomym of *sharīᶜah.* It is obvious that this synonym has been selected for tactical and diplomatic reasons.

If this is so, the Shaykh's frequent and popular sermons do contribute to the creation of a religiously fevered atmosphere in which the application of Islamic Law becomes a more and more exciting subject to talk about, to think about, and perhaps, finally, to act upon. In this atmosphere, the genesis of a more or less moderate mass organization that has a further application of Islamic Law as one of its aims is only natural. It is also only natural when such a mass organization every now and then produces terrorist cells.

It is illustrative that the Shaykh seems to think that every legal amendment *(taᶜdīl)* ever proposed has resulted in bringing the law of the land closer to the law of God.[78] This is no doubt untrue for the world as such, but it may have some truth where Egypt is concerned. In Egypt, and in other Muslim countries, small and gradual amendments of the existing laws have fulfilled some of the Muslim aspirations. Within the existing social and legal framework, one might say, Islam has undeniably made some progress. Why shouldn't it progress further yet?

The question of whether preachers like Shaykh Al-Shaᶜrāwī encourage bloodshed, murder, and assassination is not really answerable. Even if the Shaykh were one of those who contribute to the creation of a climate in which religious violence is becoming commonplace, it remains doubtful as to whether the specific acts of violence that this climate elicits can be said to be "encouraged" by his preaching.

Does Shaykh Al-Shaᶜrāwī accept the existing social and legal framework as it functions in Egypt? Does Shaykh Al-Shaᶜrāwī's thinking leave room for the secular concepts from which his own government derives its authority? Does Shaykh Al-Shaᶜrāwī accept the separation between politics and religion preached by Sadat?

Someone who wants to answer these three questions with "yes, he does" finds little support in, for example, the careless and nonchalant way in which the Shaykh talks about the material and scientific blessings of the West. The Shaykh is certainly not a supporter of the conceptuality of the Western Enlightenment. The scientific information with which he amply supplies his readers is rarely accurate. For instance, the term microbe is used indiscriminately to designate entities that are not microbes at all: human sperm, to mention one example. As the "inventor" of microbes, the reader gets introduced to a "seventeenth-century scholar" called Pasteur.[79] The Shaykh, moreover, assures the believers that all scientific inventions came about by accident and hence in reality came from God.[80] Not only the particulars of science, but also details from history fall in the sphere of his utter indifference: for instance, the medieval churchman Anselm is called "someone from Germany."[81] These illustrations of the Shaykh's attitude may be made complete by his attacks on Muḥammad ᶜAbduh and Al-ᶜAqqād (both rationalists in their own way) and his sneers on the value of logic and the weakness of the human intellect.[82]

It seems obvious that Shaykh Al-Shaᶜrāwī does not share certain basic assumptions of the Western Enlightenment. Moreover, he scorns its material fruits. Yet he lives under a government that embodies several Enlightenment values, including the separation of religion and politics, church and state. This, no doubt, generates tensions, but it does not make the Shaykh a theoretician of terrorism. It is not reasonable to accuse the Shaykh of doing more than having a certain attitude. Moreover, why should he do more? Although later generations may have great difficulty in understanding his charisma, his admirers today probably argue that nobody serves the cause of Islam better than he does. Few people so eloquently make Islam seem so important.

God, so we read in one of the Shaykh's pamphlets, "manages human affairs."[83] In English such a statement looks innocent enough. The original Arabic wording, however, runs: *yunaẓẓim al-Ḥaqq siyāsat al-bashar.* Literally, this phrase says that God "arranges the *siyāsah* of humanity." It is impossible to overlook the word *siyāsah* in this context. The word *siyāsah* is usually translated as politics, for example, in Sadat's slogan *lā siyāsah fi-'l-dīn wa-lā dīn fi-'l-siyāsah,* "No politics in religion and no religion in politics." If God is the One who is really responsible for the management of the *siyāsah* of humanity, as Shaykh Al-Shaᶜrāwī seems to maintain, this slogan about the separation of religion and *siyāsah* becomes meaningless. The provocative way in which the word *siyāsah* is used in this passage makes the underlying difference of opinion fairly conspicuous.

After Sadat's assassination, a long interview with Shaykh Al-Shaᶜrāwī was printed in *Al-Ahrām* in the November 8, 16, and 18, 1981, issues. It is almost unnecessary to mention that, like almost all the words the Shaykh utters, this interview, too, was reprinted as a booklet.[84] In the interview the Shaykh makes little effort to hide his personal dislike for the assassinated President. Under the circumstances it can hardly be called nice to draw attention (as the Shaykh does) to the fact that Islam allows killing for reasons of retaliation or "depravity" (*qiṣāṣ* and *fasād fi-'l-arḍ*),[85] especially not when one realizes that a politician's depravity can be proven by a press photographer who publishes a picture in which the politician under attack is shown drinking champagne in celebration of the conclusion of a treaty like the one signed at Camp David.

However, worse is to follow. The Shaykh evades answering whether he has friends or relatives in the extremist cells,[86] and then adds that he is especially "against them," *ḍiddahum,* because they — as some indeed do — regard anything that did not exist in the days of the Prophet as questionable. It almost looks as if the Shaykh feels hurt that some of the extremists might not approve of the way in which the Shaykh uses the television screen to further the cause of Islam, because the Prophet did not use television in order to spread Islam.

The interviewer's next question, almost at the end of the interview, makes evasion difficult. The Shaykh is asked what he would have told the murderer of Sadat if he had come to the Shaykh and had told him of this intended crime. To this the Shaykh answers that the murderer and his accomplices are not *anṣār al-Islām,* which means that (according to the Shaykh) they are not helpers of Islam.[87] In other words, their deed has not helped the cause of Islam. One does not have to be excessively trained in semantics to understand the ambiguity of the remark. The initiated might understand that the assassination did not help the cause of Islam because the new government is as un-Islamic as the old one and because the assassins did not do enough, whereas an innocent listener might simply understand that the assassination was not a duty prescribed by Islam.

The rest of the phrase does not help to remove the ambiguity. The murderers, so we read, are enemies of the existing order *(niẓām).* This does not surprise anyone since they murdered the head of state, but the question is rather whether they were enemies of Islam. Is, perhaps, the existing order hostile to Islam? Isn't the enemy of my enemy my friend?

The Shaykh tells his interviewer that, according to him, Sadat's murderers aimed at coming to power by exploiting religion and Islam. But, he warns, "Take this as a rule: if they had been real *anṣār,* helpers, of Islam, and if God had consented to their plans, no power, no police, no army could have stopped them." Logic compels one to conclude from these carefully chosen words that, according to Shaykh Al-Sha^crāwī, God may not have wanted Egypt to be ruled by the murderers of Sadat, but that God did consent to see him killed. (Critics of Shaykh Al-Sha^crāwī did not fail to point out[88] that the extreme consequence of this variety of belief in God's omnipotence implies logically that in the Arab-Israeli conflict God is on the Israeli side.)

Sadat's murderers failed, the Shaykh exclaims, in carrying out a coup d'état. "It is true that they assassinated a man that was heavily protected — this brings to mind the verse from the Qur'ān, "Wherever ye may be, death will overtake you, even though ye were in strongly built towers."[89] For those that are slow to understand, the Shaykh adds: "Were not these military forces and guards that surrounded him (at the fatal parade) 'strongly built towers'? Yet they killed him. . . . But their aim was not only to assassinate him. . . . Wasn't the real aim of this whole operation that they wanted to seize power in Egypt?"

NOTES

[Shaykh Muḥammad Mutawallī Al-Shaᶜrāwī's name is abbreviated as SMMS; *Tafsīr Sūrat* is abbreviated as *TS*.]

1. See especially SMMS, *Al-Qaḍā' wa-'l-Qadar,* Cairo/Beirut (Dār al-Shurūq), 1979, p. 7; and SMMS, *Al-Isrā wa-'l-Miᶜrāj,* Cairo/Beirut (Dār al-Shurūq), 1979, p. 25. *Nūr ᶜalā Nūr:* Qur'ān 24.35. When in early 1982 the Shaykh was for some time absent from the screen, at once rumors started that he had fallen into disgrace and was "boycotted" by the Egyptian media, see, e.g., the magazine *Ṣabāḥ al-Khayr,* nr. 2802, February 22, 1982, frontpage: *Laysa ṣaḥīḥan anna hunāka muqāṭaᶜah li-'l-Shaykh al-Shaᶜrāwī.*
2. See FĀṬIMAH AL-SAHRĀWĪ, *Al-Shaykh . . . Al-Shaᶜrāwī, Mishwār Ḥayātī, Arā' wa-Afkār,* Cairo (Al-Mukhtār al-Islāmī), n.d. (1979?), pp. 9–17; DR. AL-SAYYID AL-JAMĪLĪ, *Al-Shaykh Al-Shaᶜrāwī, Ḥayātuhu wa-Fiqhuhu,* Cairo (Al-Mukhtār al-Islāmī), 1980, pp. 11–17; DR. SAYYID AL-JAMĪLĪ, *Al-Shaykh Al-Shaᶜrāwī, ᶜĀlim ᶜAṣrihi,* Cairo (Makt. Al-Thaqāfah al-Jadīdah), 1981, p. 87. All these statements by the Shaykh are essentially autobiographic.
3. Cf. p. 36 in Chapter 2.
4. These Ramaḍān/August 1980 sermons were collected as SMMS, *Allāh wa-'l-Kawn,* Cairo (Dār al-Muslim al-Muᶜāṣir), 1980, 80 pp.
5. SMMS, *Anta Tas'al wa-'l-Islām Yujīb,* Cairo (Dār al-Bayān), 1981, p. 5: "His style is a mixture of classical and colloquial Arabic," and "Colloquial words have been replaced by classical ones."
6. SMMS, *T.S. Al-Ikhlāṣ,* p. 29.
7. SMMS, *T.S. Al-ᶜAṣr,* p. 22.
8. E.g., DR. AL-SAYYID AL-JAMĪLĪ, *Qalbī, Yā Duktūr, Amrāḍ al-Qalb wa-ᶜIlājuhā,* Cairo (Makt. Ja'far al-Ḥadīthah), 1981, 80 pp.
9. SMMS, *Al-Fatāwā, Kull mā Yuhimm al-Muslim . . . , aᶜadda wa-ᶜallaqa ᶜalayhi wa-qaddama lahu Dr. Al-Sayyid al-Jamīlī,* Cairo (Al-Mukhtār al-Islāmī), 1981, vol. 1, 136 pp., and further volumes.

10. SMMS, *Taskhīr al-Jinn wa-Karāmāt al-Awliyā',* n.p., n.d. (Cairo January 1981); repr. Cairo (Dār al-Muslim), February 1981. These two booklets are identical. They both contain 32 pages.
11. HAVA LAZARUS-YAFEH, "Muhammad Mutawallī Al-Sha'rāwī, a portrait of a contemporary 'Ālim in Egypt" (Paper read at the International Conference on Islam, Nationalism and Radicalism in Egypt and Sudan in the 20th Century held in Haifa in December 1981), quoted from the abstract distributed at the Conference.
12. On the *jinn,* see, e.g., Qur'ān 15.27 and similar passages.
13. SMMS, *Taskhīr* . . . , p. 18.
14. Ibid., pp. 16 and 19.
15. FĀṬIMAH AL-SAHRĀWĪ, *Al-Shaykh,* p. 44.
16. SMMS, *Taskhīr* . . . , p. 31.
17. DR. AL-SAYYID AL-JAMĪLĪ, *Al-Shaykh Al-Shaᶜrāwī, ᶜĀlim ᶜAṣrihi,* p. 90.
18. Cf., in the New Testament, the Epistle of James, iv, 13 – 15; and the article "In Shā' Allāh" in the *Encyclopaedia of Islam,* second ed., iii, 1196 (L. Gardet).
19. *Al-Daᶜwah,* 20, January 1978, p. 70: "Liqā' ᶜAṣif maᶜa al-Shaykh Al-Shaᶜrāwī." Critical remarks on Shaykh Al-Shaᶜrāwī's behavior in parliament: ᶜADIL ᶜĪD (AL-MUḤĀMĪ), *Al-Maḍābiṭ tatakallam,* n.p., n.d., (date of preface: Alexandria, 1984), pp. 174 and 206ff.
20. See especially the interesting chapter by Dr. Zakī Najīb Maḥmūd on Shaykh Al-Shaᶜrāwī, in Z.M. MAḤMŪD, *Qiyam min al-Turāth,* Cairo/Beirut (Dār al-Shurūq), 1984, p. 154.
21. EDWARD MORTIMER, *Faith and Power: the Politics of Islam,* London, 1982, p. 59.
22. THE EARL OF CROMER, *Modern Egypt,* London, 1908, ii, 180 – 181.
23. See my "'I believe that my friend Abdu . . . was in reality an Agnostic,'" in P.W. PESTMAN, ed., *Acta Orientalia Neerlandica,* Leiden, 1971, pp. 71 – 74.
24. MUḤAMMAD ḤUSAYN AL-DHAHABĪ, *Al-Tafsīr wa-'l-Mufassirūn,* Cairo (Dār al-Kutub al-Ḥadīthah), 1962, iii, 220 – 239.
25. MUḤAMMAD ᶜABDUH, *Tafsīr Juz' ᶜAmmā,* on Qur'ān 78.12.
26. See my "Shaykh al-Shaᶜrāwī's interpretation of the Qur'ān," in R. HILLENBRAND, ed., *Proceedings of the 10th Congress of the Union Européenne des Arabisants et Islamisants,* Edinburgh, 1982, p. 24.
27. Cf. MORTIMER, *Faith and Power,* e.g. p. 87.
28. FĀṬIMAH AL-SAHRĀWĪ, *Al-Shaykh,* 17.

29. Ibid., pp. 15–16.
30. Ibid., p. 15.
31. ṢALĀḤ MUNTAṢIR, *Ḥiwār ma^ca al-Shaykh Al-Sha^crāwī ^cani-'l-Ḥukm wa-'l-^cAdl wa-^cl-shabāb,* Cairo (Dār al-Ma^cārif), *Kitabuka* series, p. 51.
32. WĀ'IL ^cUTHMĀN, *Ḥizb Allāh fī Muwājahat Ḥizb al-Shayṭān,* Cairo (Maṭb. Nahḍat Miṣr), 1975, 2d ed., 120 pp. "*Taqdīm Faḍīlat al-Shaykh al-Sha^crāwī.*" On the title see, e.g., Qur'ān 5.56: "The party of God — they are the victors."
33. WĀ'IL ^cUTHMĀN, *Ḥizb,* p. 11.
34. Ibid., p. 19.
35. Ibid., pp. 25–26.
36. Ibid., p. 27.
37. Ibid., p. 30.
38. Ibid., p. 30.
39. Ibid., p. 32.
40. Ibid., p. 68.
41. Ibid., p. 7.
42. WĀ'IL ^cUTHMĀN, *Asrār al-Ḥarakah al-Ṭullābīyah 1968–75,* Cairo, (Maṭābi^c Madkūr), 1976, 168 pp.
43. Chapter 1, p. 11.
44. See p. 127.
45. SMMS, *T.S. Al-^cAṣr,* p. 26, and *T.S. Al-Takwīr,* p. 38.
46. SMMS, *T.S. Al-Infiṭār,* p. 30.
47. SMMS, *T.S. Al-Qāri^cah,* p. 22.
48. SMMS, *T.S. Al-Ikhlāṣ,* p. 34.
49. Ibid., pp. 23–33.
50. See B. LEWIS, "The Return of Islam," repr. in M. Curtis, ed., *Religion and Politics in the Middle East,* Boulder, Colorado, 1981, pp. 9–29.
51. SMMS, *T.S. Al-Ihklāṣ,* p. 61.
52. SMMS, *Al-Qaḍā' wa-'l-Qadar,* p. 135.
53. SMMS, *T.S. Al-Naba',* p. 62.
54. Qur'ān 81.19; SMMS, *T.S. Al-Ikhlāṣ,* p. 6; idem, *T.S. Al-Takwīr,* p. 48.
55. Qur'ān 47.2.
56. SMMS, *T.S. Iqra',* p. 6; *T.S. ^cAbasa,* pp. 21 and 24; idem, *T.S. Al-Ikhlāṣ,* p. 36.

57. SMMS, *T.S. Al-Māᶜūn*, p. 48.
58. Ibid., p. 22.
59. SMMS, *T.S. Al-Naba'*, p. 12.
60. SMMS, *T.S. Al-ᶜAṣr*, pp. 19 and 37; idem, *T.S. Al-Fīl*, p. 5; idem, *T.S. Al-Māᶜūn*, pp. 29 and 44; idem, *T.S. Al-Muṭaffifīn*, p. 33.
61. SMMS, *T.S. Al-Naba'*, p. 11; idem, *T.S. Al-Ikhlāṣ*, p. 10.
62. SMMS, *T.S. Al-Infiṭār*, p. 9.
63. SMMS, *T.S. Al-Māᶜūn*, p. 36.
64. SMMS, *T.S. Al-ᶜAṣr*, p. 23; idem, *T.S. Al-Infiṭār*, p. 25.
65. SMMS, *T.S. Al-Fīl*, p. 41.
66. SMMS, *T.S. Iqra'*, p. 37.
67. See my "Shaykh Al-Shaᶜrāwī's interpretation of the Qur'ān," in HILLENBRAND, *Proceedings*, p. 25.
68. SMMS, *T.S. Al-Naba'*, p. 5.
69. SMMS, *T.S. Al-Nāziᶜāt*, p. 17 & 27.
70. SMMS, *T.S. Al-Naba'*, p. 35; *T.S. Al-Burūj*, p. 69.
71. SMMS, *T.S. Al-Qāriᶜah*, p. 19.
72. SMMS, *T.S. Al-Fīl*, pp. 50–53.
73. TH.W. JUYNBOLL, *Handleiding tot de Kennis van de Mohammedaansche Wet*, Leiden, 1930, p. 45, especially n. 2.
74. J.M. LANDAU, "Islamism and Secularism: The Turkish Case," in *Studies in Judaism and Islam*, The Magnes Press, 1981, p. 378.
75. Ibid., p. 376.
76. SAYYID QUṬB, *Maᶜālim fi-'l-Ṭarīq*, Cairo, 1982, 89–90.
77. SMMS, *T.S. Al-ᶜAṣr*, p. 38 and 40; idem, *T.S. Al-Fīl*, p. 48; and the passages listed in my "Shaykh Al-Shaᶜrāwī's interpretation," in HILLENBRAND, *Proceedings*, n. 19.
78. SMMS, *T.S. Al-Ikhlāṣ*, p. 9.
79. SMMS, *T.S. ᶜAbasa*, p. 40; idem, *T.S. Al-Fīl*, p. 27.
80. SMMS, *T.S. Al-Fīl*, p. 30.
81. SMMS, *T.S. Al-Māᶜūn*, p. 29.
82. SMMS, *T.S. Al-Fīl*, pp. 23 and 32; idem, *T.S. Al-Naba'*, p. 52; idem, *T.S. Al-Māᶜūn*, p. 16.
83. SMMS, *T.S. Al-Muṭaffifīn*, p. 36.
84. MUNTAṢIR, *Ḥiwār maᶜa al-Shaykh al-Shaᶜrāwī*, pp. 51–52.
85. Ibid., p. 50.

86. Ibid., p. 51.
87. Ibid., p. 52.
88. DR. YŪSUF AL-QARḌĀWĪ, *Al-Ṣaḥwah al-Islāmīyah bayn al-Juḥūd wa-'l-Taṭarruf,* Cairo, 1984, p. 96.
89. Qur'ān 4.78.

Conclusion

THE RELIGIOUS DISCUSSIONS going on in Egypt in the seventies and the early eighties were dominated by a set of ideas that are expressed openly in one source only: a document that in Arabic is entitled *Al-Farīḍah al-Ghā'ibah,* "The Neglected Duty," the creed of Sadat's assassins. All participants in these discussions, so it appears, were aware of at least some of these ideas if not of the actual document itself. Nevertheless they referred to these ideas only obliquely. Much of the religious discussions in Egypt—and elsewhere in the Muslim world—might well have remained incomprehensible to an outsider had not the *Farīḍah* document become known.

There are three possible reasons why many Muslim readers have been so impressed by the document entitled *Al-Farīḍah al-Ghā'ibah.* First, they may have been impressed by the virtuosity and fearlessness with which the group associated with the *Farīḍah* managed to assassinate President Sadat. Since it is quite common, both in the East and in the West, for autocratic political leaders to be unpopular, sympathy for tyrannicides as well as admiration for their courage in facing an almost certain death may play their role and contribute to the interest with which modern Muslims read the *Farīḍah*.

Second, Muslim readers may be affected by the arguments with which the *Farīḍah* makes its views plausible or even convincing. These arguments are derived from the Qur'ān, the Traditions that go back to Muḥammad and the writings of important *patres* — if one may use this Christian term when speaking about Muslim scholars like Ibn Taymīyah and Ibn Kathīr. The traditionally recognized four "roots" *(uṣūl)* of Islamic Law (Qur'ān, Tradition, Consensus, and Analogy) are all invoked in constructing the comprehensive theory of the *Farīḍah*. When even a non-Muslim reader of the *Farīḍah* has every now and then the impression that everything he ever read from the Qur'ān, the Tradition, and the books of *fiqh* suddenly falls into place, how much more will the text of the *Farīḍah* evoke this feeling with Muslim readers? The *Farīḍah* strongly suggests that it offers a comprehensive view of the history of Islam which is based on all relevant sources, and it does so impressively.

Third, since the fifties of this century,[1] there may be a strong oral tradition in which the arguments that figure in the *Farīḍah* are repeated and reproduced, in otherwise innocent conversations and meetings of concerned citizens who discuss their many social predicaments. An important factor in the effect of the *Farīḍah* on Muslim readers may be that they suddenly see a consistent exposé in which theories are unfolded that, in part, have a familiar ring but that they have never seen systematically explained, if only because of the many official and practical limitations put upon the freedom of the printing press in large parts of the world.

When such an oral tradition exists it is, of course, important to determine when and from where it originates. A certain Dr. Yūsuf al-Qarḍāwī, from the circle around the monthly *Al-Da^cwah* and ^cUmar al-Tilimsānī, recently made an interesting suggestion on the origin of this modern theory which accuses the ruler of unbelief and hence implicitly also of apostasy from Islam, the *takfīr al-ḥākim* theory. (*Takfīr* as such, has, of course, always been known in Islam, if only from the Khārijī episodes,[2] but logic compels that *takfīr* of the ruler of the modern state can not have preceded the existence of modern states.)

According to Dr. Al-Qarḍāwī[3] the *takfīr* theory took its present shape during the cruel persecutions that the Muslim Brothers suffered at the hands of the Nasser government. Dr. Al-Qarḍāwī writes that this *takfīr* theory arose out of five questions that the imprisoned Brothers asked themselves.

The first question, so Dr. Al-Qarḍāwī says, was: "Why are we punished so severely for saying that God is our Lord *(Rabbínā)*, Islam our Way of Life *(manhajnā)*, and the Qur'ān our Constitution *(dustūrnā)*. Is it really possible that it is a crime in an Islamic country to work for the cause of Islam?"

The second question, so we read, was: "Are these interrogators and prison camp commanders, who make our lives such a misery, really Muslims? Did not one of them once say, 'Get that Lord of yours and I'll put him behind bars' *(hātū rabbúkum w-ana aḥuṭṭúhu fi-z-zinzāna)*? What is infidelity *(kufr)*, if we have to regard these monsters *(wuḥūsh)* as Muslims?"

The third question, Dr. Al-Qarḍāwī writes, ran as follows: "When these people who torment us day and night cannot be regarded as Muslims, what should we by implication think of the people who appointed them and who ordered them to treat us this way? The people in authority who are responsible for the appointment of these interrogators and prison camp commanders are worse pagans, *ashadd kufran*, than the people who only execute their orders. These rulers do not rule by what God sent down, hence they are *kāfirūn* and apostates from Islam!"

The fourth question, according to Dr. Yūsuf al-Qarḍāwī, was: "Is someone who disagrees with our view that these rulers are infidels and apostates not an apostate himself? Does not such a person have doubts whether an infidel is really an infidel? Does not such doubt disqualify the doubter as a Muslim and make him almost automatically an apostate too?" In the *Farīḍah*, the same point is made in slightly different words: "The Rulers of this age have rebelled against the religion of Islam in multiple ways to such a degree that there is little doubt as to [how to judge] people who follow the ways of these [Rulers]."

The fifth and last question, according to Dr. Al-Qarḍāwī, ran: "The masses that obey these rulers who do not rule by what God sent down, are they too not *kuffār*, infidels and apostates, like these rulers themselves? Do they not [literally] applaud these Rulers?

Wa-riḍā bi-'l-kufr kufr wa-lā shakk!!" ("to approve *kufr*—unbelief—is without doubt also a form of *kufr*").

It is from this starting point, according to Dr. Al-Qarḍāwī, that the present wave of *takfīr* spread. From this basic idea, so Dr. Al-Qarḍāwī maintains, other extremist views ramified, *tafarra^cat*, but its beginning must be traced to the harsh atmosphere of the prison camps. Nevertheless, these ideas did not remain in the isolation of the prison camps where the Muslim Brothers were held for long.

From the discussions on modern Islam that were described in the preceding chapters a picture emerged in which all participants in these discussions show a certain familiarity with the arguments that we find systematically expounded only in the text of the *Farīḍah*. It might be wise to reread and reinterpret older material, no matter how innocent it looks, in the light of the theories we now are familiar with thanks to the clarity of the *Farīḍah* document.

An example of what this means may be found when we look, for instance, at an official slogan from the Sadat period. On thousands of posters in Sadat's Egypt one could see a portrait of the President—the blue mark allegedly caused by multiple prosternations during prayer clearly visible on his forehead—above the caption "The Believing President," *Al-Ra'īs al-Mu'min*. The "Believing President" slogan was also heard and seen in many other ways. It is, however, not to be doubted that this alluded to another phrase that was rarely seen in print but often murmured by the pious who yearned for nothing less than a Muslim Ruler, *Al-Ḥākim al-Muslim*. There can be no doubt that Egyptian officials attempted, during the Sadat period, to counter the call for a *Ḥākim Muslim* with their emphasis on the fact that Egypt already had a Believing President, a *Rā'īs Mu'min*. The only result of these attempts was probably that the alleged need for a ruler applying the laws of Islam was brought more forcefully under the attention of the public.

When it is true that the fundamentalists are getting stronger, it must also be true that the liberal Muslims are getting weaker. The fate of the liberals—if one may use that word—certainly deserves more attention than it gets at the moment, but the summary list of the facts and names that follows may help to prove that it is indeed true that the liberals are leaving town.

In 1950 a certain Khālid Muḥammad Khālid published a book *Min Hunā Nabda'* (From Here We Start). This book (often reprinted) was perhaps the most spectacular example of the liberal attitude that wanted to interpret Islam in a nontheocratic way, but perhaps the book found more admirers in the West than in the Middle East itself. The book was translated into English (*Our Beginning in Wisdom,* Washington, 1953).

It is ironic that the same Khālid Muḥammad Khālid revoked his liberal views in January 1981 in a book entitled *Al-Dawlah fi-'l-Islām,* The State in Islam.[4] In this book Khālid Muḥammad Khālid publicly subscribes to the *Dīn wa-Dawlah* slogan of the Muslim Brothers. On page 16 we read for instance: "In the light of my new conviction that Islam is both a religion and a state. . . ."

Something similar can be observed in the case of Muṣṭafā Maḥmūd, an extremely prolific writer on many subjects, who published an article in *Al-Ahrām* (September 23, 1979)[5] in which he argued that an Islamic State could only gradually be established, and not by a sudden revolution. The way in which he spoke on the same subject on Egyptian television may have been meant also as an attack on the views of the fundamentalists, but, as an observer put it, the only result of his talks was that he convinced his public that the foundation of an Islamic State was an extremely urgent and important, possibly even imminent, affair.

The case of the novelist and playwright Tawfīq al-Ḥakīm can also be used to illustrate the weakening of the position of those modern Muslims who want to separate religion from politics. In 1977 Tawfīq al-Ḥakīm published an abbreviated version of the Qur'ān commentary by Al-Qurṭubī (d. 1273).[6] This important commentary is mainly devoted to legal questions. Tawfīq al-Ḥakīm's abbrevation of it consists of more than 900 pages, but the "Whosoever does not rule by what God sent down" verses (Qur'ān 5.44 – 48) are not discussed.

A final illustration is taken from the work of Muḥammad Saᶜīd al-ᶜAshmāwī, who is an Egyptian judge about whose secularist ideas both P.J. Vatikiotis and R. Wielandt recently published articles. Between 1974 and 1979, Mr. Al-ᶜAshmāwī published several "liberal," nontheocratic studies on Islam, but he was unable to find a publisher for his last book, *Rūḥ al-ᶜAdālah,* The Spirit of Justice (privately printed, Cairo, 1982).[7]

Saᶜd al-Dīn Ibrahīm, the famous sociologist of the American University in Cairo, wrote in *Al-Ahrām*[8] in November 1981 that the extremists do not come from the planet Mars, but from the heart of Egyptian society. Is there anyone, he writes, who has not seen a member of his family turn to the *jamāᶜāt* or start to wear the conspicuous Islamic dress?

It appears that the liberals are losing ground: their position has become weak and is getting weaker still. The consensus that Islamic Law has to be applied universally and at whatever cost is getting stronger. This may have unexpected and far-ranging political and social consequences.

NOTES

1. The *takfīr al-ḥākim* theory cannot be earlier than the fifties. In a book entitled *Al-Islām wa-Awḍāᶜunā al-Qānūnīyah* ("Islam and our legal situation") by ᶜABD AL-QĀDIR ᶜAWDAH, first published in 1951, before the Nasser-Naguib coup d'état and before the systematic persecutions of the Muslim Brothers, one may constantly feel the beginnings of the modern *takfīr* theory between the lines of the text. Yet on p. 147 of this book we read that *aghlab rijāl al-ḥukūmāt*, and *akthar al-ḥukkām al-muslimīn*, most Muslim rulers, are pious Muslims, *muslimūn mutadayyinūn*, who simply do not know enough of Muslim Law and the true character of the theocratic demands of Islam. No matter how much one wants to read between the lines, this book does not yet contain the modern *takfīr* theory, as this kind but condescending remark about the rulers indicates.
2. See my "The Early Islamic Movement of the Khārijīs and Modern Moslem Extremism: Similarities and Differences," to be published in the journal *Orient*, 1986.
3. DR. YŪSUF AL-QARḌĀWĪ, *Al-Ṣaḥwah al-Islāmīyah bayn al-Juḥūd wa-'l-Taṭarruf*, Cairo/Beirut, 1984, p. 128.
4. KHĀLID MUḤAMMAD KHĀLID, *Al-Dawlah fi-'l-Islām*, Cairo (Dār Thābit), January 1981, 168 pp.
5. "Al-Ḥukm al-Islāmī . . . Matā . . . wa-Kayf?," repr. in MUṢṬAFĀ MAḤMŪD, *Nār Taḥt al-Rumād*, Cairo (Dār al-Maᶜārif), 1979, pp. 17–26. (The newspaper version reads *rubbamā*, "perhaps," where the Dār al-Maᶜārif version reads *bi-dūn shakk*, "no doubt," p. 24).

6. See my "Tawfīq al-Ḥakīm on the Rigidity of Moslem Law," in *Bibliotheca Orentalis,* xxxviii, 1981, pp. 13–16.
7. P.J. VATIKIOTIS, "Islamic Resurgence: A Critical View," in A.S. CUDSI and A.E.H. DESSOUKI, eds., *Islam and Power,* London, 1981, pp. 186–191; and R. WIELANDT, "Zeitgenössische Ägyptische Stimmen zur Säkularisierungsproblematik," in *Welt des Islams,* N.S. XXII, 1982, p. 125; M.S. AL-ᶜASHMĀWĪ, *Ḥiṣād al-ᶜAql,* Beirut, 1974; *Ḍamīr al-ᶜAṣr,* Cairo/Beirut, second ed., 1979; *Risālat al-Wujūd,* Cairo/Beirut, 1977; *Uṣūl Al-Sharīᶜah,* Cairo/Beirut, 1979.
8. November 20, 1981.

Translation of Muḥammad ᶜAbd al-Salām Faraj's Text Entitled Al-Farīḍah al-Ghā'ibah

PRELIMINARY REMARKS to the translation.

1. Those parts of the text that are unclear and/or corrupt are put between *asterisks*.
2. The translator's additions to the text are put between parentheses.
3. The many proper names from Islamic history that the text contains can be looked up in for example, H.A.R. Gibb, J.H. Kramers, E. Levi-Provençal, and J. Schacht, eds., *The Encyclopaedia of Islam*, Leiden, 1960, and later years, and in similar reference works.
4. The text of the *Farīḍah* is an internal document which was not written for outsiders. It addresses the initiated only. Those who have to consult an English translation of the *Farīḍah* are probably outsiders, and have to be prepared to read paragraphs that will sometimes look strange to them.

The Neglected Duty

In the name of God the Most Compassionate

(§1)Is it not high time for those who have believed
to humble their hearts to the Reminder of God
and to the truth which He has sent down;
and that they should not be like those
to whom the Book was formerly given,
and for whom the time was long,
so that their hearts became hard,
and many of them are reprobates?

(This Qur'ān quotation is taken) from Surah 57 (verse 16).

ᶜAbdallāh ibn al-Mubārak said: "Ṣāliḥ al-Murrī told us on the authority of Qatādah on the authority of Ibn ᶜAbbās: 'God deemed the hearts of the believers to be slow and he reproached them for this (already as early as) the beginning of (the year[1]) 13 after the beginning of the Revelation of the Qur'ān.' He then said 'Is it not high time for those who have believed, . . .' (and the rest of) the verse (quoted above)."

In the Name of God the Most Compassionate
Preface

(§2) Glory to God. We praise Him, we ask for His help, we ask Him to forgive us, we ask Him to give us guidance. We seek protection with God against the wickedness of our souls and against the evilness of our acts. If God sends someone on the right path, no one can send him astray. If God sends someone astray, no one can guide him. I acknowledge that there is no god but God alone, He has no associate, and I acknowledge that Muḥammad is His Servant and His Apostle.

The most reliable Speech is the Book of God, and the best guidance is the guidance of Muḥammad, may God's peace be upon him. The worst of all things are novelties, since every novelty is an innovation *(bidᶜah)* and every innovation is a deviation, and all deviation is in Hell.

(§3) *Jihād* (struggle) for God's cause, in spite of its extreme importance and its great significance for the future of this religion, has been neglected by the *ᶜulamā'* (leading Muslim scholars) of this age. They have feigned ignorance of it, but they know that it is the only way to the return and the establishment of the glory of Islam anew. Every Muslim preferred his own favorite ideas and philosophies above the Best Road, which God — Praised and Exalted He is — drew Himself (a road that leads back) to (a state of) Honor for His Servants.

(§4) There is no doubt that the idols of this world can only be made to disappear through the power of the sword. It is therefore that (the Apostle Muḥammad) — God's peace be upon him — said: "I have been sent with the Sword at this Hour, so that God alone is worshipped, without associate to Him, He put my daily bread under the shadow of my lance, He brings lowness and smallness to those who disagree with what I command. Whosoever resembles a certain group of people will be counted as a member of that group." (This Tradition is) reported by Imām Aḥmad (ibn Ḥanbal) on the authority of Ibn ᶜUmar.

(§5) Ibn Rajab says: The saying of (the Apostle Muḥammad) — God's peace be upon him — "I have been sent with the Sword" means that God sent him to call with the sword for (acknowledgment of) God's unity after he had called (for this) with arguments. Whosoever did not comply (and accept) the unity (of God), (being called upon to do so) by (the text of) the Qur'ān, by arguments and by proof, would then be called upon with the sword.

(§6) His Guidance to (the Apostle Muḥammad) — God's Peace be upon Him — in Mecca

The Apostle of God — God's peace be upon him — addressed the idols of Mecca while he was still in Mecca (saying): "Listen, Oh ye (from the tribe) Quraysh, as to Him Who has the soul of Muḥammad in His hand, I bring you slaughter." The people who stood there took his words seriously and they were all silent with awe, even the strongest of them, who then addressed him (Muḥammad) with the best words he could find, even saying: "Please, go away, O rightly guided (Muḥammad) Abū Qāsim." By God, how ignorant I (Muḥammad ᶜAbd al-Salām Faraj) have been while the Apostle of God — God's peace be upon him —, by his saying "I bring you the sword," had already pointed to the straight road, about which there should be no discussion and no dissimulation with the Masters of Unbelief *(kufr)* and the Leaders of Error, and this while he was still within (pagan) Mecca.

(§7) Islam Approaches

The establishment of an Islamic State and the reintroduction of the Caliphate were (not only) already predicted by the Apostle of God — God's peace be upon him — (but) (they) are, moreover, part of the Command of the Lord — Majestic and Exalted He is — for which every Muslim should exert every conceivable effort in order to execute it.

(§8) a) (The Apostle) — God's peace be upon him — says: "God showed me all corners of the earth. I saw its East and its West, and (I saw) that my Community will possess of it what He showed me from it." (This Tradition) is transmitted by Muslim, Abū Dāwud, Ibn Mājah, and Al-Tirmidhī. This has not until now come about, since there are countries which the Muslims have not conquered in (any) age which has passed up to the present. (However,) it shall come about if God permits.

(§9) b) (The Apostle) — God's peace be upon him — says: "This matter will be as the day and the night: God will make this religion enter into every house of every inhabitant of the deserts, of villages, of towns, of cities, with glory or with disgrace. God will give glory to Islam, and God will bring disgrace upon Unbelief." (This Tradition) is transmitted by Aḥmad (ibn Ḥanbal) and Al-Ṭabarānī. Al-Haythamī said that the men (who transmit) it are men who (only transmit) reliable (Traditions). (The uncommon Arabic word) *madar* (which is used in this Tradition) means "someone who lives in a village or a town," and (the uncommon Arabic word) *wabar* (which is used in this Tradition) means "someone who lives in the desert or a city or a village."

(§10) c) A reliable Tradition reports that (a certain) Abū Qabīl says: We were with ᶜAbdallāh, the son of ᶜAmr ibn al-ᶜĀṣ,[2] and he was asked "Which of the two cities will be conquered first, Constantinople or Rome?" Then ᶜAbdallāh called for a box which had rings attached to it and he took a book from it. Then ᶜAbdallāh said: When we were around God's Apostle — God's peace be upon Him — we wrote down when God's Apostle — God's peace be upon Him — was asked "Which of the two cities will be conquered first, Constantinople or Rome?" God's Apostle — God's peace be upon Him — answered: "The city of Heraclius will be conquered first, Constaninople." (This Tradition) is transmitted by Aḥmad (ibn Ḥanbal) and Al-Dārimī. (The uncommon Arabic appellation) *Rūmiyah* (which the text of the Tradition employs) stands for Rome, according to the (geographical dictionary) *Muᶜjam al-Buldān*. It is the capital of Italy today.

(§11) The first conquest came about at the hands of Muḥammad the Conqueror, the Ottoman (Sultan), and this more than 800 years after the Prophet's — God's peace be upon him — prediction of the conquest. The second conquest will also be realized if God permits. There is no doubt that you will hear, after a (certain) period, of its announcement.

(§12) d) "The Prophethood will be amongst you as long as God wills that it is amongst you, then He will take it away when He wants to do so. Next there will be a Caliphate equal (in righteousness) to the Prophethood, it will be as long as God wills it to be, then He will take it away when He wants to do so. Next there will be a King Who Hinders, who shall be there as long as God wants him to be there, then He will take him away when He wants to do so. Next there will be a King Who Compels, who shall be there as long as God wants him to be there, then He will take him away when He wants to do so. Next there will (again) be a Caliphate equal (in righteousness) to the Prophethood. It will make people act according to the Example of the Prophet, and Islam will become firmly established on earth. Those who live in heaven and those who live on earth will rejoice about this. Every single drop from heaven will be abundant rain, and every single plant or blessing which springs from the earth will prosper greatly." (This Tradition) is transmitted by Ḥudhayfah who traces it back to the

Apostle Muḥammad, and the Tradition scholar al-ᶜIrāqī[3] transmits it from Aḥmad (ibn Ḥanbal), who says that this is a good and reliable (Tradition).

"The King Who Hinders" is (already) done with, and "the King Who Compels" is (a reference to rulers who derive their authority) from (military) coups that bring those who participate in them to power, against the will of the people. . . .

(§13) The Tradition is one of the predictions of the return of Islam in the present age following this Islamic Awakening, and it prophesies that they (who participate in it) have a brilliant future both economically and agriculturally.

(§14) The Response to Those Who Despair

Some people have fallen into despair and they counter this Tradition and these predictions with a Tradition from the Prophet—God's peace be upon him—which was transmitted through Anas: "Be patient, because every time which comes is worse than the one before it until you meet your Lord. I heard this from your Prophet, may peace be upon him." Al-Tirmidhī says that (this is) a good and reliable (Tradition). (These people) say: "there is no reason to waste effort and time on dreams." Here we quote the saying of the Prophet—God's peace be upon him—: "My community is a blessed community. You do not know whether the first of it is the best, or the last of it." (This Tradition) is transmitted by Ibn ᶜAsākir on the authority of ᶜAmr ibn ᶜUthmān. Al-Suyūṭī pointed out that it is a good (Tradition). There is no contradiction between the two Traditions since the address of the Prophet—God's peace be upon him—was directed to his own generation until they met their Lord. The Tradition is not (intended to be understood) in a general way, but it is (meant as) a general saying (which has to be understood to apply to only a) specific (group). Another proof (for the correctness of this understanding of this Tradition) are the Traditions about the Messiah *(Mahdi)* who will appear at the end of time, and (who) will fill the world with fairness and justice after it has been filled with injustice and oppression.

(§15) God gave a promise to a group of believers in His—

Glorious and Majestic He is — word: "God has promised to those of you who have believed and wrought the works of righteousness, that He will surely make them successors (to power) in the land as He made those before them successors, and he will surely establish for them their religion which He has approved for them, and after their fear will give them in exchange security; 'They shall serve Me not associating anything with Me.'" (This Qur'ān quotation) is taken from verse 55 of Surah 24. God does not break His promises. We ask Him — Majestic and Supreme He is — that He make us one of them (who are mentioned in the beginning of this Qur'ān quotation).

(§16) The Establishment of an Islamic State

This is a duty which is rejected by some Muslims and neglected by others although the proof for the obligatory character of the establishment of a state is clear, and made obvious by the (text of the) Book of God — Blessed and Supreme He is, — for God — Glory to Him — says: "and that you must rule between them according to what God sent down," and He says: "Whosoever does not rule by what God sent down, those, they are the unbelievers." He says — Glorious and Majestic He is — in (the first verse of) Surah 24 (of which we quoted verse 55 in the previous paragraph), about the obligatory character of the prescripts of Islam: "a Surah which we sent down and which we made obligatory." From this (verse) (it follows) that the establishment of the Rule of God over this earth (mentioned in verse 55 of this Surah) must be considered to be obligatory for the Muslims. God's prescripts are an obligation for the Muslims. Hence, the establishment of an Islamic State is an obligation for the Muslims, for something without which something which is obligatory cannot be carried out becomes (itself) obligatory. If, moreover, (such a) state cannot be established without war, then this war is an obligation as well.

(§17) Muslims are agreed on the obligatory character of the establishment of an Islamic Caliphate. To announce a Caliphate must be based on the existence of a (territorial) nucleus (from which it can grow). This (nucleus) is the Islamic State. "Whosoever dies without having taken upon himself (the obligation of) a pledge of allegiance does not die as a Muslim." So, it is obligatory for every Muslim to seriously strive for the return of the Caliphate in order not to fall into the category of people (mentioned in the) Tradition (quoted in this paragraph). By "pledge of allegiance" (the text of the Tradition) means "allegiance to the Caliphate."

(§18) The House in Which We Live

Here a question appears: Do we live in an Islamic State? One of the characteristics of such a state is that it is ruled by the laws of Islam. The Imām Abū Ḥanīfah gave as his opinion that the House of Islam changes into the House of Unbelief if three conditions are fulfilled simultaneously: 1. if it is ruled by other laws than those of Islam, 2. the disappearance of safety for the Muslim inhabitants, 3. its being adjacent or close . . . and this (means) that the House (of Islam) is close to the House of Unbelief to such an extent that this is a source of danger to the Muslims and a cause for the disappearance of their safety.

(§19) The Imām Muḥammad and the Imām Abū Yūsuf, both (jurists) from the school of Abū Ḥanīfah, gave as their opinion that a House must be categorized according to the laws by which it is ruled. If (a House) is ruled by the laws of Islam, then it is the House of Islam. If (a House) is ruled by the laws of Unbelief, it is the House of Unbelief. (This opinion can be found in a book entitled) *Badā'iᶜ al-Ṣinā'iᶜ*, vol. 1.

(§20) The *Shaykh al-Islām* Ibn Taymīyah, in his Fatwā collection, vol. 4, the book on *jihād:* "When he was asked about a town called Mārdīn which had been ruled by the Rule of Islam, but in which the situation had then changed and people had established the rule of Unbelief, whether (such a town) constitutes a House of War or House of Peace, he answered that these two concepts had become combined in it, and hence it could neither be categorized as a House of Peace which is ruled by the Laws of Islam nor as a House of War the inhabitants of which are infidels. It had become, however, a third category: a Muslim in it should be treated according to what is due to him, and someone who has rebelled against the Law of Islam should (in his turn) be treated according to what is due to him. . . ."

As a matter of fact we do not find (any) contradiction between the opinions of these Imāms, because Abū Ḥanīfah and the two (jurists) from his school did not mention that its inhabitants were infidels. . . . So, peace to whom peace is due, and war to whom war is due. . . . The State (of Egypt in which we live today) is ruled by the Laws of Unbelief although the majority of its inhabitants are Muslims.

(§21) The Ruler who Rules by Other (Laws) than (the Laws) Which God Sent Down

The laws by which the Muslims are ruled today are the laws of Unbelief, they are actually codes of law that were made by infidels who then subjected the Muslims to these (codes) although God—Praised and Exalted He is—says in Surah 5 (of the Qur'ān): "Whosoever does not rule *(yaḥkum)* by what God sent down, those are the Unbelievers *(kāfirūn)*." (This quotation is taken from Qur'ān) 5.44. After the disappearance of the Caliphate definitively in the year 1924, and (after) the removal of the laws of Islam in their entirety, and (after) their substitution by laws that were imposed by infidels, the situation (of the Muslims) became identical to the situation of the Mongols, as the Qur'ān commentary of Ibn Kathīr corroborates (in its comment) on Qur'ān 5.50: "Do they then desire the (mode) of judgment of the un-Islamic World *(Jāhilīyah)?* But who is better than God (Himself) in Judgment, to a people who are convinced?"

(§22) (In his comment on this verse) Ibn Kathīr says: "God disapproves of whosoever (firstly) rebels against God's laws, (laws) that are clear and precise *(muḥkam)* and that contain everything which is good and that forbid everything that is bad, and (secondly) turns away (from these laws) in order to follow other (mere human) opinions, ideas and conventions, that were made by humans who had no recourse to the Law of God, like the erroneous and mistaken ideas and opinions which the people of the period before the Coming of Islam had created for themselves as

jahilia

laws by which they used to live. Similarly, the Mongols rule themselves by royal decrees *(siyāsāt)* which were derived from their King Genghis Khan who made for them the *Yāsiq*. (The Mongol word *yāsiq*) is an expression (which designates) a book which contains (legal) rules which he (Genghis Khan) had derived from different systems of (revealed) law *(sharā'i^c)*, not only from Christianity and Judaism but also from the Islamic Community and others. It contains many legal rulings which he simply made up himself because he liked them. Yet it became a system of law that is applied and that they (the Mongols) prefer above the Rule by the Book of God and the Example *(sunnah)* of the Apostle of God— God's Peace be upon Him—. Whosoever does so is an infidel (and not a Muslim) and he must be fought *(yajib qitāluhu)* until he returns to the Rule of God and His Apostle, and until he rules by no other law than God's law." (This quotation is taken from the Qur'ān commentary by) Ibn Kathīr, vol. 2, p. 67.

(§23) The Rulers of this age have rebelled against the religion of Islam in multiple ways to such a degree that there is little doubt as to (how to judge) people who follow the ways of these (Rulers). (To their many transgressions of the laws of Islam) one should, moreover, add the question of the (un-Islamic) laws (which they impose on their Muslim subjects).

(§24) *Shaykh al-Islām* Ibn Taymīyah says in his book *Al-Fatāwā al-Kubrā*, in the section on *jihād*, p. 288, vol. 4: "About the religion of the Muslims it is known—(not only) through *logical necessity* *(iḍṭirār)* (but) also through agreement amongst all Muslims — that someone who makes it possible to follow another religion than the religion of Islam or to follow another law than the law of Muḥammad—God's Peace be upon him—(that such a person) is an infidel *(kāfir)*. (His Unbelief) is like the Unbelief of whosoever believes in part of the Book and does not believe in other parts. Likewise God—Exalted He is—says: 'Those who disbelieve in God and His Apostles and wish to make a distinction between God and His Apostles, and say: 'We believe in some, but disbelieve in others,' and wish to take between (this and) that a way—these are the unbelievers *(kāfirūn)* in very truth, and We have prepared for the unbelievers a humiliating punishment.' (These) two verses are from Surah 4, verses 150 and 151."

(§25) The Rulers of the Muslims Today are in Apostasy from Islam

The Rulers of this age are in apostasy from Islam. They were raised at the tables of imperialism, be it Crusaderism, or Communism, or Zionism. They carry nothing from Islam but their names,[4] even though they pray and fast and claim *(iddaᶜa)* to be Muslim. (")It is a well-established rule of Islamic Law that the punishment of an apostate will be heavier than the punishment of someone who is by origin an infidel (and has never been a Muslim), and this in many respects. For instance, an apostate has to be killed even if he is unable to (carry arms and) go to war. Someone, however, who is by origin an infidel and who is unable to (carry arms and) go to war (against the Muslims) should not be killed, according to leading Muslim scholars like Abū Ḥanīfah and Mālik and Aḥmad (ibn Ḥanbal). Hence, it is the view of the majority (of the jurists) that an apostate has to be killed, and this is in accordance with (the opinions held in) the Schools of Law of Mālik, Al-Shāfiᶜī and Aḥmad (ibn Ḥanbal). (Other examples of this difference are) that an apostate cannot inherit, cannot conclude a legally valid marriage, and to eat from the meat of animals which he slaughtered is forbidden. No such rules exist concerning someone who is by origin an infidel (and has never been a Muslim). When apostasy from a religion is worse than having always been an infidel, then apostasy from the prescripts (of a religion) is (also) worse than having always been an infidel. So, apostasy is worse than rebellion against the prescripts of a religion which comes from someone who has always been outside (this religion).(")

Ibn Taymīyah says on p. 293:

(§26) "It is a well-established rule of Islamic Law that the punishment of an apostate will be heavier than the punishment of someone who is by origin an infidel (and who has never been a Muslim), and this in many respects. For instance, an apostate has to be killed in all circumstances, he does not have the right to profess his new religion against the payment of the head tax, and there can be no Convenant of Protection (between an ex-Muslim and the Muslim authorities) unlike the case with someone who has always been an infidel (non-Muslim, e.g., a Christian or a Jew). For instance, an apostate has to be killed even if he is unable to (carry arms and) go to war. Someone, however, who is by origin an infidel and who is unable to (carry arms and) go to war (against the Muslims) should not be killed, according to leading Muslim scholars like Abū Ḥanīfah and Mālik and Aḥmad (ibn Ḥanbal). Hence, it is the view of the majority (of the jurists) that an apostate has to be killed, and this is in accordance with (the opinions held in) the Schools of Law of Mālik, Al-Shāfiᶜī and Aḥmad (ibn Ḥanbal). (Other examples of this difference are) that an apostate cannot inherit, cannot conclude a legally valid marriage, and to eat from the meat of animals which he slaughtered is forbidden. No such rules exist concerning someone who is by origin an infidel (and has never been a Muslim). When apostasy from a religion is worse than having always been an infidel, then apostasy from the prescripts (of a religion) is (also) worse than having always been an infidel. So, apostasy is worse than rebellion against the prescripts of a religion which comes from someone who has always been outside (this religion)."

What, then, is the position of the Muslims in relation to these people?

(§27) Ibn Taymīyah also says, in the same chapter on p. 281: "Any group of people that rebels against any single prescript of the clear and reliably transmitted prescripts of Islam has to be fought, according to the leading scholars of Islam, even if the members of this group pronounce the Islamic Confession of Faith. If such people make a public formal confession of their (Islamic) Faith (by pronouncing the double formula 'There is no god but God, and Muḥammad is His Apostle') but, at the same time, refuse to carry out the five daily prayer ceremonies, then it is obligatory to fight them. If they refuse to pay (the religious tax called) *zakāt*, it is obligatory to fight them until they pay the *zakāt*. Similarly, if they refuse to keep the Fast of the Month of Ramaḍān or (to perform the Pilgrimage) to the Ancient House (the Kaᶜbah), and similarly if they refuse to forbid abominations or adultery or gambling or wine or anything else that is forbidden by the laws of Islam. Similarly, if they refuse to apply on matters of life and property, or merchandise and commodities of any kind the Judgment of the Book and the Example (of the Prophet). Similarly if they refuse to compel to what is good and to prohibit what is bad (and refuse to) fight the infidels *(jihād al-kuffār)* until they surrender (to the Muslims) and humbly pay the head tax (prescribed for non-Muslims by Islamic Law). Similarly if they introduce innovations that are contrary to the Book and the Example (of Muḥammad) and that are not consistent with (the example of) the Pious Forefathers, like introducing deviating opinions concerning the Names of God, or His Signs, or disbelieving in the Signs of God and His Properties, or disbelieving His Omnipotence, or disbelieving anything on which the Community of Muslims agreed in the period of the rightly guided Caliphs, or attacking (the great personalities from) the earliest generations (of Muslims), the Immigrants (who went with Muḥammad from Mecca to Medina in 622 AD) and the Helpers (from Medina who supplied the Prophet with assistance in the period after 622) and those that imitate them by doing good works, or (like) fighting the Muslims until they (the Muslims) obey them (these people) when (these people) order (the Muslims) to rebel against the Laws of Islam. (Similarly) in all cases that are equivalent to these things. God — Exalted He is — says: "Fight them until there is no dissension *(fitnah)* and the religion is entirely God's" (Qur'ān 7.39) and because of this God — Exalted He is — says: "O ye who have believed, show piety towards God, and abandon usury which remains (unpaid) if ye are believers. If ye do it not, be apprised of war from God and His messenger" (Qur'ān 2.278–279).

(§28) These verses were revealed with reference to the people of (the town) Ṭā'if. When they became Muslims, they took it upon themselves to pray and to fast, but refused to give up usury. Then God made it clear that they would be at war with Him, and His Apostle, when they would not refrain from usury. Usury is the last thing which God declared (to be) forbidden. It is anything which is not taken with the consent of its owner. When (already) these (people in the town of Ṭā'if) had to be fought *(yajib jihāduhum)* because they were at war with God and His Apostle (only because they continued to ask for the payment of usury agreed upon before the Muslim conquest of their town), how much more (should the Muslims fight) those who omit (to carry out) many of the rites of Islam, or (perhaps) most of them, like the Mongols.

The leading scholars of Islam agree that a group of people who refuse to carry out part of the clear and reliably transmitted duties of Islam have to be fought *(yajib qitāluhā)* when they (publicly confess to be Muslim) by pronouncing the Islamic Confession of Faith ("There is no god but God and Muḥammad is His Apostle") but (at the same time) refuse to carry out the prayer ceremonies and (to pay) the *zakāt* tax, and (to keep) the Fast of the Month of Ramaḍān, or to (carry out) the pilgrimage to the Ancient House (the Kaᶜbah), or to judge between themselves according to the Book (of God) and the Example (of the Prophet), or (refuse) to forbid abominations or wine, or conclude marriages between persons whose consanguinity precludes a marriage according to Muslim law, or freely take life and property without having a right to do so, or (take) usury, or gamble, or (refuse to) fight the infidels, or (refuse to) impose the head tax on the People of the Book (Jews and Christians) and similar points from the prescripts of Islam — then they have to be fought on these points until the whole religion belongs to God.

(§29) The Comparison between the Mongols and Today's Rulers

1. It is clear from what Ibn Kathīr says in his Commentary on His word — Exalted He is —: "Do they then desire the (mode) of judgment of the un-Islamic world *(Jāhilīyah)?* But who is better than God (Himself) in Judgment, to a people who are convinced?" (Qur'ān 5.50), see page 6 (of the original version) of this book (cf. §§21 – 22 of this translation) — (from these words by Ibn Kathīr it is clear) that he does not distinguish between, on the one hand, those who rebel against God's Judgment whoever they are, and, on the other hand, the Mongols. . . . There is no doubt that the Mongol Yāsā is less of a sin than the laws which the West has imposed (on countries like Eygpt) and which have no connection with Islam or any other revealed religion.

(§30) 2. In a question directed to the *Shaykh al-Islām* Ibn Taymīyah by a concerned Muslim, the questioner says, describing their (the Mongol's) situation to the Imām (Ibn Taymīyah): "These

Mongols who come again and again to Syria and who have pronounced the double Islamic Confession of Faith and who have not remained in the state of Unbelief in which they originally found themselves — have they to be fought and how must someone who has been forced to join their armies to be judged? — (This question is relevant because) they attached Muslim (units) to the ranks of their army by force, "obligatory conscription" — and how must the (Muslim) scholars, jurists, mystics, etc., who are in their camp be judged, and what can be said about those who allege that they are Muslims, and that those who fight them are Muslims as well, and that both of them are wrong *(ẓālim)* and that one should not serve in the army of any one of these two groups?" This is the same difficulty *(shubhah)* which exists now and it will be cleared up if God permits. (See the book entitled) *Al-Fatāwā al-Kubrā,* pp. 280–281, question 516.

(§31) 3. In his description of the Mongols Ibn Taymīyah says: "Everyone who is with them in the state over which they rule has to be regarded as belonging to the most evil class of men. He is either is an atheist *(zindīq)* and hypocrite who does not believe in the essence of the religion of Islam — this means that he (only) outwardly pretends to be Muslim — or he belongs to that worst class of all people who are the people of the *bida*ᶜ (heretical innovations) like (the members of sects like) the *Rawāfiḍ,* the Jaḥmīyah, the Ittiḥādīyah, etc. — These are all groups who commit themselves to *bida*ᶜ —, or they are from that most criminal and sinful group who although they are quite able to perform the pilgrimage to the Ancient House (the Kaᶜbah) do not perform this pilgrimage, even though there are amongst them some who perform the prayers and fast, but the majority (of them) does not perform the prayers or pay the (Muslim religious) *zakāt* tax. . . ." Is this not (exactly) what is the case (in Egypt today)?

(§32) 4. They fight under the banners of Genghis Khan — the name of their King —. Whosoever enters into their obedience becomes their client even if he is an infidel. Whosoever rebels against their authority is regarded as their enemy even if he were from amongst the best of Muslims. They do not fight under the banners of Islam and they do not impose the head tax (on Jews and Christians). Many of the Muslim army commanders and viziers in their camps even have it as their aim that in their (the Mongols') esteem a Muslim should be equal to the nonmonotheist *(mushrikūn)* Jews and Christians to whom they give high positions. (This is quoted from) *Al-Fatāwā*, p. 286.

NOTE: Are not these characteristics the same characteristics as those of the Rulers of this age, and their entourage of clients as well? (Do the members of their entourage not) glorify the Ruler more than they glorify their Creator?

(§33) 5. On p. 287 *Shaykh al-Islām* Ibn Taymīyah adds to his description of the clients of Genghis Khan. He writes on those who outwardly profess to be Muslims that "they place Muḥammad (in a position) equal to (the position of) Genghis Khan; and if (they do) not (do) this they—in spite of their pretension to be Muslims—not only glorify Genghis Khan but they also fight the Muslims. The worst of these infidels even give him their total and complete obedience; they bring him their properties and give their decisions in his name. When they disagree with what he orders them this is like rebellion against an Imām. Above all this they fight the Muslims and treat them with the greatest enmity. They ask the Muslims to obey them, to give them their properties, and to enter (the obedience of the rules) which were imposed on them by this infidel polytheist King who so resembles the Pharaoh or Nimrod and their likes. He is, however, a greater pest than both of these two."

(§34) 6. Ibn Taymīyah says in addition: "Whosoever enters into their obedience (and obeys their) un-Islamic (prescripts) *(ṭā^catahum al-jāhilīyah)* and their pagan customs is their friend; whosoever disagrees with them is their enemy even if he were the best of God's Prophets, Apostles or Saints." (This quotation is taken from) p. 288.

(§35) 7. Speaking about the judicial system in the age of the Mongols *Shaykh al-Islām* (Ibn Taymīyah) says moreover: "Similarly their foolish vizier (the well-known Persian historiographer) called Rashīd (al-Dīn) ruled over these kinds (of people) (who were in the Mongol camp) and put the worst Muslims like the *Rawāfiḍ* and (other) heretics above the best Muslims, people of science and faith. The office of High Judge even fell into the hands of someone who is closer to atheism *(zandaqah)*, heresy and unbelief in God and His Apostle (than to Islam). . . . He puts agreement with infidel and hypocritical Jews, Qarmathians, heretics and *Rawāfiḍ* above agreement with anyone else. (These people) only outwardly carry out that part (of the prescripts) of Islam which they have to (carry out) for the sake of the Muslims who are with them. Their vizier, this wicked heretical hypocrite, even wrote a work which purports to say that 'the Prophet—God's Peace be upon Him—had no objections *(raḍiya)* against the religion of the Jews and the Christians, did not disapprove of them, did not blame them, did not want them to give up their religion, and did not order them to come over to Islam. The ignorant *(jāhil)* and wicked (Rashīd al-Dīn) inferred this from the Word of God—Exalted He is—in (the Qur'ān), Surah 109:' Say: 'O ye unbelievers, I serve not what ye serve, and ye are not servers of what I serve; I am not a server of what ye have served, nor are ye servers of what I serve; Ye have your religion, and I have mine.' He alleges that this verse implies that he (Muḥammad) had no objections against their religion. He also says that this verse is well established *(muḥkam)* and not abrogated *(mansūkh)*. . . ." (This passage is taken from) p. 288 and 289 (of the book entitled) *Al-Fatāwā al-Kubrā*,[5] and Praise be to God. Is not (the purport of) the work of this Mongol vizier exactly the same as (what we see in the modern concepts)[6] "Religious Brotherhood" and "Unity of Religions"? The latter is even worse and even more wrong than the former.

(§36) Ibn Taymīyah's Collection of Fatwās is Useful in the Present Age

Hence we think it proper that we should quote some of Ibn Taymīyah's fatwās on how to judge these people. We already mentioned his fatwā on the town of Mārdīn which the Mongols ruled by (a system of) laws which combined the laws of the Jews and the Christians (on the one hand) and part of Islam (on the other hand) and (lastly) part of (laws made up on the basis of their own) reasoning and fancies. On this he said: "Whether it is a House of War or a House of Peace is a complicated (question). Both concepts (can be found) in it. It is neither a House of Peace which is ruled by the laws of Islam because its soldiers are Muslims, nor a House of

War the inhabitants of which are infidels. It became, however, a third category: a Muslim in it should be treated according to what is due to him and someone who rebels against the Law of Islam should (in his turn) be treated in accordance to what is due to him."

(§37) How to Judge Helping and Supporting Them?

Shaykh al-Islām Ibn Taymīyah says in answer to this question, p. 280, the chapter on *Jihād:* "To help those who rebel against the laws of the religion of Islam is forbidden, both to the people of Mārdīn and to anyone else. Someone who lives there (in Mārdīn) must emigrate *(hijrah)* from it, if he is unable to carry out his religious obligations (there). If he is not (unable to do so) it is (nevertheless) recommendable (to leave Mārdīn), but it is not obligatory. To support an enemy of the Muslims with personal military service or with money is forbidden. They are under the obligation to avoid doing so with all available means: by going away, resisting, or bribery. If this can only be done by emigrating, then this emigration is a personal obligation." To this Ibn Taymīyah adds, talking about the people of Mārdīn who helped the Mongols, that is, the ruling Power: "It is, generally, not allowed to denounce them as hypocrites. Denouncing someone as (a hypocrite) and accusing him of hypocrisy is only permissible on the basis of the characteristics that are mentioned in the Qur'ān and the Tradition. Some of the people of Mārdīn fell into this category, and others did not." This means that not all of them were (hypocrites).

(§38) How to Judge Muslim Soldiers who Refuse Service in the Army of the Mongols?

Page 280, question 513, on a soldier who did not want to serve. The answer: When it is useful for the Muslims and he is able to bear it, he should not leave his post without benefit (from his desertion) to the Muslims. . . . To be, however, in the forefront during the *jihād* which God and His Apostle have called for is better than voluntary acts of worship like voluntary prayer, the pilgrimage, and voluntary fasting. God, however, knows best.

(§39) How to Judge their Possessions?

Question 514. When the Mongols entered Syria and plundered the possessions of the Christians and the Muslims, and next the Muslims plundered the Mongols and stripped their dead of arms and clothing—is it then permissible to take things from their properties? The answer: "A fifth may be taken from everything which is captured from the Mongols and to profit from it is permitted." The meaning of the expression "to take a fifth" refers to the spoils.

(§40) How to Judge Fighting Them?

Ibn Taymīyah says, p. 298, question 217: "To fight the Mongols who came to Syria *(Al-Shām)* is a duty prescribed by the Book (of God) and the Example (of the Prophet). God says in the Qur'ān (2.193): Fight them until there is no dissension *(fitnah)* and religion becomes God's. "Religion" (here) means "obedience." When part of the religion is God's, and another part of it is not, the fighting is obligatory until the whole religion is God's, and hence God—Exalted He is—says (Qur'ān 2.278–279): 'O ye who have believed, show piety towards God, and abandon usury which remains (unpaid) if ye are believers. If ye do it not, be apprised of war from God and His Messenger.' These verses were revealed with reference to the people of (the town) Ṭā'if. When they became Muslims, they took it upon themselves to pray and to fast, but refused to give up usury. Then God made it clear that they would be at war with Him, and His Apostle, when they would not refrain from usury. When (already) these (people in the town of Ṭā'if) had to be fought *(yajib jihāduhum)* because they were at war with God and His Apostle (only because they continued to ask for the payment of usury agreed upon before the Muslim conquest of their town), how much more (should the Muslims fight) those who omit (to carry out) many of the rites of Islam, or (perhaps) most of them, like the Mongols.

The leading scholars of Islam agree that a group of people who refuse to carry out part of the clear and reliably transmitted duties of Islam have to be fought *(yajib qitāluhā)* when they (publicly confess to be Muslim) by pronouncing the Islamic Confession of Faith ("There is no god but God and Muḥammad is His Apostle") but (at the same time) refuse to carry out the prayer ceremonies and (to pay) the *zakāt* tax, and (to keep) the Fast of the Month of Ramaḍān, or to (carry out) the pilgrimage to the Ancient House (the Kaᶜbah), or to judge between themselves according to the Book (of God) and the Example (of the Prophet), or (refuse) to forbid abominations or wine or conclude marriages between persons whose consanguinity precludes a marriage according to Muslim law, or freely take life and property without having a right to do so, or (take) usury, or gamble, or (refuse to) fight the infidels, or (refuse to) impose the head tax on the People of the Book (Jews and Christians) and similar points from the prescripts of Islam — then they have to be fought on these points until the whole religion belongs to God (cf. §28).

It is certain from the (two Tradition collections entitled) *Al-Ṣaḥīḥ* (by Al-Bukhārī and Muslim) that (the first Caliph) Abū Bakr said to (his successor, the second Caliph) ᶜUmar, when the latter saw how (concerned) Abū Bakr was about those who refused to pay the *zakāt* tax: "How should I (Abū Bakr) not fight those who neglect (some of) the obligations which God and His Messenger imposed on them even when they have become Muslims, like (for instance) the *zakāt* tax? Abū Bakr then said to ᶜUmar: "The *zakāt* tax is one of these obligations. By God, if they refuse me (even a thing as insignificant as) the cord used for hobbling the feet of a camel which they used to bring to the Apostle of God — God's Peace be upon Him —, I will certainly fight them on account of this refusal."

(§41) ᶜUmar then said: "When I heard this, I saw at once that God had opened the breast of Abū Bakr (and had inspired him) to go to war (on account of the refusal to pay the *zakāt* tax), and I realized that he was right."

It is certain that in the Traditions (that go back to Muḥammad) it is said more than once that the Prophet — God's Peace be upon Him — mentioned the (sects of the) Khārijīs and said about them: "Some of you will think slightly of the prayers (which they perform) together with their prayers, and the fast (which they perform) together with their fast, and the recitation of the Qur'ān (which they recite) together with their recitation. These people recite the Qur'ān but it does not go further than their throats (i.e., it does not enter their hearts). They go out of Islam the way an arrow goes out of the bow. Wherever you meet them, kill them for a recompense with God (which He shall give) at the Day of Resurrection to those who have killed them. Whenever you get hold of them, kill them the way (the tribe of) ᶜĀd was killed (according to the stories told in the Qur'ān).

(§42) The (Pious) Forefathers and the (leading authorative) Imāms have always agreed that these people have to be fought. The first one who did so was (Caliph) ᶜAlī Ibn Abū Ṭālib — May God be Pleased with Him. All through the Umayyad and Abbasid Caliphates Muslim army commanders have continued to do so, even when they were unjust (and not good Muslims). (For instance) Al-Ḥajjāj and his lieutenants were amongst those who fought them. All Muslim Imāms command to fight these (Khārijīs). The Mongols and their likes — the equivalent of our rulers today — are (even) more rebellious against the laws of Islam than those who refused the *zakāt* tax, or the Khārijīs, or those from the people of (the town) Al-Ṭā'if who refused to abandon usury. Whosoever doubts whether they should be fought is more ignorant of the religion of Islam. Since fighting them is obligatory they have to be fought, even though there are amongst them some who have been forced (to join their pagan ranks)."

(§43) Is To Fight Them (the same as) Fighting the (Group of Rebels Traditionally Called) Al-Bughāh?[7]

Ibn Taymīyah says on p. 283, the Chapter on *Jihād:* "Some people presume that these Mongols are (to be regarded as) belonging to (the group of rebels traditionally called) *Al-Bughāh* who deprecate

Religion and reduce it to symbols and allegories *(Al-Muta'awwilūn),* and should be judged accordingly, and that also the people who refuse the *zakāt* tax and the Khārijīs are to be classified as such. We shall make clear the error of this presumption, if God permits."

Ibn Taymīyah says on p. 296: *"Similarly the Prophet—May God's Peace be upon Him— says (and this is reported) in a reliable Tradition: 'Whosoever is killed is a martyr even when his possessions are left intact; whosoever is killed is a martyr even when he did not personally participate in the battle; whosoever is killed is a martyr even when his family is saved from the enemy.'"

(If this is so,) how (much more should we regard it as justified) to fight these people who rebel against the prescripts of Islam and who fight God and His Apostle? Their violence and their rebellion is the smallest (of their sins)! To fight people who are violent and aggressive is well established (as an Islamic duty) by the Example (of the Prophet) and the Consensus (of the Muslims and the Muslim scholars). These people indeed are violent and aggressive against the persons, the properties and the families and the religion of the Muslims. (An attack on any of these four points mentioned in the previous line) makes it permissible to fight someone who attacked one of them. Whosoever is killed when only one of these (four is attacked) is a martyr. How (much more should we respect) someone who fights for all (four) of them?

They (the Mongols) are from amongst the worst rebels and allegorizers, and they are unjust. However, whosoever alleges that they (the Mongols) have to be fought in the way the allegorizing (rebels traditionally called) *Al-Bughāh* have to be fought, makes a terrible mistake and goes far astray, because the smallest of the sins of the allegorizing (rebels traditionally called) *Al-Bughāh* is that they believe in cheap allegories through which they became heretical. They say that their Imām communicates with them. They mention legal reasons for not doing certain things which he would have explained to them, and they mention injustice which he took away. What legal reason could there possibly be for not fighting these people (the Mongols) who are at war with God and His Apostle, who spread corruption in the land, who rebel against the prescripts of the religion? It is perfectly clear that they (the Mongols) do not (even) say that they are better Muslims as far as their religious practice or their religious scholarship is concerned than this sect (referred to as *Al-Bughāh*).*

(§44) How to Judge Someone Who Becomes Their Client Against the Muslims?

Ibn Taymīyah says on p. 291 of the Chapter on *Jihād:* "Every army commander and every soldier who goes over to them is to be judged like them. They are as much apostates from the prescripts of Islam as they (themselves) are apostates from the prescripts of Islam. When the Pious Forefathers used to call apostates the people who refused to pay the *zakāt* tax although they kept the Fasts and Prayers and did not fight the Muslim community, how (much more must we regard as apostates) those who became (in the same camp as) the enemies of God and His Apostle and who kill Muslims?"

(§45) Ibn Taymīyah also says, p. 293: "This makes it clear that whoever was originally a Muslim is worse than the Turk(ic tribes which joined the Mongol armies), who were originally pagans, since someone who is by origin a Muslim and who apostacized from some of the prescripts of Islam is in a worse position than those who had not yet entered into (the obedience of) those prescripts, whether he be a *fiqh* scholar, or a Ṣūfī, or a merchant, or a professional secretary, or something like this. These people are more wicked than the Turk(ic tribes) who had not entered into obedience of these prescripts and who persisted in their paganism. It is for this reason that Muslims suffer injury to their religion from these people what they do not suffer from the others. Those (the tribes) (actually) submit to more of Islam and its prescripts and obedience to God and His Apostle than these people who apostacized from part of the religion and simulate to go along with another part of it, even if they pretend to be affiliated with (Islamic) scholarship and faith."[8]

(§46) How to Judge Those Who Are Forced to Go Out and Fight in Their Ranks?

Ibn Taymīyah also says, on p. 292: "Only a hypocrite or an atheist *(zindīq)* or a sinful criminal who only pretends outwardly to be a Muslim will join their ranks voluntarily. When they (the Mongols) make someone go out with their army against his will, then such a person has to prove his intention (of not wanting to fight against Islam and the Muslims). We on our side cannot but fight the whole army and can not differentiate between someone who is forced (into that army) and someone who is not. . . ."

A warning to someone who is forced: Ibn Taymīyah says, warning someone who is forced, on p. 295 of the Chapter on *Jihād:* "Someone who is forced to fight in a (Muslim) civil war has the duty not to fight. He has the duty to destroy his armor and to endure that he is, unrightfully, killed. How (much more) someone who is forced to fight the Muslims under the banners of a group which rebels against the prescripts of Islam, like the people who refuse to pay the *zakāt* tax, and apostates, and similar people? There is no doubt that when he is forced into their army he has the duty not to fight even if (this means that) the Muslims will kill him. If they force him (by threatening) to kill him, is it (then) not better that his soul is saved by being innocently killed, than the opposite? For he has the duty not to be unjust to others, so he will be killed, and if (this is not so) he will kill himself."

(§47) Ideas and Misunderstandings

In the Islamic world there are several ideas about the elimination of these Rulers and the establishment of the Rule of God—Exalted and Majestic He is—. To what extent are these ideas correct?

(§48) Benevolent Societies

There are those who say that we should establish societies that are subject to the State and that urge people to perform their prayers and to pay their *zakāt* tax and to do (other) good works. Prayer, *zakāt* and good works are (all equally) commands of God—Exalted and Majestic He is—which we should not at all neglect. However, when we ask ourselves: "Do these works, and acts of devotion, bring about the establishment of an Islamic State?"—then the immediate answer without any further consideration must be "No." Moreover, these societies would in principle be subject to the State, be registered in its files, and they would have to follow (the State's) instructions.

(§49) Obedience, Education and Abundance of Acts of Devotion

There are those who say that we should occupy ourselves with Obedience to God, with educating the Muslims, and with exerting ourselves in acts of devotion, because the backwardness in which we live overpowered us on account of our sins and our (own) works. They sometimes prove this with a maxim which says on the authority of Mālik Ibn Dīnār: God—Exalted and Majestic He is—says: "I am God, the King of Kings; the hearts of the Kings are in My hand; When someone obeys Me, I make (the Kings) (My instrument of) mercy towards him; When someone disobeys Me, I make (the Kings) (My instrument of) revenge towards him. Do not occupy yourselves with kings, but turn in repentance to the Most Compassionate King you have."

(§50) The truth is that someone who thinks that this maxim abrogates the two duties of (1) *jihād* and (2) ordering to do what is reputable and forbidding to do what is not destroys himself and those who obey him and listen to him. . . .

Whoever really wants to be occupied with the highest degrees of obedience and wants to reach the peak of devotion must commit himself to *jihād* for the cause of God, without, however, neglecting the other (prescribed) pillars of Islam.

The Apostle of God—God's Peace be upon Him—once described *jihād* as the best of the summit of Islam, saying: "Someone who does not participate in any way in the raids (against the enemies of Islam), or someone whose soul does not talk to him encouraging him to wage a fight on behalf of his religion, dies as if he had never been a Muslim, or (he dies) like someone who, filled with some form of hypocrisy, only outwardly pretended to be a Muslim."

Therefore (a certain) ᶜAbdallāh ibn Mubārak, someone who waged *jihād* for God's cause, said (the following two lines of poetry) that make the eminent weep:

O (Ruler,) servant of the two Holy Places (Mecca and Medina)
If ye looked at us well
Then you would realize that you only play with what is devotion

Some people make their cheeks wet with tears
in great quantities
but our chests and throats become wet
by torrents of our blood

(§51) Some people say that to occupy oneself with politics hardens the heart and keeps people away from remembering *(dhikr)* God. The likes of these people do not understand the word of the Prophet—May God's Peace be upon Him—: "The best form of *jihād* is a word of truth (spoken to) a tyrannical Ruler." The truth is that whoever adheres to such philosophies is either not interested in Islam or he is a coward who does not wish to stand up for the Rule of God with firmness.

(§52) The Foundation of a Political Party

There are those who say: "We must establish an Islamic political party (and add this party) to the list of extant political parties." It is true that this is better than benevolent societies, because a party at least talks about politics. However, the purpose of the foundation (of such a party) is the destruction of the infidel State (and to replace it by an Islamic theocracy). To work through a political party will, however, have the opposite effect, since it means building the pagan State and collaborating with it. . . . (Moreover, such an Islamic political party) will participate in the membership of legislative councils that enact laws without consideration for God's Laws.

(§53) To Exert Oneself in Order to Obtain Important Positions

There are those who say that the Muslims should do their best in order to obtain (socially) important positions. Only when all important centers are filled with Muslim doctors and Muslim engineers, will the existing pagan order perish automatically and the Muslim Ruler *(Al-Ḥākim al-Muslim)* establish himself. . . . Someone who hears this argument for the first time will think it is a fantasy or a joke, but there are, as a matter of fact, people in the Muslim world who embrace such philosophies and arguments, although there is nothing in the Book (of God) or the Example (of the Prophet) which supports or proves the(se arguments). Moreover, reality prevents (such aspirations) from ever coming true. . . . No matter how many Muslim doctors and Muslim engineers there are, they too will help to build the (pagan) State. Moreover, things will never go so far as to permit a Muslim personality to reach a ministerial post when he is not a 100 percent supporter of the existing order.

(§54) (Nonviolent) Propaganda Only, and the Creation of a Broad Base

Some of them say that the right road to the establishment of an (Islamic) State is (nonviolent) propaganda *(daᶜwah)* only, and the creation of a broad base. This, however, does not bring about the foundation of an (Islamic) State. Nevertheless, some people make this point the basis for their withdrawal from (true) *jihād*. The truth is that an (Islamic) State can only be founded by a believing minority. . . . Those who follow the straight path that is in accordance with the Command of God and the Example of the Apostle of God—May God's Peace be upon Him—are always a minority. Scriptural proof of this is found in the Word of God—Exalted and Majestic He is—: "Few among my servants are thankful" (Qur'ān 34.12) and in His Word—He be Praised—: "If thou obey the majority of those who are in the land they will lead thee astray from the Way of God" (Qur'ān 6.116). This is the Custom of God

(Sunnat Allāh) with regard to His World. . . . From where will we get this hoped-for majority? (Did not God) also say: "Most of the people, even though thou shouldst be zealous, are not believers"? (Qur'ān 12.103).

(§55) Islam does not triumph by (attracting the support of) the majority. Did not God — Praised and Exalted He is — say: "How many a small band has, by the permission of God, conquered a numerous band?" (Qur'ān 2.249)? And also: "(God has already helped you on many fields) and on the Day of Ḥunayn when ye prided yourselves on your numbers but they did not benefit you at all, and the land, wide as it was, became too narrow for you" (Qur'ān 9.25).

(§56) (The Apostle) — May God's Peace be upon Him — says: "God will certainly take away from the hearts of your enemies all awe (which will make them poor fighters), and he will put weakness (and fear) in your hearts (which will make you effective fighters)." This (he said in response to a question) which they asked Him — May God's Peace be upon Him —: "Shall we, on that day, be a minority, O Apostle of God?" He then said: "No, you shall be many on that day, but (looking insignificant) like rubbish swept by a torrent."

(§57) But then, how can (nonviolent) propaganda be widely successful when all means of (mass) communication today are under the control of the pagan and wicked (State) and (under the control) of those who are at war with God's religion? The (only) really effective method could be to liberate the media from the control of these people. It is well known that compliance will only come about through a convincing victory. Does not God — Praised and Exalted He is — say: "When comes the victory of God, and the Conquest, thou seest the people entering into the religion of God in crowds" (Qur'ān 110.1–2).

(§58) In connection with this point we ought to answer those who say that people have to be Muslims in order to have Muslim Law applied to them, in order to be obedient to that Law, and in order that we should not fail in applying it. Someone who is so foolish as to say this, however, accuses Islam of imperfection and incapability, without realizing (that he implicitly makes this accusation). For this religion is well applicable, in all times and all places, and it is capable of arranging (the affairs) of Muslims and infidels, of sinners and the righteous, of scholars and fools. . . . When people have been able to live under the rules of Unbelief *(aḥkām al-kufr),* what will their position be when they find themselves under the rule of Islam which is all justice?

(§59) Some people have misunderstood what I say and have taken it to mean that we should refrain from (nonviolent) propaganda altogether. "Propaganda" here means "Calling upon people to become Muslims." Here it is basic to take Islam as a whole. This, however, is the refutation of those who see it as their aim to create a broad base and (in doing so) forget about (true) *jihād,* or even hinder or obstruct (true *jihād*) in order to realize this (peaceful aim of theirs).

(§60) Emigration *(Hijrah)*

There are some who say that the true road to the establishment of an Islamic State is *hijrah,* emigration, to another locality and to establish the (new Islamic) State out there. Then they (want to) return again, as conquerors. These people must, in order to save their efforts (from being wasted on impossible tasks), (first) establish an Islamic State in their (new) *balad* ("town," "country," or "locality") and then they will leave it as conquerors. . . .

Is this (form of) Emigration in accordance with God's laws or not? To answer this question we have to study the different forms of "Emigration," which are transmitted in the (Collections of) Traditions (from Muḥammad), that are to be found in the Commentary on the Tradition "Someone who emigrates to God and His Apostle really emigrates to God and His Apostle, but someone who emigrates because of worldly possessions or because of a woman he wants to marry, emigrates to whatever he emigrates to (without further religious, or other, merit)." Ibn Hajar says: "To emigrate to something is to move over to it away from something else." In religion it means: "To refrain from something which God has forbidden." *Hijrah,* "emigration," occurs in Islam in two ways:

(§61) First, by moving over from the House of Unbelief to the House of Safety, like the two *hijrahs* to Ethiopia and the beginning of the *hijrah* from Mecca to Medina.

(§62) Second, the *hijrah* from the House of Unbelief to the

House of Faith. This (variety of *hijrah*) occurred after the Prophet — God's Peace be upon Him — had established himself safely in Medina, and those Muslims who could emigrated to him. *There is nothing odd in this. There are, however, those who say that they will emigrate to the desert and then come back, and have a confrontation with the Pharaoh*, as Moses did, and then God will make the ground swallow the Pharaoh up, together with his army. . . . All these strange ideas only result from having forsaken the only true and religiously allowed road towards establishing an Islamic State. So, what is this true road? God — Exalted He is — says: "Fighting is prescribed for you, though it is distasteful to you. Possibly ye may dislike a thing, though it is good for you, and possibly ye may love a thing, though it is bad for you" (Qur'ān 2.216). (God) — Praised He is — also says: "Fight them until there is no dissension, and religion becomes God's."

(§63) To Be Occupied with the Quest for Knowledge

There are some who say that at present the true road is the quest for knowledge. "How can we fight when we have no knowledge (of Islam and its prescripts)? The quest for knowledge is an obligation *(farīḍah)*, too." But we shall not heed the words of someone who permits the neglect of a religious command or one of the duties of Islam for the sake of (the quest for religious) knowledge, certainly not if this duty is the duty of *jihād*. How could we possibly neglect a personal individual duty (like *jihād*) for the sake of a collective duty (like the quest for knowledge)?

How can it have come about that we got to know the smallest (details of the Islamic doctrine of duties like) recommendable and desirable acts, and call upon people to perform these acts, but at the same time neglect a duty which the Apostle — May God's Peace be upon Him — glorified?

How can someone who has specialized in (Islamic) religious studies and who really knows all about small and great sins not have noticed the great importance of *jihād*, and the punishment for postponing or neglecting it?

Someone who says that (the quest for) knowledge (also) is (a form of) *jihād* has to understand that the duty (which is indicated by the Arabic word *jihād*) entails the obligation of fighting, for God—Praised and Exalted He is—says: "Prescribed for you is fighting" (Qur'ān 2.216).

It is well known that a man (once) pronounced the double Islamic Confession of Faith in the presence of the Apostle—May God's Peace be upon Him—and then at once went to the battlefield. He fought (for Islam) till he was killed before he had had the opportunity to occupy himself with anything from either the theory or the practice of Islam. Then the Apostle of God—God's Peace be upon Him—announced that the works of this man had been few, but that his reward would be great.

(§64) It is an essential characteristic of knowledge that someone who has knowledge of the obligatory character of the prayer ceremony has the obligation to pray. Similarly, someone who has knowledge of the obligatory character of the Fast must keep the Fast. Whoever has knowledge of the obligatory character of *jihād* must fight. Whoever frankly admits that he has no knowledge of the way in which Islam regulates *jihād* must know that the regulations of Islam are simple and easy for someone who sincerely dedicates his intentions to God. Such a person must consciously formulate the inner intention of fighting for God's cause, and from that moment on the regulations of *jihād* can easily and simply be studied, and in a very, very short time. The matter then has no need for[9] *much study.*

When someone wants to increase his knowledge above this (elementary) level (he can freely do so), for there is no monopoly on knowledge. Knowledge is available to all, but to postpone *jihād* for the sake of the quest for knowledge is the line of reasoning of someone who has no case (worth considering).

There have been people who participated in *jihād (mujāhidūn)* since the beginning of the Call to Islam by the Prophet—God's Peace be upon Him—. In the ages that followed, until recently, they (the participators in *jihād*) have not been scholars (*ᶜulamā'*). Nevertheless, God conquered many towns at their hands. These people never excused themselves (from participation in *jihād*) by (saying that they were preoccupied with) the quest for knowledge, or by study of the Traditions, or the Science of Deriving Legal

Rules from the Qur'ān, the Tradition, etc. (i.e., the *ᶜIlm Uṣūl al-Fiqh*). On the contrary, God — Praised and Exalted He is — gave at their hands victories to Islam which were not equalled by the scholars of al-Azhar on the day when Napoleon and his soldiers entered al-Azhar on horseback. What did their knowledge help them against this comedy?

Scholarship is not the decisive weapon which will radically put an end to paganism. This can only be done with the weapon which the Lord — Exalted and Majestic He is — mentioned in His word: "Fight them and God will punish them at your hands, will humiliate them and aid you against them, and will bring healing to the breasts of people who are believers" (Qur'ān 9.14). We do not have a low opinion of the importance of scholarship. On the contrary, we emphasize it(s importance). We do, however, not excuse ourselves (by appealing to the need for scholarship) from carrying out the obligations which God prescribed.

(§65) Explanation why the Islamic Community Differs from Other Communities as far as Fighting is Concerned

God — Exalted He is — made it clear that this Community differs from the other (religious) Communities as far as Fighting is concerned. In the case of earlier communities God — Praised and Exalted He is — made His punishment come down upon the infidels and the enemies of His religion by means of natural phenomena like eclipses (of the moon), floods, shouts[10] and storms. . . . With regard to the Community of Muḥammad — God's Peace be upon Him — this differs, for God — Praised and Exalted He is — addressed them saying: "Fight them and God will punish them at your hands, will humiliate them and aid you against them, and will bring healing to the breasts of people who are believers" (Qur'ān 9.14).

This means that a Muslim has first of all the duty to execute the command to fight with his hands. (Once he has done so) God — Praised and Exalted He is — will then intervene (and change) the laws of nature. In this way victory will be achieved through the hands of the believers by means of God's — Praised and Exalted He is — (intervention).

(§66) Revolt against the Ruler

In (the Collection of Traditions entitled) *Al-Ṣaḥīḥ* made by Muslim, with the commentary to it by Al-Nawawī (we read a Tradition reported) on the authority of Junādah ibn Abī Umayyah, who said: "Once we visited ᶜUbādah ibn Ṣāmit while he was ill, and we said: 'Tell us—May God Give you back your Health—a Tradition by which God beneficially gave us guidance which you heard from the Apostle of God—May God's Peace be upon Him—.' He then said: 'The Apostle of God—May God's Peace be upon Him—once called us and we gave Him our oath of allegiance. (In this oath the Apostle) imposed on us to swear that we would listen to him and obey him irrespective of whether we liked (His commands) or not or whether it was difficult or easy for us. He impressed us with this, and (added) that we should not fight for the command (of the Community) with His people, saying 'except when you see Unbelief publicly displayed—You will have proof from God with you for this." (The relatively unusual Arabic word) *bawāḥan* (which the text of this Tradition here uses) means: "publicly displayed." With (the word) Unbelief (the text) here means "sins" *(maᶜāṣī)*. The meaning of "you will have proof from God with you for this" is that you will know it from (the prescripts of) the religion of God.

Al-Nawawī says in his commentary on this Tradition: "The Qāḍī ᶜAyyāḍ says: 'The leading Muslim scholars agree that the (duties of) Leadership (of the Community) can not be given to an infidel, and that when (a Leader) suddenly becomes an unbeliever, his leadership comes to an end. The same is the case when he neglects to perform the prayer ceremonies, or to urge (others to perform) them. The majority (of the scholars) also holds (this to be true) when (this leader introduces) a **bidᶜah** (innovation).[11]

Some of the scholars from Basra say, however, that (the leadership nevertheless) is given to him, and continues because he is (only) guilty of allegorizing.

The Qāḍī says: "When he suddenly becomes an unbeliever, or changes God's Law, or introduces an innovation *(bidᶜah)*, he has no longer the qualifications needed in a Leader, to obey him is no longer necessary, and the Muslims have the duty to revolt against him and to depose him, and to put a Just Imām in his place when they are able to do so. When this occurs to a group of people, they have the duty to revolt and depose the infidel." (This passage is quoted from the Collection of Traditions entitled) *Al-Ṣaḥīḥ* by Muslim, the Chapter on *Jihād*.[12]

This chapter is also the refutation of those who say that it is only permissible to fight under a Caliph or a Commander *(taḥt khalīfah aw amīr).*

(§67) Ibn Taymīyah says: "Any group of people that rebels against any single prescript of the clear and reliably transmitted prescripts of Islam has to be fought, according to the leading scholars of Islam, even if the members of this group pronounce the Islamic Confession of Faith." (This quotation is taken from) *Al-Fatāwā al-Kubrā,* the chapter on *jihād,* p. 281.

(§68) The Enemy who is Near and the Enemy Who is Far

It is said that the battlefield of *jihād* today is the liberation of Jerusalem since it is (part of) the Holy Land. It is true that the liberation of the Holy Land is a religious command, obligatory for all Muslims, but the Apostle of God—May God's Peace be upon Him—described the believer as "sagacious and prudent" *(kayyis faṭin),* and this means that a Muslim knows what is useful and what is harmful, and gives priority to radical definitive solutions. This is a point that makes the explanation of the following necessary:

(§69) First: To fight an enemy who is near is more important than to fight an enemy who is far.

Second: Muslim blood will be shed in order to realize this victory. Now it must be asked whether this victory will benefit the interests of an Islamic State? Or will this victory benefit the interests of Infidel Rule? It will mean the strengthening of a State which rebels against the Laws of God. . . . These Rulers will take advantage of the nationalist ideas of these Muslims in order to realize their un-Islamic aims, even though at the surface (these aims) look Islamic. Fighting has to be done (only) under the Banner of Islam and under Islamic Leadership. About this there is no difference of opinion.

(§70) Third: The basis of the existence of Imperialism in the Lands of Islam are (precisely) these Rulers. To begin by putting an end to imperialism is not a laudatory and not a useful act. It is only a waste of time. We must concentrate on our own Islamic situation: we have to establish the Rule of God's Religion in our own country first, and to make the Word of God supreme. . . . There is no doubt that the first battlefield for *jihād* is the extermination of these infidel leaders and to replace them by a complete Islamic Order. From here we should start.

(§71) The Answer to Those Who Say that in Islam Jihād is Defensive Only

Concerning this question it is proper that we should refute those who say that *jihād* in Islam is defensive, and that Islam was not spread by the sword. This is a false view, which is (nevertheless) repeated by a great number of those who are prominent in the field of Islamic missionary activities. The right answer comes from the Apostle of God — God's Peace be upon Him — when he was asked: "What is *jihād* for God's cause?" He then said: "Whosoever fights in order to make the Word of God supreme is someone who (really) fights for God's cause." To fight is, in Islam, to make supreme the Word of God in this world, whether it be by attacking or by defending. . . .

Islam spread by the sword, *and under the very eyes of these Leaders of Unbelief who conceal it from mankind. After the (removal of these Leaders) nobody has an aversion (to Islam). . . .*

It is obligatory for the Muslims to raise their swords under the very eyes of the Leaders who hide the Truth and spread falsehoods. If (the Muslims) do not do this, the Truth will not reach the hearts of Men. Read with me the Letter of the Prophet — God's Peace be upon Him — to Heraclius, which is reported on the authority of Ibn ᶜAbbās in the (Collection of Traditions entitled) *Al-Ṣaḥīḥ* by Al-Bukhārī. Its text runs as follows:

(§72) In the Name of God, the Most Compassionate. From Muḥammad, the Servant and Apostle of God, to Heraclius, the Ruler of the Byzantine Empire. Peace upon whomever follows the (divine) Guidance. I call upon you to accept Islam. Become Muslim and be saved. God will bring you your reward twofold. When you turn away (from this Call), the sins of (your subjects), the *arīsīyyīn,*[13] will be held against you. "Say: 'O people of the Book, come to a word which is fair between us and you, to wit that we serve no one but God, that we associate nothing with Him, and that we do not take one the other as Lords apart from God'; if they then turn away, say ye: 'Bear witness that we are Muslims.'" (Qur'ān 3.64)

We add the text of the Letter of the Prophet — God's Peace be upon Him — to Khosrau as well:

(§73) In the Name of God, the Most Compassionate. From Muḥammad, the Apostle of God, to Khosrau, the Ruler of the Persian (Sasanid) Empire. Peace upon whomever follows the (divine) Guidance and believes in God and His Apostle and testifies that there is no god but God alone, He has no associate, and (testifies) that Muḥammad is His Servant and His Apostle. I call upon you from God, for I am the Apostle of God to all mankind, to warn those who are alive. True is the word to the infidels: Become Muslim and be saved. When you refuse, the sins of (your subjects), the *Majūs,*[14] will be upon you." (This Tradition is reported) by Ibn Jarīr (Al-Ṭabarī) on the authority of Ibn Isḥāq.

(§74) Al-Bayhaqī quotes the text of the Letter which the Apostle sent to the (Christians) of Najrān:

In the Name of the God of Abraham, Isaac and Jacob. From Muḥammad, the Prophet and Apostle of God to the Bishop and the people of Najrān. Peace upon you. I praise the God of Abraham, Isaac and Jacob. I call upon you to serve God, and not to serve men. I call upon you to let yourselves be ruled by God, and not by men. When you refuse, then a head tax. When you refuse (this, too), be apprised of war. A greeting of Peace.

(§75) (Muḥammad) — God's Peace be upon Him — sent similar Letters to *Al-Muqawqis* (the Ruler of Egypt), to the King of Yamāmah (in Arabia), to Al-Mundhir ibn Sāwī, the Ruler of Bahrein, to Al-Ḥārith ibn Abī Shimr the Ghassanid (King in Northern Arabia), to Al-Ḥārith ibn ᶜAbd al-Kalāl, the Ḥimyārī (King of Southern Arabia), to the King of Oman, and to others.

(§76) The Verse of the Sword (Qur'ān 9.5)

Most Koran commentators have said something about a certain verse from the Koran which they have named the Verse of the Sword (Qur'ān 9.5). This verse runs: "Then when the sacred months have slipped away, slay the polytheists wherever ye find them, seize them, beset them, lie in ambush for them everywhere."

The Qur'ān scholar Ibn Kathīr noted in his commentary on this verse: "Al-Ḍaḥḥāk ibn Muzāḥim said: 'It cancelled every treaty between the Prophet — God's Peace be upon Him — and any infidel, and every contract and every term.' Al-ᶜŪfī said about this verse, on the authority of Ibn ᶜAbbās: 'No contract nor covenant of protection was left to a single infidel since (this) dissolution (of treaty obligations) was revealed.'"

(§77) The Qur'ān scholar Muḥammad ibn Aḥmad ibn Muḥammad ibn Juzayy al-Kalbī, the author of (a Qur'ān commentary entitled) *Tafsīr al-Tashīl li-ᶜUlūm al-Tanzīl,* says: "The abrogation of the command to be at peace with the infidels, to forgive them, to be (passively) exposed to them and to endure their insults preceded here the command to fight them. This makes it superfluous to repeat the abrogation of the command to live in peace with the infidels at each Qur'anic passage (where this is relevant). (Such a command to live in peace with them) is found in 114 verses in 54 surahs. This is all abrogated by His word: "Slay the polytheists wherever ye find them" (Qur'ān 9.5) and "Fighting is prescribed for you" (Qur'ān 2.216).

Al-Ḥusayn ibn Faḍl says: "This is the verse of the sword. It abrogates every verse in the Qur'ān in which suffering the insults of the enemy is mentioned." It is strange indeed that there are those who want to conclude from Qur'ān verses that have been abrogated that fighting and *jihād* are to be forsworn.

(§78) The Imām Abū ᶜAbdallāh Muḥammad Ibn Ḥazm who died in *456* AH says in (his book entitled) *Al-Nāsikh wa-'l-Mansūkh* (The Abrogating and the Abrogated Passages from the Qur'ān), in the Chapter "On Not Attacking the Infidels": "In 114 verses in 48 surahs everything is abrogated by the Word of God —

Exalted and Majestic He is —: 'Slay the polytheists wherever ye find them' (Qur'ān 9.5). We shall discuss this whenever we come across it, if God — Exalted He is — permits." End of quotation.

(§79) The scholar and Imām Abū al-Qāsim Hibbat Allāh ibn Salāmah says on "Slay the polytheists wherever ye find them": "The third verse is indeed the third verse, and it is this verse which is the verse which abrogates. But it abrogates 114 verses from the Qur'ān and then the end of it abrogates the beginning of it, because the verse ends with: 'If they repent and establish the Prayer and pay the Zakāt, then set them free' (Qur'ān 9.5, end of the verse)." (This quotation is taken from) a book (entitled) *Kitāb al-Nāsikh wa-'l-Mansūkh*.

(§80) "So When You Meet Those Who Have Disbelieved, Let There Be Slaughter" (Qur'ān 47.4)

Al-Suddī and Al-Ḍaḥḥāk say: "The Verse of the Sword was abrogated by: 'So when you meet those who have disbelieved, (let there be) slaughter until ye have made havoc of them, bind them fast, then (liberate them) either freely or by ransom' (Qur'ān 47.4). This verse is harsher on the infidels than the Verse of the Sword." Al-Qatāda, however, has the opposite opinion, and I do not know anyone who disagrees with the opinion that it is abrogated except Al-Suyūṭī who says in his book (entitled) *Al-Ittifāq*: "At the time when the Muslims were weak and few in number the command was to endure and to suffer. Then this command was abrogated by making fighting obligatory. In reality this is, however, not really abrogation, but it is to be regarded as 'causing to forget.' Did not God — Exalted He is — say (in Qur'ān 2.106): '. . . or We cause (the Messenger) to forget?' "

The thing that is forgotten is the command to fight, until the time when the Muslims are strong. When, however, the Muslims are weak, the legal ruling is that it is obligatory to endure insults. This weakens a view about which so many are so enthusiastic, namely, that the verse (Qur'ān 47.4) on this point is abrogated by the Verse of the Sword (9.5). It is not like that. On the contrary, it is caused to be forgotten.

(Al-Suyūṭī) also said: "Some mention that verses like (Qur'ān 2.109 which runs): 'So overlook and pay no attention until God interveneth with His Command' do not address a specific group of people at a specific time and with a specific aim. Hence (the command embodied in this verse) is not abrogated but it is postponed until a certain time." Here ends the quotation from Al-Suyūṭī.

(§81) In spite of Al-Suyūṭī's disagreement with all the preceding opinions, there is no room for doubt that to adopt the first opinion is correct. Moreover, whoever thinks that the view that nonabrogation of the verses of pardon and forgiveness (like 2.109) means that we are free to neglect the two duties of (1) *jihād* and (2) urging to what is reputable and prohibiting what is not, is mistaken.

It certainly also does not mean that the duty of *jihād* has come to an end, because the Apostle of God — God's Peace be upon Him — says: "*Jihād* continues *(māḍin)* until the day of Resurrection." Professor Dr. ᶜAbd al-Wahhāb Khallāf says in his book (entitled) *ᶜIlm Uṣūl al-Fiqh* (The Science of the "Roots" of the Islamic Legal System) on p. 227: "Since it continues until the Day of Resurrection this indicates that it will remain (a duty) as long as the World remains."

To do away with *jihād* with the argument that it was caused to be forgotten does not only put an end to fighting for this religion but it also puts an end to the intention *(nīyah)* of fighting for this religion. The danger of that is apparent from the saying of the Apostle of God — God's Peace be upon Him —: "Someone who does not fight for his religion, or someone whose soul does not talk to him encouraging him to fight for his religion, dies as a pagan."

It is, moreover, generally agreed upon that in order to wage *jihād* the Muslims must have strength. But how can this strength be realized when you abolish the duty of *jihād?* Does not God — Praised and Exalted He is — say: "If they intended to go forth, they would make some preparation for it; but God is adverse to their being stirred up and hath made them laggards" (Qur'ān 9.46). The fact that you are not willing to go forth has as a consequence your neglecting to prepare (for it). From where now will a Muslim who has abolished the duty of *jihād* get the means for obtaining strength? Does not the Apostle of God say: "When people yearn for money and wealth, and conclude their bargains upon credit, and neglect the waging of *jihād* for God's cause, and hold on to the tails of their cows, then God will send a plague upon them from heaven, and He will not remove it from them until they return to their religion?"

(§82) Muslim Positions on Fighting

Muslim armies in the course of the centuries have been small and ill-prepared, encountering armies double their size. Some argue that this was a prerogative of the Apostle of God — God's Peace be upon Him —, and His Noble Companions. The refutation of this view is that God promised victory to the Muslims, lasting as long as the Heavens and the Earth last. Maybe you know about what happened (centuries after the days of the Apostle) to Ẓahīr al-Dīn Bābar who faced the Hindu King Rānā Sanjā[15] with an army of 20,000 while the army of the Hindu King was 200,000. The Muslim Commander was victorious after he repented from drinking wine. . . . There are many others like him.

(§83) The Meccan and the Medinan Society

There are those who allege that we live in a Meccan society, thereby endeavoring to obtain for themselves the permission to abandon the waging of *jihād* for God's cause. Whoever puts himself in a Meccan society in order to abandon the religious duty of *jihād*, must also refrain from fasting and prayer (since the Revelations about these duties were only given after the Apostle had emigrated from Mecca to Medina in 622 AD), and he must enrich himself by asking usury since usury was not forbidden until the Medinan period.

The truth of the matter is that (the period in) Mecca is the period of the genesis of the Call (to Islam). The Word of God — Praised and Exalted He is — (Qur'ān 5.3): "Today I have perfected your religion for you, and have completed my goodness towards you, and have approved Islam as your religion," abrogates these defeatist ideas that have to be substantiated by the argument that we are Meccans. We are not at the beginning of something, as the Prophet—God's Peace be upon Him—was at the beginning (of the establishment of Islam), but we (have to) accept the Revelation in its final form.

We do not live in a Meccan society, and neither do we live in a Medinan society. When you wish to know in what kind of society we live, consult the paragraph on "The House in Which We Live" (§18).

(§84) Fighting is Now a Duty upon All Muslims

When God—Praised and Exalted He is—made fasting obligatory, he said (Qur'ān 2.183): "Fasting is prescribed for you." In regard to fighting He said (Qur'ān 2.216): "Fighting is prescribed for you." This refutes the view of whoever says that *jihād* is indeed a duty and then goes on by saying: "When I have fulfilled the duty of engaging in missionary activities for Islam *(da^cwah)*, then I have fulfilled the duty (of *jihād*), because (engagement in missionary activities for Islam) is *jihād* too." However, the (real character of this) duty is clearly spelled out in the text of the Qur'ān: It is fighting, which means confrontation and blood.

The question now is: When is *jihād* an individual duty? *Jihād* becomes an individual duty in three situations:

(§85) First, when two armies meet and their ranks are facing each other, it is forbidden to those who are present to leave, and it becomes an individual duty to remain standing, because God—Exalted He is—says: "O ye who have believed, when ye meet a hostile party, stand firm, and call God frequently to mind" (Qur'ān 8.45) and also: "O ye who have believed, when ye meet those who have disbelieved moving into battle, turn them not your backs" (Qur'ān 8.15).

Second, when the infidels descend upon a country, it becomes an individual duty for its people to fight them and drive them away.

Third, when the Imām calls upon a people to fight, they must depart into battle, for God—Exalted He is—says (Qur'ān 9.38–

39): "O ye who have believed, what is the matter with you? When one says to you: 'March out in the way of God,' ye are weighed down to the ground; are you so satisfied with this nearer life as to neglect the Hereafter? The enjoyment of this nearer life is in comparison with the Hereafter only a little thing. If ye do not march out He will inflict upon you a painful punishment, and will substitute (for you) another people; ye will not injure Him at all; God over everything has power." The Apostle — God's Peace be upon Him — says: "When you are called upon to fight, then hasten."

With regard to the lands of Islam, the enemy lives right in the middle of them. The enemy even has got hold of the reins of power, for this enemy is (none other than) these rulers who have (illegally) seized the Leadership of the Muslims. Therefore, waging *jihād* against them is an individual duty, in addition to the fact that Islamic *jihād* today requires a drop of sweat from every Muslim.

(§87) Know that when *jihād* is an individual duty, there is no (need to) ask permission of (your) parents to leave to wage *jihād*, as the jurists have said; it is thus similar to prayer and fasting.

(§88) The Aspects of Jihād are Not Successive Phases of Jihād

It is clear that today *jihād* is an individual duty of every Muslim. Nevertheless we find that there are those who argue that they need to educate their own souls, and that *jihād* knows successive phases; and that they are still in the phase of *jihād* against their own soul. They offer as proof the doctrine of Imām Ibn al-Qayyim, who distinguished three aspects in *jihād:*

1. *Jihād* against one's own soul
2. *Jihād* against the Devil
3. *Jihād* against the infidels and the hypocrites

(§89) This argument shows either complete ignorance or excessive cowardice, because Ibn Al-Qayyim (only) distinguished *aspects* in *jihād,* he did not divide it into successive phases. Otherwise we would have to suspend the waging of *jihād* against the Devil until we finished the phase of *jihād* against our own soul. The reality is that the three (aspects) are aspects (only) that follow a straight parallel course. We, in our turn, do not deny that the strongest of us in regard to faith, and the most zealous of us in regard to waging *jihād* against his own soul is the one (of us) who is the most steadfast.

Whoever studies the Biography (of Muḥammad) will find that whenever (a state) of *jihād* was proclaimed, everybody used to rush off for God's cause, even perpetrators of great sins and those who had (only) recently adopted Islam.

It is reported that (once) a man embraced Islam during the fighting and fell in the battle, thus dying a martyr, and the Apostle — God's Peace be upon Him — said: "A small work, a great reward."

(§90) (There is also) the story about Abū Miḥjan al-Thaqafī (who was guilty of a great sin since he was) addicted to wine, while his bravery in the war against Persia was famous.

Ibn al-Qayyim also made mention that the Tradition: "'We returned from the Small *Jihād* to the Great *Jihād*' — and then someone said: 'What is the Great *Jihād*, O Apostle of God?' — and then (Muḥammad) said: 'The *jihād* against the soul,'" is a fabricated Tradition, see *(the book by Ibn Al-Qayyim entitled *Kitāb*) *Al-Manār**.

The only reason for inventing this Tradition is to reduce the value of fighting with the Sword, so as to distract the Muslims from fighting the infidels and the hypocrites.

(§91) Fear of Failure

It is said that we fear to establish the State (because) after one or two days a reaction will occur that will put to an end everything we have accomplished.

The refutation of this (view) is that the establishment of an Islamic State is the execution of a divine Command. We are not responsible for its results. Someone who is so stupid as to hold this view — which has no use except to hinder Muslims from the execution of their religious duty by establishing the Rule of God—forgets that when the Rule of the Infidel has fallen everything will be in the hands of the Muslims, whereupon *(bi-mā)* the downfall of the Islamic State will become inconceivable. Furthermore, the Laws of Islam are not too weak to be able to subject everyone who spreads corruption in the land and rebels against the Command of God. Moreover, the Laws of God are all justice and will be welcomed by everyone, even by people who do not know Islam.

In order to clarify the position of the hypocrites in their enmity towards the Muslims and to put at peace the hearts of those who fear (this) failure (we quote) the Word of the Lord in Surah 59, (verses 11 and 12): "Hast thou not seen those who have played the hypocrite saying to their brethren the People of the Book who have disbelieved: 'Surely, if ye are expelled, we shall go out with you, we shall never obey anyone in regard to you, and if ye are attacked in war, we shall help you?' God testifieth that they are lying. If they are expelled, they will assuredly not go out with them, and if they are attacked in war, they will help them, and if they do not help them, they will certainly turn their backs in flight and then they will not be helped (and gain a victory)."

This is God's promise. When the hypocrites see that the power is in the ranks of Islam they will come back in submission, so we will not be deceived by these voices that will quickly fade away and be extinguished. . . . The position of the hypocrites will be equal to that of the enemies of Islam. God—Exalted He is—says: "(O ye who have believed), if ye help God He will help you (and give you victories) and He will set firm your feet" (Qur'ān 47.7).

(§92) The Command

There are some who excuse themselves (from participating in *jihād*) because of the lack of a commander who will lead the course of *jihād*. There are also people who make (the execution of) the divine command to *jihād* dependent upon the presence of a commander or a Caliph. . . .

The people who hold these opinions are the same people who have made (proper) leadership impossible and who have stopped the course of *jihād*. Yet the Apostle — God's Peace be upon Him — urges the Muslims, according to the texts of His Traditions, to entrust the (military) leadership to one of them.

Abū Dāwud transmits in the chapter on *jihād* (in his Collection of Traditions) that the Apostle — God's Peace be upon Him — says: "When three (of you) go out on a journey, then make one of them the commander *(amīr)*." From (the text of) this (Tradition) one can conclude that the leadership over the Muslims is (always) in their own hands if only they make this manifest. (The Apostle) — God's Peace be upon Him — says: "Whosoever is put at the head of a group in which there is someone who is more agreeable to God than him himself, is disloyal to God and His Apostle and the Muslim Community." This Tradition is transmitted by Al-Ḥākim. Its reliability is pointed out by Al-Suyūṭī.

(§93) (This means that the command) must go to the best Muslim. (The Apostle) — God's Peace be upon Him — says to Abū Dharr: "You are weak. This is (to our) security!" (The command) must be in the hands of the strongest, which is a relative matter. Our conclusion is that the leader of the Muslims. . . .[16]

Whoever alleges that the (proper) leadership has been lost has no case, because the Muslims can (always) produce leaders from amongst themselves. If there is something lacking in the leadership, well, there is nothing that cannot be acquired. It is (simply) impossible that the leadership disappears (from amongst us).

(§94) Sometimes we may find a *fiqh* scholar who does not know anything about modern circumstances and (military) command and organization; and sometimes we find the opposite, but all this[17] does not discharge us of the duty from organizing proper leadership, by getting the most suitable from amongst us into the position of leadership, through mutual consultation *(shūrā)*. The qualities which such a leader may lack can be supplemented.

So now there can be no valid excuse for any Muslim for neglecting the duty of *jihād* which has been thrown upon his shoulder. We must seriously begin to organize *jihād* activities to return Islam to this nation and to establish an Islamic State, and to exterminate the idols who are only human and who have not (yet) found in front of them anyone who has subdued them with the Command of God — Praised and Exalted He is.

(§95) The Oath of Allegiance to Fight until Death

Al-Bukhārī reports on the authority of (Abū) Salmah—May God be Pleased with him—that he said: "I gave an oath of allegiance to the Prophet—May God's Peace be upon Him—and afterwards I went off to the shade of a tree. When people crowded around Him He said: 'O Ibn al-Akwaᶜ, don't you give the oath of allegiance?' I said: 'But I did, O Apostle of God.' He said: 'Again.' Then I gave Him my oath of allegiance for a second time. I said to him: 'O Abū Salmah, what was the content of your oath of allegiance, on that day?' He said: '(To obey the Apostle) till death.'" (This Tradition) is also transmitted by Muslim and Al-Tirmidhī.

Al-Bukhārī also transmits,[18] p. 415, on the authority of ᶜAbdallāh ibn Zayd—May God be Pleased with him—that he said: "In the period of (the Battle of) Al-Ḥarrah[19] someone came and said: 'Ibn Ḥanẓalah makes people swear an oath of allegiance (to obey him) till death.' Then he said: 'I shall not give such an oath to anybody after (I gave it to) the Apostle of God—God's Peace be upon Him—.'" Muslim transmits (this Tradition), too, in exactly the same words, on p. 5,[20] and so does Al-Bayhaqī.

(§96) The report mentioned before (in §95) informs (us) of the permissibility of the Oath of Allegiance till Death. We shall, in this context, not study the exact case of ᶜAbdallāh ibn Zayd.

There is (however), a difference between the Oath of Allegiance till Death and the Absolute Oath of Allegiance to only the Caliph. This does not mean that the commander of an army does not have to be obeyed, because the Apostle of God—God's Peace be upon Him—says: "Whoever obeys me, obeys God. Whosoever disobeys me, disobeys God. Whoever obeys his commander, obeys me. Whoever disobeys his commander, disobeys me." There is no disagreement (on the reliability of the Tradition).

(§97) On the authority of Ibn ᶜAbbās (who transmits a Tradition concerning) the Word of God: "Obey God and obey the Apostle and those of you who have the command" (Qur'ān 4.59): This verse was revealed with regard to ᶜAbdallāh ibn Ḥudhāfah whom the Prophet put at the head of a body of troops, that is, he was Commander (in a battle that has to be regarded as) *jihād (kān amīr jihād).*

(§98) Incitement to Jihād for the Cause of God

A Muslim has the duty to prepare himself for *jihād* for God's cause only, for the Apostle of God — God's Peace be upon Him — says: "God turns towards whomever goes out for His cause. He will not send someone out but to wage *jihād* for His cause and for belief in Him[21] and for accepting the truthfulness of His Apostle. He guarantees that He will (either) make him enter Paradise or will make him come back to his home from which he went out with whatever reward or booty he obtained." There is no disagreement (on the reliability of this Tradition).

(§99) (The Apostle) — God's Peace be upon Him — says: "Whoever truthfully asks for martyrdom will be put in the (heavenly) abodes of the martyrs even if he dies in his bed." (This Tradition is) reported by Muslim and Al-Bayhaqī on the authority of Abū Hurayrah.

"(Once) a man came to the Apostle of God and said to Him: 'Show me a work which equals *jihād*.' The Apostle of God answered: 'There is none.' He said: 'Are you capable of entering your place of prayer to stand up (and pray) without pause and to fast without breaking this fast during the whole period the Fighter for the cause of God *(mujāhid)* has gone out?' He said: 'Who would be able to do so?' Then Abū Hurayrah said: 'The horse of someone who participates in *jihād* — whenever it prances in its tether this is booked as a good deed.'" (This Tradition is) transmitted by Al-Bukhārī.[22]

(The Apostle) — God's Peace be upon Him — says: "A martyr has six virtues in the eyes of God. He will be forgiven upon the first drop of blood. His seat will be in Paradise. He will be free from the punishment of the grave. He will be safe from the Great Fright. He will be dressed in the garb of faith. He will marry the heavenly dark-eyed virgins. He will intercede for 70 of his relatives." (Transmitted by) Al-Tirmidhī.[23]

(§100) The Punishment for Neglecting Jihād

Neglecting *jihād* is the cause of the lowness, humiliation, division and fragmentation in which the Muslims live today. The word of the Lord—Exalted and Majestic He is—about them has come true: "O ye who have believed, what is the matter with you? When one says to you: 'March out in the way of God,' ye are weighed down to the ground; are you so satisfied with this nearer life as to neglect the Hereafter? The enjoyment of this nearer life is in comparison with the Hereafter only a little thing. If ye do not march out He will inflict upon you a painful punishment, and will substitute for you another people; ye will not injure Him at all. God over everything has power." (This quotation is taken) from Surah 9 (verses 38–39).

(§101) Ibn Kathīr says in his commentary to these verses: "This passage was revealed in order to reprimand those who stayed behind and did not go out with the Apostle of God—God's Peace be upon Him—in the Raid of Tabūk when the harvest was ready. (Yet) He went out *(inṭalaq)* in extreme heat at the height of the summer. Then God—Exalted He is—said: "O ye who have believed, what is the matter with you? When one says to you: 'March out in the way of God,' ye are weighed down to the ground";—this means that when you are called to *jihād* for the cause of God 'ye are weighed down to the ground,' and this means 'you were lazy and turned away to an abode of ease and rest and ripe fruits.'

"'Are you so satisfied with this nearer life as to neglect the Hereafter?' means 'What is the matter with you? Did you act like this[24] out of love for the World, instead of (love for) the Hereafter?' Next God urges them to abstain from the world and reminds them of the pleasures of the Hereafter, saying: 'The enjoyment of this nearer life is in comparison with the Hereafter only a little thing.' Next God—Exalted He is—threatens those who neglect *jihād* saying: 'If ye do not march out He will inflict upon you a painful punishment.' Ibn ᶜAbbās said: 'Once the Apostle of God—God's Peace be upon Him—convoked a tribe of bedouins to war but they found this burdensome and turned away from Him. Then God withheld all water from them, and this was their punishment.'"

"'He will substitute for you another people': that is (another people which will work) for the victory of His Prophet and the establishment of His religion. God also says (Qur'ān 47.38): 'If ye turn away, He will substitute for you another people; and then they will not be like you.' "Ye will not injure Him at all" means that you will not at all harm God by turning away from *jihād* and by your unwillingness to follow Him.'"

(§102) (The Apostle) — God's Peace be upon Him — says: "When people yearn for money and wealth and conclude their bargains upon credit, and neglect to participate in *jihād,* and hold on to the tails of their cows, then a Plague from Heaven will be sent upon them, and this Plague will not be lifted from them until they turn back to their religion."

A Muslim must not be content today to be in the ranks of women. Did the Apostle of God — God's Peace be upon Him — not say about women that their *jihād* is the Greater and the Smaller Pilgrimage?

(§103) Legal Difficulties and their Refutation

There are some who fear to enter into this kind of fighting, arguing that those with whom they will be confronted are armies in which there are Muslims and infidels. So, how can we fight the Muslims? Does the Apostle of God — God's Peace be upon Him — not say that both the one who kills and the one who is killed will go to the Fire?

Shaykh al-Islām Ibn Taymīyah discusses the same problem, in one of the questions (he gives an answer to) in his *Al-Fatāwā al-Kubrā,* no. 517 (p. 298): "On Soldiers Who Refuse to Fight the Mongols, saying that there are amongst them soldiers who are forced to go out (to fight)." In his answer Ibn Taymīyah says (p. 299, line 4): "Whoever doubts whether he has to fight them is most ignorant of the religion of Islam. Since fighting them is obligatory, they have to be fought, even if there is amongst them someone who has been forced to join their ranks. On this the Muslims are in agreement. Al-ᶜAbbās (once) said, when he was taken prisoner on the Day of the Battle of Badr: 'O Apostle of God, I was forced to go out.' Then the Apostle of God said: 'Outwardly you were against us. Only God knows what is in your heart.'

(line 7) The leading scholars of Islam agree that when an army of infidels protects itself[25] by using the Muslim prisoners it took, and the Muslims (in the army of the infidels) fear that harm may befall them when they do not fight, then they must fight even if this leads to the killing of the Muslims who were made prisoners of war and were enlisted in the army of the enemy, even if (the army of infidels is not strong enough and) the Muslims have nothing to fear (from it).

(line 10) The scholars of Islam have two well-established opinions on the permissibility of the fighting which causes the killing of these Muslims (who are enlisted in the army of the infidels). When they are killed, these Muslims are martyrs, and the prescribed *jihād* must not be neglected on account of those who are killed as martyrs. When the Muslims fight the unbelievers, a Muslim who is killed is a martyr, and someone who is killed while he is in reality a Muslim who cannot show this and who hence does not deserve to be killed on account of his religion, is (also) a martyr.

(§104) (line 13) There is a reliable Tradition which is transmitted in (both the Collections entitled) *Al-Ṣaḥīḥ*, on the authority of the Prophet—May God's Peace be upon Him—that He said: 'This house is raided by an army. When this army is in the desert the moon will eclipse upon them.' Then they said to Him: 'O Apostle of God, there are some amongst this army who have been forced to join them.' Then He said: 'They will be called (on the Last Day) according to their intentions. When the punishment which God sends down upon the army (of the infidels) who raid the Muslims comes down upon those amongst them who are forced and upon those of them who are not, how (much more will this be the case with) the punishment which God sends them through the hands of the believers?' Does God not say (Qur'ān 9.52): 'Do ye wait for anything in our case but one of the two goods (i.e., victory or death leading to future reward), while in your case we wait for God afflicting you with punishment, either from Himself or at our hands?'

(line 18) We cannot know who are the ones who were forced into the army of the infidels. We cannot differentiate between those who are and those who are not. When we kill them in accordance with the Command of God we are both rewarded and excused. They, however, will be judged according to their intentions. Whoever is forced into an army of infidels is not able to withdraw from fighting. He will be reunited with his fellow Muslims on the Day of Resurrection. So, when such a person is killed for standing by his religion, this is not greater than the killing of someone from the camp of the Muslims.

(line 21) When someone flees (from the army of infidels) some people regard fighting him in the same category as fighting the rebels designated as *Al-Bughāh* who are guilty of allegorizing religion.

(§105) Is it permissible when part of the army of these people is potentially refractory, to pursue those amongst them who run away from the battlefield, to kill the prisoners of war taken from them and to kill their wounded? About this question there are two well-established views amongst the scholars of Islam. Some say that this must not be done because a herald from the army of ᶜAlī Ibn Abū Ṭālib announced on the Day of the Battle of the Camel that someone who fled from the battlefield would not be pursued, the wounded would not be finished off and the prisoners of war would not be killed. Others say (however) that this must be done, because the Battle of the Camel (is not a good precedent to follow) because there was no potentially refractory group in the army (of ᶜAlī's enemies).

(p. 300, line 1) With "fighting" is meant: to push them back. When they have been pushed back already, there is no need to continue to do, as is the case when someone attacks *(ṣā'il).* It is reported that at the Battle of the Camel and at the Battle at Ṣiffīn their situation was not like this, and those who regard them as (the rebels designated as) *Al-Bughāh* who are guilty of allegorizing religion make these two views (mentioned before) applicable to them. However, they (the Mongols) are not (to be regarded) as (the rebels designated as) *Al-Bughāh* who are guilty of allegorizing religion. They are, on the other hand, to be classified in the same category as the dangerously heretical Khārijīs and the people who refused to pay the *zakāt* tax, and the people of the town al-Ṭā'if,[26] and others like them who have to be fought on account of their rebellion against the prescripts of Islam. This position has not been clear to many of the scholars of Islam." (Here ends the passage quoted from Ibn Taymīyah).

(§106) The Proper Method of Fighting

With the advance of time and the development of mankind emerges a question we must ask ourselves. There is no doubt that the modern methods of fighting differ to a certain extent from the methods of fighting in the time of the Prophet— God's Peace be upon Him —. What is the Muslim's method of fighting in this day and age? Can he use his own intellect and his own individual judgment?

(§107) Deceiving the Infidels: One of the Arts of Fighting in Islam

(The Apostle) says: "War is deceit," and Al-Nawawī remarks in his commentary on this Tradition: "Scholars are agreed on the permissibility of deceiving the infidels in war however possible, except when this would imply a breach of a treaty or of a promise of safety (from attack), for then it is not allowed (to deceive them)." It is, however, a fact that there is no treaty between us and them since they wage war against the religion of God—Praised and Exalted He is—and (therefore) Muslims are free to choose the most suitable method of fighting so that deception, which is victory with the fewest losses and by the easiest means possible, is realized.

(§108) The Method of Fighting in the Attack of the Aḥzāb

After the Jewish leaders were successful in inciting unbelieving groups *(al-aḥzāb)* against the Prophet— God's Peace be upon Him — and His Call to Islam, and the situation had become dangerous, the Muslims quickly conceived a unique plan of which the Arabs had not heard before, for they knew only of fighting on exposed battlefields. This plan was suggested by (Salmān) al-Fārisī[27] and it was to dig a deep trench which would encircle Medina from the side of the plain and make a division between the defenders and the attackers. (Thus) the method of fighting is not a revelation nor (is it) an established custom *(sunnah)* but the Muslim has the right to use his own intellect, to organize and to deliberate.

(§109) Lying to the Enemy

The permissibility of lying is clear from the Tradition, in three cases. "Al-Ṭabarī said: 'In respect to lying in war, oblique modes of speech[28] are permitted, that is, without in fact lying, which is not allowed.' This is what he said, and it is evident that lying is essentially permitted, but it is better to limit oneself to speaking ambiguously, and God knows best." (This quotation is) taken intact from Al-Nawawī's commentary.

(§110) Islamic Planning

By studying the night expeditions (wherein the Muslims marched at night and lay in concealment during the day) the Muslims can extract Islamic plans and battle deceptions whose principles were practiced by many Muslims, and we mention by way of example:

1) the night expedition to murder Kaᶜb ibn al-Ashraf in the year 3 of the Hijrah, transmitted in the *Ṣaḥīḥ* of Al-Bukhārī on the authority of Jābir ibn ᶜAbdallāh: "The Apostle — God's Peace be upon Him — said: 'Who will go for Kaᶜb ibn al-Ashraf, for he has wronged God and His Apostle?' Then Muḥammad ibn Maslamah stood and said: 'O Apostle of God, do you wish me to kill him?' He said: 'Yes.' (Muḥammad ibn Maslamah then) said: 'Allow me to say something'—that is, he asked permission of the Prophet, God's Peace be upon Him, to say things contradictory to the belief in God so as to feign disbelief in front of Kaᶜb ibn al-Ashraf, and He gave him this permission.

(§111) (The Apostle) — God's Peace be upon Him — said: 'Say (what you want),' so Muḥammad ibn Maslamah went to Kaᶜb ibn al-Ashraf and said that this man—meaning the Prophet, God's Peace be upon Him—has asked us for a tithe and is burdening us.[29] The literal sense of this is to refuse the tithe and to transgress against the Prophet— God's Peace be upon Him—and this is

Unbelief. This conveys the meaning that a Muslim may pretend to genuine friendship with the enemy in war, even if the matter goes so far that idolatry and disbelief are feigned as well.

(§112) 'I have come to you to ask you for a loan.' (Ka^{c}b) said: 'You too then became weary[30] of him.' (Muḥammad ibn Maslamah) said: 'We have followed him (i.e., Muḥammad) and we wish not to leave him until we see what becomes of him, so we wanted you to lend us a camel's load or two (of dates).' Ka^{c}b agreed, saying: 'Give me a security,' whereupon they[31] said: 'What do you want?' He said: 'Give me your wives as security.' They said: 'How can we give our wives as security when you are the handsomest of the Arabs?' He said: 'Give me your sons as security?' They said: 'How can we give you our sons as security? They will be reviled when people would say that they were given as security for a camel's load or two of dates. That is a disgrace for us, but we will give you our *cuirasses*,' that is, arms. Thereupon he made an appointment with Ka^{c}b to come to him. He went at night, taking with him Abū Nā'ilah, the foster brother of Ka^{c}b, and Ka^{c}b summoned them to the fort and he too went there.

His wife said to him: 'Where are you going at this hour?' and he said: 'It is only Muḥammad ibn Maslamah and my brother Abū Nā'ilah. Another (transmitter) than ^{c}Amr said that she said to him: 'I hear a voice as if *blood* were dripping from it.' He said: 'It is only my brother, Muḥammad ibn Maslamah, and my foster brother Abū Nā'ilah. Verily, if someone noble is summoned to attack at night, he does not refuse.'

(§113) (So the transmitter of this Tradition) says, and (Ka'b) admitted Muḥammad ibn Maslamah with two men who were said to belong to Sufyān. ^{c}Amr names them as Al-Ḥārith ibn Aws and ^{c}Abbād ibn Bishr.[32] ^{c}Amr (then continues) saying: 'Then Muḥammad ibn Maslamah said: 'When he comes I will make a motion with his hair to smell it, so when you see me get a hold of his head, then take him and strike at him.'—That was a way to get into a position to kill him since he was large-bodied and sturdy—."

In this story are useful lessons in the great art of fighting. Some orientalists have claimed, along with those in whose hearts is the sickness of doubt (cf. Qur'ān 2.9), that the murder of Ka^{c}b ibn al-Ashraf was perfidious and treacherous to him. The refutation to them is that that infidel had broken his pledge and devoted all his efforts to harm the Muslims.

"The Jews came to the Prophet — God's Peace be upon Him — after the murder of Kaᶜb ibn al-Ashraf, and said: O Muḥammad, something happened to our friend this night,' — that is, he was killed —, 'but he was one of our chiefs, now killed by assassination, without a crime or misdeed of which we know.' (The Apostle) — God's Peace be upon Him — replied: If he had remained still like the others with the same opinions remain still, then he would not have been assassinated. He, however, wronged Us and mocked Us with poetry, and not one of you has ever done this without having the sword as punishment! (Quoted from a book entitled) *Al-Ṣārim al-Maslūl ᶜalā Shāṭim al-Rasūl* by Ibn Taymīyah, p. 71.

2) (§114) The night expedition of ᶜAbdallāh to Abū Sufyān, which was in the year 4 of the Hijrah. The occasion of this was that the news had reached the Prophet that Shaᶜbān ibn Khālid al-Hudhallī was residing in *ᶜUranah* and that he was assembling crowds to wage war against the Muslims. Then the Apostle of God — God's Peace be upon Him — ordered ᶜAbdallāh ibn Unays al-Jihnī to kill (Shaᶜbān). ᶜAbdallāh said that he said: "O Apostle of God, describe him to me so that I know him." Then the Apostle — God's Peace be upon Him — said: "When you see him, the Devil will remind you. That will be the sign of what is between you and him." He said: "I asked permission of the Apostle of God — God's Peace be upon Him — to say (to him whatever was needed) — this is the same permission Muḥammad ibn Maslamah asked — and He permitted me. Then He said to me: "Tell him that you are from the tribe of Banū Khuzāᶜah." — This was a lie but that is allowed —.

(§115) ᶜAbdallāh said: "I knew him by the description which the Apostle of God — God's Peace be upon Him — had given me and I was afraid of him. I said to myself that the Apostle of God had been right." ᶜAbdallāh further said: "It was time for the afternoon prayer, he had entered already when I saw him and I feared that there would be an exchange of words between me and him which would keep me from my prayer, so I performed my prayer while walking towards him gesturing with my head. When I reached him, he said: 'From which tribe is this man?' I said: 'From Banū Khuzāᶜah. I heard of your gathering to attack Muḥammad so I came to be with you.'—In this expression is a feigning of friendship—. He said: 'Sure, I am assembling to attack him.' ᶜAbdallāh said: 'Then I walked with him and talked to him and he liked my talk, and I recited (poetry) for him and said: What a strange new religion Muḥammad has created, it separates us from our forefathers and calls their virtues stupidities.—This speech is Unbelief.

Abū Sufyān said that he (Muḥammad) had not (yet) met anyone who resembled *him,* and, leaning on a walking stick, he crushed the ground, until he reached his tent. His companions then left him for homes nearby which encircled (his tent). Then he said: 'Come on, brother of Khuzāᶜah,' and I neared him and he said: 'Sit down.' "

ᶜAbdallāh (continued his story) saying: "So I sat with him until, when the people had become quiet and slept, I surprised him and killed him. I cut off his head and left, leaving his women[34] bent over him. When I reached Medina, I found the Apostle of God—God's peace be upon him—and the moment He saw me He said: 'May you thrive!' I said: 'May you thrive, O Apostle of God!' Then I placed the head in front of Him and told Him my story."

3) (§116) The story of Nuᶜaym ibn Masᶜūd in the attack of the *Aḥzāb* (the coalition of anti-Muḥammad tribes). When Nuᶜaym ibn Masᶜūd *became Muslim, he was ordered to conceal his conversion* and was sent back to the infidels in order to sow dissension between them.

Nuᶜaym went to (the Jewish Medinan tribe) Banū Qurayẓah and said to them (pretending to give) friendly advice: "Do not fight together with those people—meaning the (Meccan pagan tribes) Quraysh and Ghaṭafān—without taking hostages from among their chiefs as security who will then be in your hands." That was after he had convinced them that (the Meccans of) Quraysh and Ghaṭafān as such did not belong to the people of Medina (as the Qurayẓah did) and, should something happen, (these Meccan tribes) would stick to their own people and leave (the Qurayẓah at the mercy of) the Prophet — God's Peace be upon Him — . They said to him: "You have a point there."

(§117) Then he went to the Quraysh and informed them that the Jews of Banū Qurayẓah regretted their alliance with them and had sent messengers to Muḥammad, saying: "Do you want us to bring to you (some of the) leaders of these two tribes (Quraysh and Ghaṭafān) so that you can behead them?" Then he went to the Ghaṭafān and said the same.

Then Abū Sufyān and the chiefs of the Ghaṭafān sent to Banū Qurayẓah (a certain) ᶜIkrimah ibn Abī Jahl at the head of a group made up of men from the Quraysh and the Ghaṭafān. These said to Banū Qurayẓah: "Go out early tomorrow morning to battle with us against Muḥammad." Thereupon Banū Qurayẓah answered: "That is a Saturday on which we can do nothing. Also we will not fight together with you (against Muḥammad) if you do not give us some of your men as hostages who will be in our hands, as a surety for us, for we fear that you will scatter to your lands should the fighting become too much for you."

When the messengers returned, the Quraysh and the Ghaṭafān said: "By God, it is true why Nuᶜaym ibn Masᶜūd spoke about. We will not hand over a single man to you." Then Banū Qurayẓah said: "The thing which Nuᶜaym mentioned is true. . . ."

In this way Nuᶜaym arranged the split in the ranks of the coalition of unbelieving *Aḥzāb.*

An Important Point

The permissibility of a Muslim penetrating into the ranks of the infidels even if that is to the advantage of the Muslims. Ibn Taymīyah says in the chapter on *Jihād,* p. 296:

(§118) "Muslim transmitted in his (Collection of Traditions entitled) *Al-Ṣaḥīḥ,* on the authority of the Prophet — God's Peace be upon Him — the story of the people of the Trench, wherein (is told of) the youth who was ordered to kill himself for the benefit of the religion, and therefore the four Imāms permit a Muslim to penetrate into the ranks of the infidels even if he considered it probable that they would kill him, when this (penetration) is to the advantage of the Muslims."

What Ibn Taymīyah (here) says means that it is permissible for a Muslim to penetrate into the ranks of the infidel army even though this will lead to his death before he can see with his own eyes the advantage of this penetration.

(§119) The Summons (to Islam) before the Battle

The permissibility of attacking without warning the infidels who have been summoned to accept Islam. The Imām Muslim narrated on the authority of Ibn ᶜAdī who said: "I wrote to Nāfiᶜ asking him about the summons (to Islam) before the battle, and he answered me, writing that that was in the beginning of Islam. The Apostle of God—God's Peace be upon Him—had attacked the Banū al-Muṣṭaliq when they were unaware and their livestock was being given water, and their warriors were killed and taken as captives, and I think Yaḥyā (an earlier transmitter of this Tradition) said that (a certain) Juwayrīyah, or Al-Battah, the daughter of Al-Ḥārith, was wounded on that day.[35]

(§120) Al-Nawawī's commentary: This Tradition demonstrates the permissibility of attacking the infidels who have been summoned to Islam without warning of attack, and concerning this issue there are three schools of thought, reported by *Al-Māzarī and the Judge.* The first: the warning of attack is absolutely necessary, Mālik and others said, and this (view) is weak.

The second: it is absolutely not necessary, and this is weaker than the first (view), or even invalid.

The third: it is necessary if the summons to Islam did not reach them, and it is not necessary if it did reach them but (in this case) it is recommended (only), and this is the correct viewpoint, pronounded by Nāfiᶜ, a client of Ibn ᶜUmar, Al-Ḥasan al-Baṣrī, Al-Thawrī, Al-Layth, Al-Shāfiᶜī, Abū Thawr, Ibn al-Mundhir, and most others. Ibn al-Mundhir said: It is the opinion of the majority of the scholars. Here ends the quotation from Al-Nawawī's commentary on Muslim.[36]

(§121) The Permissibility of Attacking the Infidels at Night and Firing at Them Even if it Leads to Killing Their Dependents. Attacking at Night.

On the authority of Ibn ᶜAbbās on the authority of Al-Ṣaᶜb ibn Jaththāmah, who said: "I said: 'O Apostle of God, when *attacking at night* we hit the dependents of the polytheists.—'Dependents': their children—. He then said: 'They are part of them.' " This Tradition is transmitted by Muslim.

The commentary: The Apostle of God—God's Peace be upon Him—was asked to give an opinion about the children of the polytheists who were *attacked at night* and some of their women and children were killed, whereupon He said: 'They are part of their fathers,' that is, there is no objection to it because the rules applying to their fathers pertain to them as well, in inheritance, marriage, retaliation, blood-money, and other things.

This means: when they do not do it on purpose without need for it (it is allowed to kill these dependents). End of the quotation from Al-Nawawī's commentary on Muslim, Chapter on *Jihād*.

(§122) To Refrain from Aiming at Killing Women, Monks, and Old Men

On the authority of Ibn ᶜUmar: "A woman was found killed on one of the military campaigns of the Prophet—God's Peace be upon Him—, whereupon the Apostle of God—God's Peace be upon Him—forbade the killing of women, children, and old men." Transmitted by all except Al-Nisā'ī.

Aḥmad (ibn Ḥanbal) and Abū Dāwud relate that in one of His expeditions the Apostle of God—God's Peace be upon Him—passed by a dead woman who had been killed by the advance guard, and they stood looking at her, that is they were astonished at her beauty, until the Apostle of God—God's Peace be upon Him—met up with them and said: "She cannot have been fighting. . . ." Then he said to one of them: "Catch up with Khālid and tell him not to kill dependents nor slaves."[38]

The previous Tradition of Ibn ᶜAbbās concerning the permissibility of killing dependents does not contradict this Tradition inasmuch as the situation in each Tradition is different from the other.

(§123) Asking a Polytheist for Help

On the authority of ᶜĀ'ishah—May God be pleased with Her—(there is a Tradition) that she once said: "The Apostle of God—God's Peace be upon Him—went out, and when He was in *Ḥarrat al-Wabarah* a man who was known for his courage and bravery came up to Him. The Companions of the Apostle of God—God's Peace be upon Him—were glad when they saw him, and when he reached Him he said *to the Apostle of God—God's Peace be upon Him—: 'I have come to follow you and fall with you.'* The Apostle of God—God's Peace be upon Him—said to him: 'Do you believe in God and His Apostle?' He said: 'No.' Then (Muḥammad) said: 'Go back, for we will never ask help from a polytheist.' Then He went on until when we came to Al-Shajarah the same man came up to us and said the same as he had said the first time. Thereupon the Prophet—God's Peace be upon Him—said to him, as He had said the first time: 'Go back, for we will never ask help from a polytheist.' Then the man went away and met us at Al-Baydā, and (Muḥammad) said to him, as He had said the first time: 'Do you believe in God and His Apostle?' Now he said: 'Yes.' Then (the Apostle)—God's Peace be upon Him—said to him: 'Then start!' " (This Tradition) is transmitted by Muslim.[39]

Al-Nawawī says: "In another Tradition it is reported that the Prophet—God's Peace be upon Him—asked Ṣafwān ibn Umayyah for help before his conversion to Islam. Therefore a group of scholars adopted unrestrictedly (the view implicit in) the first Tradition, and Al-Shāfiᶜī and others say that if the infidel has a good opinion about the Muslims and need requires that he be asked for help then he should be asked, otherwise it is disapproved.

(§124) The two Traditions (mentioned before) refer to these two situations. If an infidel is present (in the Muslim army) with (proper) permission then he should be given something, but not a real share of the booty as is given to Muslims. This is the opinion of the schools of Mālik, Al-Shāfiᶜī, Abū Ḥanīfah and the majority. Al-Zuhrī and Al-Awzāᶜī say, however, that (such an infidel) should be given his share, and God knows best." Here ends the quotation from Al-Nawawī's commentary on Muslim, the chapter on *Jihād*.[40]

Mālik says regarding the permissibility of asking polytheists and infidels for help: "On the condition that they are servants to the Muslims; then it is allowed."

Abū Ḥanīfah says that they can be asked for help, and they can help unrestrictedly when (the law of) Islam is usually applied to them, but when they usually follow the laws of polytheism, then it is disapproved.

(§125) Al-Shāfiᶜī says that it is allowed under two conditions, the first of these is that there are few Muslims and many polytheists, and the second is that these polytheists are known to have a good opinion of Islam and be inclined to it, and when one asks them for help, one should give them a small something but no share, that is, one gives them a compensation (for their trouble) but does not share with them in the shares of the booty given to the Muslims.

(§126) Is it Permitted to Fell and Burn the Trees of the Infidels?

The Imām Muslim relates, on the authority of Nāfiᶜ on the authority of ᶜAbdallāh ibn ᶜUmar, that the Apostle of God — God's Peace be upon Him — burned the date trees of Banū al-Naḍīr and felled them, at Buwayrah. Qutaybah and Ibn *Rumḥ* added in their Traditions: "Whereupon God — Exalted and Majestic He is — revealed (Qur'ān 59.5): 'What palm trees ye cut down, or left standing on their roots was by the permission of God, that He might disgrace the wicked doers.'" Quoted from Al-Nawawī's commentary on Muslim, vol. 12.

Al-Nawawī says in his commentary on Muslim's Tradition

Collection: "This Tradition contains the license to fell the trees of the infidels and burn them." Cf. the chapter on *jihād* in Al-Nawawī's Commentary on Muslim.[41]

(§127) Should Whoever is Frightened of Capture Surrender *or* Fight Until He is Killed?

On the authority of Abū Hurayrah: "The Apostle of God — God's Peace be upon Him — sent *ten men on an expedition* as spies. He put ᶜĀṣim ibn Thābit al-Anṣārī in charge, and they set off until they were in Al-Had'ah, which is between ᶜUsfān and Mecca, and said to belong to the (tribe called) Liḥyān. Then close to 200 men, all of them archers, made them rush away. (These archers also) followed their tracks. When ᶜĀṣim and his companions saw them, they took refuge in a tract of desert land, and there they were surrounded by these people, who said to them: 'Dismount and surrender. You have our pledge and word of honour that *we* will not kill any of you.'

"ᶜĀṣim ibn Thābit, commander of the expedition, said: 'As for me, by God, I will not dismount today into the care of an infidel. O God, inform your Prophet about us.' Thereupon they shot at them and killed ᶜĀṣim *who was at the head of seven men.* Three men dismounted, going by their pledge and their word of honor: Khubayb al-Anṣārī, Ibn *Dathīnah* and another man, and when they had seized them they loosed the strings of their bows and bound them with them.

"The third man said: 'This is the first *perfidious act* and by God, I am not accompanying you for I have in these dead an example (which warns me) that you want dead men.'

"They dragged him and struggled with him (trying to get him) to accompany him but he resisted, so they killed him and set off with Khubayb and Ibn *Dathīnah* until they sold them in Mecca after the Battle of Badr."

Then (Abū Hurayra went on with) the story of the murder of Khubayb, and said: "God answered ᶜĀṣim ibn Thābit's prayer on the day he was hit, because the Prophet of God — God's Peace be upon Him — told His Companions their news and what happened to them." (This is an) extract from Aḥmad (ibn Ḥanbal), Al-Bukhārī and Abū Dāwud.[42]

(§128) The Tactics of a Muslim Army

On the authority of ᶜAmmār ibn Yāsir: "The Apostle of God — God's Peace be upon Him — used to recommend to the men to fight under the banners of their own tribes." Transmitted by Aḥmad (ibn Ḥanbal).[43]

On the authority of Al-Barā' ibn ᶜĀzib: "The Apostle of God — God's Peace be upon Him — said: 'You will meet the enemy tomorrow and if your watchword is *ḥā'-mīm* (cf. the first verse of the surahs 40 – 46) they will not be victorious.'" Transmitted by Aḥmad (ibn Ḥanbal).[44]

On the authority of Al-Ḥasan on the authority of Qays ibn ᶜAbbād who said: "The Companions of the Apostle of God — God's Peace be upon Him — used to disapprove of the sound of the voice during the battle." Transmitted by Abū Dāwud.

(§129) The Recommended Times for Going out on a Military Expedition

On the authority of Kaᶜb ibn Mālik: "The Prophet — God's Peace be upon Him — went out on a Thursday on the military expedition to Tabūk, and He used to like to go out on a Thursday." (This Tradition) is generally agreed upon.

On the authority of Nuᶜmān ibn *Muqarran:* "When the Prophet — God's Peace be upon Him — was not fighting in the early part of the day, He used to postpone the battle until the sun was set and the winds blew and victory would be sent down." Transmitted by Aḥmad (ibn Ḥanbal) and Abū Dāwud. Al-Bukhārī has a different version, saying: "He waited until the winds blew and the prayers had been attended to."[45]

Recommendation to Pray for Victory When Meeting the Enemy, and Prayers for Battle

(We here quote) from the Prayers for Battle of the Prophet—God's Peace be upon Him—: "O God, Revealer of the Book, Giver of Rain, Router of Enemy Parties, Thou routest them and grantest us victory over them." (Taken from) Muslim's *Al-Ṣaḥīḥ*.[46]

(§130) An Important Matter Which Requires Attention

Complete devotion to *jihād* for the cause of God: "Complete devotion" *(ikhlāṣ)* can be defined as "removing all imperfections from the aspiration of getting closer to God—Exalted and Majestic He is—." It is also said that it can be defined as "forgetting the outward appearance of things created by looking uninterruptedly towards the Creator."

In his chapter on "Satan's *Deceiving* the Fighters," Al-Imām Ibn al-Jawzī mentions: "Satan deceived many people so that they went out to wage *jihād,* their intention being vainglory and pride, hoping that it would be said that So-and-so is a Fighter for God. Probably, however, the real intention was that (they hoped that) people would say that So-and-So was a hero, or in pursuit of booty. Deeds, however, are (to be judged) according to their intentions."

On the authority of Abū Mūsā, who said: "A man came to the Prophet—God's Peace be upon Him—and said: 'O Apostle of God, did you see the man fighting with valor and the one fighting with ardor and the one fighting in pride? Which of these fights for God's cause? (The Apostle)—God's Peace be upon Him—said: 'Whoever fights in order to make the word of God supreme. He is the one fighting for God's cause."[47] Both (Muslim and Al-Bukhārī) transmit (this Tradition).

On the authority of Ibn Masᶜūd—May God be pleased with him—, who said: "Be careful not to say: 'So-and-So died a martyr, or was killed as a martyr,' for there is the man who fights for booty and the man who fights to be remembered and the man who fights so that his standing will be seen."[48]

There is also a Tradition with a chain of authorities transmitting it, going back to the authority of Abū Hurayrah—May God be pleased with him—who said: "The first group of people who will be judged on the Day of the Resurrection consists of three men. The first was a man who had died in battle. He was brought forward and then He informed him of His favors. This he understood. (God) said: 'What did you do for them?' (The man) said: 'I fought in Your name until I was martyred.' (God) said: 'You lie, instead you fought so that it would be said that you are courageous, and so it was said.' Then it was ordered that he be dragged on his face until he was thrown into the fire.

"The second man had studied and taught religion, and he had recited the Qur'ān. He was brought forward, and He informed him of His favors. This he understood. (God) said: 'What did you do for them?' The man said: 'I studied and taught in Your name and recited the Qur'ān.' (God) said: 'You lie, instead you studied so that it would be said that you were learned, and so it was said. You recited the Qur'ān so that it would be said that you were a Qur'ān reciter, and so it was said.' Then it was ordered that he be dragged on his face until he was thrown into the fire.

(§131) "The third man was someone to whom God had been generous and He had given him every possible possession. He was brought forward, and (God) informed him of His favors. This he understood. (God) said: 'What did you do for them?' He said: 'I did not stray from the path on which You desire that there be charity, and I was only charitable in Your name.' (God) said: 'You lie, instead you did that so that it would be said that you were generous, and so it was said.' Then it was ordered that he be dragged on his face until he was thrown into the fire." Muslim alone included this Tradition in his Collection (Vol. 13, p. 50, Trad. 152).

There is also the report with a chain of authorities going back to Muḥammad on the authority of Abū Ḥatim Al-Rāzī, who said: "I heard ᶜAbduh ibn Sulaymān say: 'We were on a military expedition with ᶜAbdallāh ibn al-Mubārak in the Byzantine empire when we unexpectedly came upon the enemy, and when the two battle lines faced each other, one of the enemy got out of line and called for a dual. A man left our line and came to him and chased him for an hour, finally stabbing and killing him. Then another contested him, and he killed him also. Then he called for a duel and a man came out to him; he chased him for an hour and then he stabbed him and killed him.'

(§132) "The people thronged to him, and I was among those who crowded around him, and there he was, his face veiled with his sleeve. I took hold of the edge of his sleeve and drew it away, and lo it was ᶜAbdallāh ibn al-Mubārak. *(I)* said: 'Is it you, Abū ᶜUmar. Why do you keep aloof from us?' Then I said: 'Look all of you, may God have mercy upon you, at this devoted man. How he feared for the sincerity of his devotion to God with everybody looking at him, and their praising him, so he veiled himself. . . .'"

There is also the story of Ibrāhīm ibn Ādām who was fighting but when they took the war booty, he did not take anything of the spoils so that his (heavenly) reward would be greater; Satan certainly deceives a fighter when he takes war booty. Perhaps he takes things he has no right to since he has little knowledge and thinks that the possessions of the infidels are permitted to whomever takes them, and he does not know that to take fraudulently more than your share from the war booty constitutes a sin.

In the two Tradition Collections known as *Al-Ṣaḥīḥ* (we read) a Tradition[49] on the authority of Abū Hurayrah, who said: "We went out with the Apostle of God — God's Peace be upon Him — to Khaybar, and God granted us victory. We took neither gold nor silver as booty but only household goods, food, and clothes. Then we set out for Wādī *al-Qurā.*

"There was a servant with the Apostle of God — God's Peace be upon Him — who, when we dismounted, began to untie the saddlebags of the Apostle of God — God's Peace be upon Him —. At that moment he was struck by an arrow which spelled his death. But when we said: 'May he enjoy this! He has attained martyrdom, O Apostle of God!,' the Apostle of God said: 'Not at all. By Him Who has the soul of Muḥammad in His hand, the cloak which he is wearing is burning him with fire for he took it from the spoils on the day of the battle of Khaybar. It was not alloted to him from the shares.'"

Abū Hurayrah continued, saying: "The people got frightened, and a man brought a sandal strap or two sandal straps, and said: 'I acquired it on the day of the battle of Khaybar.' The Apostle of God — God's Peace be upon Him — said: 'One sandal strap of fire' or 'Two sandal straps of fire.'"

(§133) Perhaps a fighter knows that it is forbidden (to take whatever he likes from the war booty) but when he sees the thing he cannot resist taking it. Perhaps he thinks that his waging *jihād* justifies whatever he does. Here it is clear that belief and knowledge have great influence (on his behavior).

It has been transmitted to us with an uninterrupted chain of authorities on the authority of *Hubayrah* ibn al-Ashaff on the authority of Abū ᶜUbaydah al-ᶜAnbarī, who said: "When the Muslims descended on Ctesiphon and collected the spoils[50] a man approached with legally acquired war booty and handed it over to the man in charge of dividing the booty. Those with him said: 'We have never seen a thing which equals *(yaᶜdil)* it, and we do not have anything which even approximates it.' Then they said: 'Did you (already) take something from it?' He said: 'No, by God, if I had I would not have brought it to you.' Then they knew that this man had character and standing and they said: 'Who are you?' He said: 'By God, I will not tell you so that you praise me nor will I tempt you so that you laud me. I praise God and am pleased with His reward.' They then followed him as one man until he reached his companions. There they asked about him and he turned out to be ᶜĀmir ibn ᶜAbd al-Qays."

(§134) There Are Those Who Have Distanced Themselves from the Right Path

Abstain! Verily some people meet with great misfortunes
Leave alone the things which passions want to seize!

The poet demands *(yaṭlub)* from them (in this verse) to abstain from temptation, and he calls upon them to declare outright their true motive which is love of comfort and avoidance of hardships, which they conceal. This is the same motive which the Qur'ān gives for those who stayed behind, in Surah 9 (verse 81) where God—Exalted He is—says: "Those who have been left behind rejoiced at their sitting still behind the Apostle of God, and have refused to strive with goods and person in the way of God; they said: 'Do not march out in the heat'; say: 'The fire of Hell will be hotter still, if they would use their intelligence.'"

(§135) "These people (who refuse today to wage *jihād*) have an example in the weakness of the zeal and the softness of the will (seen in the people mentioned in the verse of the Qur'ān quoted in the previous paragraph). Many are those who shirk hardship and flee from effort, and prefer cheap comfort to noble toil, base safety to sweet danger, and they collapse exhausted behind the marching fighting ranks who are in earnest, knowing the burdens of missions that serve to further the cause of Islam. These fighting ranks remain in their path which is filled with obstacles and thorns, because they are aware with an innate knowledge that fighting the obstacles and thorns is natural to man and that it is more pleasant and more beautiful than the sitting and staying behind, or the spiritless comfort that is in (these) men." (Quoted from Sayyid Quṭb's Qur'ān commentary entitled) *Fī Ẓilāl al-Qur'ān*, 10, 26.

"These are the people who prefer comfort to struggle in the hour of difficulty and who stayed behind from the riding party the first time; these people are not suited for strife. Their participation in *jihād* is not hoped for, nor is it allowed to force them to participate. The glory of *jihād* should not be given to these people who stayed behind and did so willingly."

"So if God bring thee back to a party of them, and they ask permission of thee to go forth, say: 'Ye shall never go forth with me, nor ever fight any enemy with me; ye were content to sit still the first time, so sit still with those who stay behind'" (Qur'ān 9.83).

"Missions which further the cause of Islam require solid, straightforward, steady, and healthy constitutions which can withstand a long and difficult strife. Military ranks which are permeated with the weak and the soft cannot effectively resist because (these weak and soft soldiers) will abandon the ranks in the hour of difficulty. They will cause failure, weakness, and confusion to spread through the ranks. It is necessary to banish those who are weak and stay behind far away from the military ranks, in order to protect these from becoming disjointed and being put to flight. Indulgence towards those (weak people) is a crime towards the whole army."

(§136) Fatwās of the Jurists Regarding the Cleansing of the Ranks

Our forefathers had much to say concerning this. An example of what the First Generations of Muslims said can be found in the exposé by Imām Al-Shāfiᶜī in his *Kitāb al-Umm* (when Al-Shāfiᶜī discusses) what happened to the Hypocrites consequent to their participation in the noble expeditions of the Prophet, and the warning (which Al-Shāfiᶜī gives) against those people in later generations of Muslims who have become known for possessing the same characteristics as these Hypocrites. These will be judged by analogy and will be punished with the same punishment.

Al-Shāfiᶜī says: "The Apostle of God — God's Peace be upon Him — went on an expedition and there was someone with him whose hypocrisy was known, and who forsook (Muḥammad) on the Day of the battle of Uḥud, taking with him 300 men. Later these were present with him on the Day of the battle of the Trench and they spoke the words which God — Exalted and Majestic He is — reported (Qur'ān 33.12): "God and His Apostle have promised us nothing but illusion."

Then the Prophet — God's Peace be upon Him — went on an expedition against Banū Al-Muṣṭaliq and (again) a number of people was present with Him on this occasion, and they said those words[51] *which God repeated (Qur'ān 63.8): "If we return to the city, the highest in dignity will assuredly expel the most abased," and other things which God reported* concerning their hypocrisy.

Then He made an expedition to Tabūk and *there was a group present* with Him which fled on the evening of the (coalition of) Al-ᶜAqabah to kill Him, but God protected Him against their evil intentions. Others who were with Him stayed behind, whereupon God revealed *during* the expedition to Tabūk, *or at his departure from there for there was no fighting in Tabūk* what they had been saying and doing: "If they intended to go forth they would make some preparation for it; but God is adverse to their being stirred up and hath made them laggards; the word has passed: 'Stay at home with the stay-at-homes'" (Qur'ān 9.46).

(§137) (On this verse, 9.46) Al-Shāfiᶜī says: "God showed his Apostle their secrets and the true position of those who listened to them, and (God showed His Apostle) their desire *(ibtighā')* to seduce those with Him with lies, false rumors, and incitement to forsake (Him). (God) informed (His Apostle) that He was adverse to stirring them up, so He had made them laggards *since* they had this intention. In this *(fīhā)* is a proof that God commanded that those who were known by what they were known by (i.e., the hypocrites) would be prevented from going on an expedition with the Muslims because their presence would be a disadvantage to them."

(§138) It is not permitted to a leader to allow to participate in fights and expeditions with him those people who are described with what the hypocrites are described with. *If he went with them on an expedition it is not allowed to give such people a share in the booty, not even something small, because God forbade such people to go on an expedition with the Muslims* because they desire to provoke dissension and incite (the Muslims) to forsake (their leader), even if they are those who obey him with indifference or because of ties of kinship or friendship, for this might be more damaging *(aḍarr)* to them than many enemies *(ᶜadūw)*."

(This quotation is taken from) Al-Shāfiᶜī's (book entitled) *Kitāb al-Umm,* vol. 4, p. 89.

(§139) Islamic jurisprudence has persisted in this view, and also Ibn Qudāmah al-Maqdisī accepted *this opinion,* saying: "A commander must not bear the presence of someone who bothers him, that is, someone who keeps people away from going forth on an expedition and induces them to abstain from going out to it and to battle by saying, for instance: 'The heat or cold is severe,' or 'The hardship is severe,' and 'The routing of the enemy army is not assured.' Nor (should a commander tolerate the presence of) someone who spreads rumors, that is, someone who says: 'The army of the Muslims has been wiped out' and 'They have no auxiliaries *(madad)'* or 'Their power is nothing compared to that of the infidels' or 'The infidels have great power and many auxiliaries and a capacity to endure hardships' and 'No one can resist them' and similar things."

"(Also a commander must not tolerate the presence of) someone who spies on the Muslims for the infidels and informs them of the deficiencies of the Muslims and writes them with news of the Muslims or shows them their deficiencies or where their spies are sheltered."

"(Also a commander must not tolerate the presence of) someone who sows the enmity and discord among the Muslims, and spreads corruption. (This all is based) on the word of God—Exalted He is—: 'But God is adverse to their being stirred up and hath made them laggards; the word has passed: "Stay at home with the stay-at-homes." If they were to go forth with you, they would add nothing to you, nothing but unsoundness; they would emphasize the rifts among you, desiring to bring sedition upon you' (Qur'ān 9.46–47). Since all these (kinds of) people (mentioned) are harmful to the Muslims, it is necessary to prevent them (from being present in the Muslim armies)." (Quoted from) *Al-Mughnī* by Ibn Qudāmah, vol. 8, p. 351.

(§140) The Vanity of a Man of Religion Makes It Impossible to Give Him the Command

We find in the wisdom (ascribed to) ᶜUmar ibn ᶜAbd al-ᶜAzīz—May God have mercy upon him—an argument which justifies keeping away (even) pious men who are all good from the responsibility (of command). When there is in him ostentatiousness or conceit, *this bars him from being a means (to our great aim).* Also, we must protect (such a man) against the possibilities of temptation, and the perpetration of a crime against himself and our Cause.

(§141) It has been transmitted that when the fifth rightly guided Caliph (i.e., ᶜUmar ibn ᶜAbd al-ᶜAzīz, known as ᶜUmar II) succeeded to the Caliphate, he sent a messenger for Abū ᶜUbayd *al-Mazajī* who was learned in Islamic jurisprudence and a great

Tradition scholar from the Schools of Mālik and Al-Awzāᶜī, and one of those on whom the (previous) Caliph Sulaymān ibn ᶜAbd al-Mālik had much relied. Nevertheless ᶜUmar said to him: "This is the road to Palestine—you are one of its people, so follow it (and go away from here)." Thereupon it was said to him: "O Commander of the Faithful, if you took a look at Abū ᶜUbayd and how he works for the Good. . . ." Then ᶜUmar said: "It is more just if we do not tempt him,[52] he is the pride of the masses." (This quotation is taken from Ibn Ḥajar al-ᶜAsqalānī's) *Tahdhīb al-Tahdhīb*, vol. 12, p. 158.

(§142) It is up to the leaders of the Muslim organizations *(jamāᶜāt al-Muslimīn)* today that they say to every propagandist (for the cause of Islam) who strives to obtain a reputation and a highly regarded social position the same that ᶜUmar said to Abū ᶜUbayd.

(§143)[53] (Also they should) make them understand: "You missed the beginning of the road to your aim and consequently you passed by regions where the Call to Islam should have been made heard. Humility, sacrifice, and persisting in the right strategy is the True Road to the regions where you should *work *(ashghālak?).** *Take that road and follow it.*

NOTES TO THE TRANSLATION

1. (§1) The word "year" *(sanah)* is not found in any version of the *Farīḍah* that I consulted. There is, however, little doubt that it has to be added to the text. In AL-WĀḤIDĪ's *Asbāb al-Nuzūl*, on the discussion of Qur'ān 57.16, we read that Qur'ān 57.16 was revealed in the first year after the Hijrah from Mecca to Medina. Traditionally the revelation of the Qur'ān is believed to have begun twelve years before the Hijrah. It then follows that Qur'ān 57.16 was revealed thirteen years after the beginning of the revelation of the Qur'ān.
2. (§10) In this context it is relevant to realize that an Egyptian reader certainly knows that ᶜAmr ibn al-ᶜĀṣ is the general who led the armies that conquered Egypt for the Islamic empire.
3. (§12) Probably Ḥāfiẓ al-Islām Zayn al-Dīn Abū Faḍl ᶜAbd al-Raḥīm ibn al-Ḥusayn al-ᶜIrāqī (d. 806 AH), the teacher of the better known Ibn Ḥajar al-ᶜAsqalānī, and the author of a commentary on the Tra-

ditions which occur in AL-GHAZĀLĪ'S *Iḥyā' 'Ulūm al-Dīn*. Since this commentary is printed at the bottom of the page of the Cairo (Muṣṭafā al-Bābī al-Ḥalabī) edition of the *Iḥyā'*, it must have been easily accessible to the author of the *Farīḍah*.

4. (§25) The reference here is to the circumstance that in the Middle East a person's name betrays his religious affiliation. Someone called George is always a Christian, someone who is called Muḥammad is always a Muslim. A person's name is the only indication by which one remembers that someone bearing a Muslim name is actually a Muslim, so the text of the *Farīḍah* here maintains.
5. (§35) The author here refers to vol. 4 of *Majmūᶜat Fatāwā Shaykh al-Islām Taqī al-Dīn Ibn Taymīyah*, ed. AL-SHAYKH FARAJ ALLĀH ZAKĪ AL-KURDĪ, Cairo (Maṭb. Kurdistān al-ᶜIlmīyah), 1329. The "*Kitāb al-Jihād*" starts on p. 279 of this volume, with question 511.
6. (§35) The word *muṣannaf* occurs twice in this sentence. The second time it appears to be a dittography.
7. (§43) The term *Al-Bughāh* is used to designate Muslims who have rebelled against a lawful Imām. Some Muslim scholars regard both *al-bughāh* and apostates as people who have to be condemned to death. (TH.W. JUYNBOLL, *Handleiding tot de Kennis van de Mohammedaansche Wet*, Leiden, 1930, p. 305). The context indicates that Ibn Taymīyah is here discussing the Shīᶜah. From this point until the end of the paragraph, the text of the *Farīḍah* omits words, phrases, and even a complete line from the text of Ibn Taymīyah's fatwā. This does not facilitate the understanding of the text. I translated here the text of Ibn Taymīyah's fatwā as printed in the original, vol. 4, p. 296, lines 13 – 21, since the printed versions of the *Farīḍah*, whatever their defects, make it obvious that this is what the author wanted.
8. (§45) Again there are small discrepancies between Ibn Taymīyah's original text and its transcript in the *Farīḍah*.
9. (§64) At this point the text breaks off in the middle of the sentence, after the preposition *ilā*, both in the Awqāf and the *Aḥrār* editions. The Amman edition continues with "*kathīr min al-dirāsah.*" Since the Amman edition has copied all the mistakes that are found in the *Aḥrār* edition, and has added many more mistakes of its own, it is probable that the addition *kathīr min al-dirāsah* is a (plausible) printer's conjecture.
10. (§65) Cf., e.g., Qur'ān 54.31: "We sent upon them one shout, and they were like the rubble of the wall builder."
11. (§66) The text of the passage quoted from Al-Nawawī's commentary

reads *bid^c^ah*, and not *mubdi^c^ah* as the printed versions of the *Farīḍah* do.

12. (§66) The text of the passage quoted from Al-Nawawī's commentary reads *tustadām*, and not *tusnid* as the printed versions of the *Farīḍah* do. The passage is taken from *Ṣaḥīḥ Muslim bi-Sharḥ al-Nawawī*, Cairo, 1349, 18 vols., vol. 12, p. 229, lines 9–13, *Bāb al-Imārah*, which immediately follows the chapter on *Jihād*. The printed texts of the *Farīḍah* leave out a few words from the original. In the translation these words have been added.
13. (§72) Cf., e.g., Al-Nawawī's commentary on Muslim quoted before, vol. 12, p. 109. The context indicates that the unusual word *arīsīyyīn* denotes the subjects of the Emperor. The word may be derived from an Arabic form of the word "orthodox," by reducing the consonant clusters in the standard Arabic word "*urthuduksīyyīn*." The translation of the Letters follows Al-Nawawī's interpretation of them since it appears that Muḥammad ^c^Abd al-Salām Faraj used Al-Nawawī's commentary on Muslim's *Ṣaḥīḥ*.
14. (§73) *Al-Majūs* is a common Arabic designation for the adherents to the official religion of the Sasanid Empire.
15. (§82) Cf. *The Encyclopaedia of Islam*,[2] s.v. Bābur; see also S. Lane-Poole, *Bābar*, Oxford, 1919, pp. 173–181.
16. (§93) The sentence breaks off in all three printed versions of the *Farīḍah*.
17. (§94) On the problems the *Farīḍah* group experienced in finding a leader, see Dr. ^c^Umar ^c^Abd al-Raḥmān, *Kalimat Ḥaqq*, Cairo (Dār al-I^c^tiṣām) 1985, pp. 83–88.
18. (§95) Cf. Al-Bukhārī, *Jihād*, nr. 110.
19. (§95) Cf. *Sharḥ Saḥīḥ al-Bukhārī li-'l-Qasṭallānī*, Cairo, 1288–1289, 10 vols., vol. 5, p. 135.
20. (§95) Cf. Al-Nawawī's commentary on Muslim quoted before, vol. 13, p. 5 (*Imārah* 81). The printed versions of the *Farīḍah* read "15," which is probably an error for "5."
21. (§98) The Amman edition reads *bihi* and *rasūlihi*, which is no doubt correct. The two other editions read *bī* and *rasūlī*.
22. (§99) The printed texts of the *Farīḍah* differ. See, however, Al-Bukhārī, *Jihād*, nr. 1 (ed. L. Krehl, Leiden, 1864, vol. 2, p. 199).
23. (§99) Cf. A.J. Wensinck, "The Oriental Doctrine of the Martyrs," in *Semietische Studiën uit de Nalatenschap van Prof. Dr A.J. Wensinck*, Leiden, 1941, pp. 90–113.

24. (§101) The text of Ibn Kathīr reads *hākadhā,* which is omitted from the text of the *Farīḍah.* (Ibn Kathīr, *Tafsīr,* Cairo [ᶜĪsā al-Bābī al-Ḥalabī], n.d., vol. 2, p. 357.)
25. (§103) Muḥammad ᶜAbd al-Salām Faraj explains the word *tatarrasū* ("they provide their prisoners of war with arms and enlist them in their army") which Ibn Taymīyah here used with *iḥtamaw* ("they protect themselves").
26. (§105) The edition of Ibn Taymīyah's Fatwās that the *Farīḍah* copies is not a critical edition. Some of its mistakes are corrected by Muḥammad ᶜAbd al-Salām Faraj. Here, for instance, the printed text of Ibn Taymīyah's fatwā reads *ḥaramīyah* ("thieves"), which should almost certainly be *Jahmīyah,* the name of a sect. The author of the *Farīḍah* did not correct this, but left the word out.
27. (§108) Cf. *Encyclopaedia of Islam,* Leiden, 1913, vol. IV, p. 124.
28. (§109) Al-Nawawī/Muslim, vol. 12, p. 45, reads *al-maᶜārīḍ,* cf. Ibn al-Athīr, *Al-Nihāyah fī Gharīb al-Ḥadīth wa-'l-Āthār,* iii, 212.
29. (§111) See Al-Nawawī/Muslim, 12, 161: "This is a permitted oblique mode of speech, indeed recommended, because its inner meaning is that (Muḥammad) has disciplined us with the morals of the Revelation which brings about exhaustion, but it is an exhaustion for the gratification of God—Praised and Exalted He is—and therefore dear to us, and the literal sense which is understood by the one addressed is hardship, which is not dear to us."
30. (§112) Al-Qastallānī/al-Bukhārī, Būlāq 1288/1871, 6, 317–319.
31. (§112) Muḥammad ibn Maslamah appears to have been accompanied by others. A change in number is not uncommon in Arabic texts.
32. (§113) Cf. Al-Bukhārī, 6, 317–319; Al-Nawawī/Muslim, 12, 162.
33. (§114) See, however, Al-Wāḥidī, *Kitāb al-Maghāzī,* ed. Marsden Jones, London, 1966, 531f and 532, n. 1.
34. (§115) Cf. Ibn Ḥanbal, *Musnad,* Cairo, 1313/1895, 3, 496f.
35. (§119) Again there are many discrepancies between the text of the *Farīḍah* and the version of the Tradition in Muslim.
36. (§120) Al-Nawawī/Muslim, 12, 35–36.
37. (§121) Ibid., 49–50, Tradition 27.
38. (§122) Ibn Ḥanbal, *Musnad,* 3, 488, lines 13–18.
39. (§123) Ḥarrat al-Wabarah was a place four miles from Medina.
40. (§124) Al-Nawawī/Muslim, 12, 198, Tradition 150.

41. (§126) Ibid., 12, 50, Tradition 29.
42. (§127) Cf. IBN ḤANBAL, 2, 294, line 10; AL-QASṬALLĀNĪ/AL-BUKHĀRI, Būlāq, 1288/1871, 5, 183, *bāb* 170. The text of the *Farīḍah* is closer to the version of Al-Bukhārī. Al-Qasṭallānī (p. 184) gives the name of the third man as ᶜAbdallāh ibn Ṭāriq al-Balwī.
43. (§128) IBN ḤANBAL, 4, 263, lines 7–10.
44. (§128) Ibid., 289, lines 25–27.
45. (§129) IBN ḤANBAL, 5, 444, line 3 from bottom until 445; AL-BUKHĀRĪ, 5, 260, line 4 from bottom until 261, line 5 from top.
46. (§129) MUSLIM, 12, 47, *bāb* 6, but here in a slightly different version.
47. (§130) AL-NAWAWĪ/MUSLIM, 13, 49, Tradition 150.
48. (§130) Ibid., 13, 50.
49. (§132) AL-BUKHĀRĪ, 9, 452; (*Aymān 33*); MUSLIM, *Aymān,* Tradition 183.
50. (§133) The first *alladhīna . . . hādhā qaṭ* is a dittography.
51. (§136) The translation follows Al-Shāfiᶜī's original text.
52. (§141) The translation follows Ibn Ḥajar's original text.
53. (§143) The text of this paragraph of the *Farīḍah* is corrupt.

Bibliography

ᶜAbd al-Laṭīf, Muḥ. Fahmī, *Al-Sayyid al-Badawī wa-Dawlat al-Darāwīsh fī Miṣr* (Cairo: Al-Markaz al-ᶜArabī li-'l-Ṣiḥafah) 1979, 192 pp., Manshūrāt Samīr Abū Dawūd.

ᶜAbd al-Raḥman, Bint al-Shaṭi' ᶜĀ'ishah, *Al-Qur'ān wa-'l-Tafsīr al-ᶜAṣrī* (Cairo) 1970.

ᶜAbd al-Raḥmān, Dr. ᶜUmar, *Kalimat Ḥaqq,* (Cairo: Dār al-Iᶜtiṣām) 1985.

ᶜAbduh, Ibr., *Wa-Min al-Nifāqi Mā Qatal,* (Cairo: Sijill al-ᶜArab) 1982, 144 pp.

ᶜAbduh, Muḥ., *Tafsīr Guz' ᶜAmmā* (Cairo) n.d.

Abū al-Khayr, ᶜAr., *Dhikrayātī maᶜa Jamāᶜat al-Muslimīn "Al-Takfīr wa-'l-Hijrah"* (Kuwayt: Dār al-Buḥūth al-ᶜIlmīyah) 1980, 208 pp.

Aḥmad, ᶜĀṭif, *Naqd al-Fahm al-ᶜAṣrī li-'l-Qur'ān* (Beirut: Dār al-Ṭalīᶜah) 1972.

Amīn, Muṣṭafā, *Min Wāḥidah li ᶜAsharah,* (Cairo: Al-Maktab al-Miṣrī al-Ḥadīth) 1977.

———, *Min ᶜAsharah li-ᶜIshrīn,* (Cairo: Al-Maktab al-Miṣrī al-Ḥadīth) 1981.

ᶜAMMĀRAH, MUḤ., *Al-Farīḍah al-Ghā'ibah: ᶜArḍ wa-Ḥiwār wa-Taqyīm,* (Cairo) 1982.

AL-ᶜASHMĀWĪ, MUḤ. S., *Uṣūl al-Sharīᶜah,* (Cairo/Beirut) 1979.

AL-ᶜASQALĀNĪ, IBN ḤAJAR, *Tahdhīb al-Tahdhīb* (Hyderabad) 1325–27, 12 vols.

AL-BANNĀ, JAMĀL, *Al-Farīḍah al-Ghā'ibah: Jihād al-Sayf am Jihād al-ᶜAql,* (Cairo: Dār Thābit) 1984, 170 pp.

BELL, R., *The Qur'ān Translated with a Critical Re-arrangement of the Surahs* (Edinburgh) 1937, 2 vols., Repr. 1960.

AL-BUKHĀRĪ: *Sharḥ Ṣaḥīḥ al-Bukhārī li-'l-Qasṭallānī* (Cairo) 1288–89, 12 vols.

BURTON, JOHN, *The Collection of the Qur'ān* (Cambridge University Press) 1977. (Essential for the understanding of *naskh,* "abrogation").

CARRÉ, O., and MICHAUD, G., *Les Frères Musulmanes 1928–1982* (Paris) 1983.

AL-DHAHABĪ, MUḤ. ḤUSAYN, *Al-Tafsīr wa-'l-Mufassirūn* (Cairo: Dār al-Kutub al-Ḥadīthah) 1962, 3 vols.

ECCEL, A.C., *Egypt, Islam and Social Change: Al-Azhar in Conflict and Accomodation* (Berlin: Klaus Schwarz) 1984.

FARAJ, MUḤ. ᶜABD AL-SALĀM, *Al-Jihād: Al-Farīḍah al-Ghā'ibah* (Amman) 1982, 32 pp. (See also footnotes 8–12 of Chapter 1)

AL-GHAYṬHĀNĪ, JAMĀL, *Muṣṭafā Amīn Yatadhakkar,* (Cairo: Madbūlī) 1983.

HOPWOOD, D., *Egypt: Politics and Society 1945–1981* (London) 1982.

IBN TAYMĪYAH: *Majmūᶜat Fatāwā Shaykh al-Islām Taqī al-Dīn Ibn Taymīyah,* ed. AL-Shaykh Faraj Allāh Zakī al-Kurdī, Cairo (Maṭb. Kurdistān al-ᶜIlmīyah) 1329.

ᶜĪD, AL-MUḤĀMĪ ᶜĀDIL, *Al-Maḍābiṭ Tatakallam,* n.p., n.d., (date of preface: Alexandria 1984)

JĀDD AL-ḤAQQ, JĀDD AL-ḤAQQ ᶜALĪ; AL-DASŪQĪ, IBR.; HAMZAH, ᶜABD AL-LAṬIF; and MAḤMŪD, JAMĀL AL-DĪN MUḤ., *Al-Fatāwā al-Islāmīyah min Dār al-Iftā' al-Miṣrīyah* (Cairo) 1980–1984, 11 vols.

JANSEN, J.J.G., "I believe that my friend Abdu (. . .) was in reality an Agnostic," in P.W. PESTMAN, ed., *Acta Orientalia Neerlandica* (Leiden) 1971, pp. 71–74.

———, *The Interpretation of the Koran in Modern Egypt,* (Leiden) 1974, Repr. 1980.

———, "The Philosophical Development of Zaki Nagib Mahmud," *Bibliotheca Orientalis,* xxxiv (1977), pp. 298–300.

———, "Ibrahim Abduh," *Bibliotheca Orientalis,* xxxvii (1980), pp. 128–132.

———, "Polemics on Mustafa Mahmud's Koran Exegesis," in R. PETERS, ed., *Proceedings of the Ninth Congres of the Union Européenne des Arabisants et Islamisants* (Leiden) 1981, pp. 110–122.

———, "Tawfīq al-Hakīm on the Rigidity of Moslem Law," *Bibliotheca Orientalis,* xxxviii (1981), pp. 13–16.

———, "Shaikh al-Shaᶜrāwī's Interpretation of the Qur'an," in R. HILLENBRAND, ed., *Proceedings of the Tenth Congres of the Union Européenne des Arabisants et Islamisants* (Edinburgh) 1982.

———, "Islamitisch Activisme: Waarom Sadat Werd Vermoord," *Intermediair* (Amsterdam) January 28, 1983.

AL-JAMĪLĪ, DR. AL-SAYYID, *Al-Shaykh al-Shaᶜrāwī: Ḥayātuhu wa-Fiqhuhu,* (Cairo: Al-Mukhtār al-Islāmī) 1980.

———, *Al-Shaykh al-Shaᶜrāwī: ᶜĀlim ᶜAṣrihi* (Makt. Al-Thaqāfah al-Jadīdah) 1981.

JUYNBOLL, TH. W., *Handleiding tot de Kennis van de Mohammedaansche Wet* (Leiden) 1930.

KEPEL, G., *Le Prophète et Pharaon* (Paris) 1984.

KHĀLID, KHĀLID MUḤ., *Al-Dawlah fi-'l-Islām* (Cairo: Dār Thābit) 1981, 168 pp.

KHOMEINI: RŪḤ ALLĀH AL-KHUMAYNĪ, *Al-Ḥukūmah al-Islāmīyah* (Cairo) 1979, *iᶜdād wa-taqdīm dr. Ḥasan Ḥanafī.*

KISHK, SHAYKH MUḤ. ᶜABD AL-ḤAMĪD: see the footnotes to Chapter 4.

KISTER, M.J., "You shall only set out for three mosques": a study of an early tradition," *Muséon,* lxxxii (1969), pp. 173–196.

KÜMMEL, W.G., *Theology of the New Testament* (London) 1974.

LANDAU, J.M., "Islam and Secularism: the Turkish Case," in *Studies in Judaism and Islam* (The Magnes Press) 1981.

LAZARUS-YAFEH, H., "Muḥammad Mutawallī Al-Shaᶜrāwī: a Portrait of a Contemporary ᶜĀlim in Egypt," paper read at the International Conference on Islam, Nationalism and Radicalism in Egypt and the Sudan in the twentieth century (Haifa) 1981.

LEWIS, B., "The Return of Islam," repr. in M. CURTIS, ed., *Religion and Politics in the Middle East* (Boulder, Colorado) 1981, pp. 9–29.

MAḤMŪD, ᶜABD AL-ḤALĪM, *Fatāwā al-Imām ᶜAbd al-Ḥalīm Maḥmūd,* (Cairo: Dār al-Maᶜārif) 1981–82, 2 vols.

MAḤMŪD, MUṢṬAFĀ, *Al-Qur'ān: Muḥāwalah li-'l-Fahm al-ᶜAṣrī,* (Cairo) 1970.

———, *Nār taḥt al-Rumād,* (Cairo: Dār al-Maᶜarīf) 1979.

MAḤMŪD, ZAKĪ NAJĪB, *Tajdīd al-Fikr al-ᶜArabī* (Beirut: Dār al-Shurūq) 1981.

———, *Qiyam min al-Turāth,* (Cairo/Beirut: Dār al-Shurūq) 1984.

Majallat al-Azhar.

Majallat al-Taṣawwuf al-Islāmī.

Majallat al-Daᶜwah

MAKHLŪF, ḤASANAYN MUḤ., *Fatāwā Sharᶜīyah wa-Buḥūth Islāmīyah,* (Cairo: Muṣṭafā al-Babī al-Ḥalabī), Second Edition, 1965, 2 vols.

MEINARDUS, O.F.A., *Christian Egypt: Faith and Life,* (Cairo: American University) 1970.

MITCHELL, R.P., *The Society of the Muslim Brothers* (London: Oxford University Press) 1969.

MORTIMER, EDWARD, *Faith and Power: the Politics of Islam,* (London) 1982.

MUNTAṢIR, ṢALĀḤ, *Ḥiwar maᶜa al-Shaykh al-Shaᶜrāwī ᶜani-'l-Ḥukm wa-'l-ᶜAdl wa-'l-Shabāb,* (Cairo: Dar al-Maᶜārif) 1982, *Kitabuka* 142.

MUSLIM: *Ṣaḥīḥ Muslim bi-Sharḥ al-Nawawī,* (Cairo: Muḥ. Tawfiq, Maṭb. Ḥijāzī) 1349, 18 vols.

NIMR, ᶜABD AL-MUNᶜIM, *Tafsīr Sūrat al-Jāthiyah* (Cairo) 1980.

AL-QARḌĀWĪ, YŪSUF, *Al-Ṣaḥwah al-Islāmīyah bayn al-Juḥūd wa-'l-Taṭarruf,* (Cairo) 1984.

QUṬB, SAYYID, *Maᶜālim fi-'l-Ṭarīq* (Cairo) 1982.

RIEDEL, W., and CRUM, W.E., *The Canons of Athanasius* (London) 1904, Repr. (Amsterdam: Philo Press) 1973.

RUSSELL, B., "Mysticism and Logic," in: id., *Mysticism and Logic* (London: Allen & Unwin) 1963, pp. 9–30.

AL-SAḤRĀWĪ, FĀṬIMAH, *Al-Shaykh Muḥ. Mutawallī Al-Shaᶜrāwī: Mishwār Ḥayātī, Arā' wa-Afkār* (Cairo: Al-Mukhtār al-Islāmī) n.d. (1979?).

SHALTŪT, MAḤMŪD, *Al-Fatāwā: Dirāsah li-Mushkilāt al-Muslim fī Ḥayātihi al-Yawmīyah al-ᶜĀmmah,* (Cairo: Dār al-Qalam), Third Edition, 1966.

AL-SHAᶜRĀWĪ, SHAYKH MUḤ. MUTAWALLĪ: see the footnotes to Chapter 5.

AL-TILIMSĀNĪ, *Ayyām ma^{c}a al-Sādāt,* (Cairo: Dar al-I^{c}tiṣām) 1984.

^{c}UTHMĀN, WĀ'IL, *Ḥizb Allāh fī Muwājahat Ḥizb al-Shayṭān* (Cairo: Maṭb. Nahḍat Miṣr), Second Edition, 1975.

———, *Asrār al-Ḥarakah al-Ṭullabīyah 1968–75,* (Cairo: Maṭābi^{c} Madkūr) 1976.

VATIKIOTIS, P.J., "Islamic Resurgence: a Critical View," in A.S. CUDSI and A.E.H. DESSOUKI, eds., *Islam and Power* (London) 1981, pp. 186–191.

WENSINCK, A.J., *Mohammed en de Joden te Medina* (Leiden) 1928.

———, "The Oriental Doctrine of the Martyrs," Repr. in *Semietische Studiën uit de Nalatenschap van Prof. Dr. A.J. Wensinck* (Leiden) 1941.

WIELANDT, R., "Zeitgenössische Aegyptische Stimmen zur Säkularisierungsproblematik," *Welt des Islams,* N.S. xxii (1982).

YOUSSEF, M., *Revolt Against Modernity: Muslim Zealots and the West* (Leiden) 1985.

Index

T

U

V

W

Y

Z

Qurān Quotations